The MINIMALIST
Cooks at HOME

Recipes that Give You More Flavor
from Fewer Ingredients in Less Time

Mark Bittman

BROADWAY BOOKS
NEW YORK

Broadway Books titles may be purchased for business or promotional use or for special sales. For information, please write to: Special Markets Department, Random House, Inc., 1540 Broadway, New York, NY 10036.

BROADWAY BOOKS and its logo, a letter B bisected on the diagonal, are trademarks of Broadway Books, a division of Random House, Inc.

"The Minimalist" columns originally appeared in *The New York Times*. Reprinted by permission. "The Minimalist" is a trademark of The New York Times Company and is used under license.

Visit our website at www.broadwaybooks.com

Library of Congress Cataloging-in-Publication Data

Bittman, Mark.
    The minimalist cooks at home: recipes that give you more flavor
from fewer ingredients in less time / Mark Bittman. — 1st ed.
        p.   cm.
    Includes index.
    1. Cookery.   I. Title.
    TX718.B575   2000
    641.5—dc21   99-36291
                                                                     CIP

FIRST EDITION

Designed by Vertigo Design, Inc.

Photographs by Ellen Silverman

ISBN 0-7679-0361-7

00 01 02 03 04 10 9 8 7 6 5 4 3 2 1

For Karen

Acknowledgments

In 1995 Trish Hall, then editor of *The New York Times* Living Section, asked me to develop a weekly column. Two years later, when the section was relaunched as Dining, that column became "The Minimalist." The column title, and indeed its theme, were the brainchildren of Rick Flaste, an inspired and inspiring editor and person. Though there are dozens of people I'm grateful to for their help and support in my work on the column and *The Minimalist Cooks at Home,* Trish and Rick are chief among them, and I'm happily in their debt for life.

My current editors at the *Times,* Michalene Busico and Regina Schrambling, are wonderful colleagues and brilliant word-and-idea people. Each column is improved by their work, and by the work of Pat Gurosky and the paper's artists, layout, and copy desk people.

Many chefs and fellow food writers, especially in the New York area but all over the world, have given me great ideas for "the Mini," and you'll find their names scattered throughout the book. But my good friend Jean-Georges Vongerichten deserves special mention; although I knew more than he thinks when we began working together, I probably knew less than I believed.

Thanks of course to Harriet Bell, my editor; Angela Miller, my agent; Ellen Silverman, who took every photograph you see here; Roberto de Vicq de Cumptich, for the jacket; Vertigo Design, responsible for the highly accessible and rather minimalist design; and all the other folks at Broadway who were so helpful along the way.

As always, a special thanks to my daily phone companion, John H. Willoughby.

Finally, there are the people I rely on most: Kate Bittman, who has come to realize that maybe it isn't so bad having a dad who cooks; Emma Baar-Bittman, who is wavering between finding it annoying and highly enjoyable; and Karen Baar, who started me on this road, gave me a push when I needed it most, and loves me even when I don't cook at all.

Contents

Introduction

The key to enjoying cooking is embracing simplicity. Simplicity in food is honesty, warmth, pleasure, modesty, even fairness. Simplicity in cooking is ease and grace.

This book is all about simplicity in cooking. Many of the recipes and all of the inspiration are drawn from my weekly *New York Times* column, "The Minimalist." The title says much. In the column, I offer recipes that require a minimum of technique and/or a minimum number of ingredients; most of them are fast as well. The approach is strictly less-is-more.

And there's another goal: I try to produce recipes that are so sophisticated, savvy, and fresh that they will inspire even experienced cooks. At the same time, I strive to make them basic and simple enough to tempt novices.

The Minimalist Cooks at Home is more than a collection of my columns, because my thinking about "The Minimalist" has evolved since I began writing the column. Nearly every recipe, I've realized, symbolizes many others. A recipe almost always offers opportunities for variations or spin-offs, techniques to be illustrated and explained in depth, lessons to be learned. I've taken advantage of the room offered in this book to expand each of the columns, to exploit the opportunities the recipes present.

A disproportionate amount of space and time in food magazines, newspapers, cookbooks, and television shows is devoted to needlessly and sometimes outrageously complex recipes. But all except the most basic recipes are moments frozen in time, experiences based on a near-random concurrence of available ingredients and cookware, the time of day, season, cook's mood, and so on. Such recipes can be faithfully recorded and reasonably well duplicated, but, in fact, the best way to cook is to understand that most individual ingredients rarely matter (aside from the obvious point that you cannot roast a chicken without a chicken), and that almost all recipes can be readily transformed.

Sometimes the success of a minimalist dish hinges on a single ingredient, but most times it does not—herbs and spices can be omitted and substituted for one another, chicken can pinch-hit for fish and pork for chicken (and vice versa), many fish are interchangeable, many vegetables can be treated the same. The cook who turns the page because she or he has broccoli and a recipe calls for cauliflower has not learned this lesson, which is one of the most valuable in all of cooking, and which expands your options infinitely.

This last point—demonstrating that cooking is not a set of dogmas but a craft that can be learned and enjoyed—is not the most common approach. When faced with the choice between iron-clad recipes or those that encourage flexibility and improvisation, authors usually opt for the former. I prefer flexibility, substitution, improvisation.

This is not a theory. I learned this the long way, not in cooking school but by cooking thousands of meals, almost always without adequate time or planning. The organized chef (or cookbook writer, for that matter) knows what he or she is going to cook and has all the ingredients at hand. The home cook decides what to prepare based on what's in the fridge, pantry, or shopping bag. Minimizing the required number of ingredients, then, is a top priority. Recognizing that some ingredients can almost always be switched or dispensed with is an important axiom.

Stripping recipes to their bare essentials and seeing ingredients as interchangeable is just part of the minimalist plan. In fact, home cooks in the United States are living through a period where we are seeing the introduction of a new set of basic recipes, not the French classics revisited or the Italian staples revealed—although these are certainly parts of the trend—but the informal, quick, everyday food of households from all over the world.

In cultures where cooking is thousands of years old, most recipes are little more than combinations of ingredients that appear seasonally. Now, for the first time in history, the standard ingredients of many of those cuisines are available in most supermarkets, opening new possibilities to both novice and experienced cooks. The result is that cooking no longer has to be complicated to be interesting and unusual. What's common to a home cook in Thailand, Brazil, or Greece is exotic to us; what's new is that the ingredients are sold in supermarkets, and the expertise needed to put them together is available in cookbooks like this one.

Thus the recipes here not only provide great weeknight dinners. They will change the repertoire of experienced cooks while demonstrating international cooking basics and teaching home cooks how to develop the sixth sense that comes with experience.

Again, it all starts with simplicity, which is not a compromise but a treasure.

Salads

Grilled Bread Salad

WORK TIME	20 minutes
PREP TIME	45 minutes
CAN BE	easily multiplied
MAKES	4 servings

BREAD SALAD IS A WAY OF making good use of stale bread. The bread is softened, usually with water, olive oil, lemon juice, or a combination, then tossed with tomatoes and a variety of seasonings. Like many old-fashioned preparations created as a way to salvage food before it goes bad (count pickles and jam among these), bread salad has an appeal of its own. This is especially true in the summer, when good tomatoes are plentiful and may lead to the rather unusual problem of waiting around for bread to become stale.

Or, of course, making it stale. I'd always solved this problem by drying bread in the oven until I realized that using the grill or broiler would not only dry the bread more quickly but, by charring the edges slightly, add another dimension of flavor to the salad. This procedure is really the same as making toast—exposing the bread to direct heat (rather than the indirect heat of the oven) to brown it as well as dry it. There's another benefit to grilling the bread in order to dry it out: The added flavor makes it possible to strip the salad to its bare minimum.

This is a substantial salad, but it's still a side dish unless you're in the mood for a very light meal. (See "With Minimal Effort" for a couple of simple ideas for changing that.) Because it's juicy, almost saucy, and pleasantly acidic, this salad makes a nice accompaniment to simple grilled meat or poultry, and has a special affinity for dark fish such as tuna and swordfish.

The only tricks here involve timing. You must watch the bread carefully as you grill or broil it; a slight char is good, but it's a short step from there to burned bread. And the time you allow the bread to soften after tossing it with the seasonings varies some; keep tasting until the texture pleases you. If your tomatoes are on the dry side, you might add a little extra liquid, in the form of more olive oil and lemon juice, or a light sprinkling of water.

1 small baguette (about 8 ounces) or other crusty bread	$\frac{1}{4}$ teaspoon minced garlic, optional
$\frac{1}{4}$ cup extra virgin olive oil	$1\frac{1}{2}$ pounds tomatoes, chopped
$\frac{1}{4}$ cup fresh lemon juice (good vinegar also works well)	Salt and freshly ground black pepper
2 tablespoons diced shallot, scallion, or red onion	$\frac{1}{4}$ cup or more roughly chopped basil or parsley

1 Start a gas or charcoal grill or preheat the broiler; the rack should be 4 to 6 inches from the heat source. Cut the bread lengthwise into quarters. Grill or broil the bread, watching carefully and turning as each side browns and chars slightly; total time will be less than 10 minutes.

2 While the bread cools, mix together the next five ingredients in a large bowl. Mash the tomatoes with the back of a fork to release all of their juices. Season to taste with salt and pepper to taste. Cut the bread into $\frac{1}{2}$- to 1-inch cubes (no larger) and toss it with the dressing.

3 Let the bread sit for 20 to 30 minutes, tossing occasionally and tasting a piece every now and then. The salad is at its peak when the bread is fairly soft but some edges remain crisp, but you can serve it before or after it reaches that state. When it's ready, stir in the herb and serve.

With MINIMAL Effort

BEFORE grilling, rub the bread with a cut clove of garlic and/or brush it with some olive oil and a sprinkle of salt.

ADD to the salad $\frac{1}{4}$ cup chopped olives, 1 tablespoon capers, and/or 2 minced anchovy fillets.

FOR a one-dish meal, grill or broil some shrimp or boneless chicken alongside the bread, then add the chunks to the salad. Or add some leftover or canned tuna (the Italian kind, packed in olive oil) to the mix.

Pear and Gorgonzola Green Salad

WORK TIME	15 minutes
PREP TIME	15 minutes
CAN BE	prepared in advance; easily multiplied
MAKES	4 servings

THIS SALAD IS A FAR CRY from iceberg lettuce and bottled dressing, but it isn't much more work. And it's a magical combination of powerful flavors made without cooking or any major challenges. No wonder it's become a turn-of-the-century classic.

| Use a melon baller to remove seeds and core in one easy step.

Simple as it is, without top-quality ingredients this salad won't amount to much. I love a good Basic Vinaigrette (page 208) made with either sherry vinegar or good balsamic vinegar. The pears must be tender and very juicy, so sample one before making the salad—it should not be crunchy, mushy, or dry. The Gorgonzola should be creamy; ask for a taste before buying it.

2 large pears, about 1 pound

1 tablespoon fresh lemon juice

4 ounces Gorgonzola or other creamy blue cheese

6 cups mixed greens, washed, dried, and torn into bite-sized pieces

About ½ cup Basic Vinaigrette (page 208) made with sherry or balsamic vinegar

1 Peel and core the pears; cut them into ½-inch chunks and toss with the lemon juice. Cover and refrigerate until needed, up to 2 hours.

2 Crumble the Gorgonzola into small bits; cover and refrigerate until needed.

3 When you're ready to serve, toss the pears, cheese, and greens together with as much of the dressing as you like. Serve immediately.

With MINIMAL Effort

Pear and Gorgonzola Salad with Walnuts: To add another dimension—crunchiness—place 1 cup walnuts in a dry skillet with the heat on medium, and toast them, shaking the pan frequently until they are aromatic and beginning to darken in color, 3 to 5 minutes. Set aside to cool while you prepare the other ingredients, then crumble them into bits over the salad. Try hazelnuts, too.

SUBSTITUTE spinach, arugula, or any other strong-flavored salad green for the mesclun.

ADD about a cup of diced cucumber or bell pepper (preferably red or yellow) to the greens when you toss them.

CRUMBLE about ½ cup of crisp-cooked bacon over the salad in place of or along with the walnuts.

OMIT the pears; just make a salad of greens and cheese. Nuts are great here too.

Asian Chicken Salad

Hold the Mayo

WORK TIME	30 minutes
PREP TIME	30 minutes (or longer if you want to serve cold)
CAN BE	prepared in advance; easily multiplied
MAKES	4 servings

THE STANDARD CHICKEN SALAD—poached chicken, mayonnaise, and celery—is about as minimalist as you can get, but I prefer one that has only one thing—chicken—in common with the familiar variety. This one features grilled chicken; a superflavorful dressing based on soy sauce, peanut or sesame butter, and spices; and cucumber for crunch. By combining the chicken and sauce while the chicken is hot, the flavors marry perfectly, and their clarity remains even after the chicken has been chilled (of course you can serve the dish hot or warm if you prefer). I like to make extra dressing and serve the chicken on top of a bed of salad greens.

If possible, use boneless chicken thighs rather than breasts; their flavor and texture are superior, they remain moist during grilling, and they brown perfectly. I prefer only a slight hint of heat and therefore limit the hot sauce to a few drops, but obviously you can add as much as you like; garlic, vinegar, and sesame oil also can be added to taste. Unless you must omit it for health reasons, you should really include the sugar, which even in this minuscule quantity adds a certain roundness that is otherwise lacking.

1½ pounds boneless, skinless chicken thighs or breasts

3 tablespoons soy sauce

1½ tablespoons peanut butter or tahini (ground sesame paste)

1 teaspoon roasted sesame oil

1 small garlic clove, peeled

A few drops of hot sauce, such as Tabasco

Salt and freshly ground black pepper

¼ teaspoon sugar

1 tablespoon rice or other mild vinegar

1 cucumber

½ cup minced cilantro leaves

1 Start a charcoal or gas grill, or preheat the broiler. Cut the chicken meat into 1/2- to 1-inch chunks and thread it onto skewers (if you're broiling you can forget the skewers and simply use a roasting pan). Put the skewers on a plate and drizzle with 2 tablespoons of the soy sauce.

2 In a blender, combine the remaining soy sauce with the peanut butter, sesame oil, garlic, hot sauce, salt and pepper to taste, sugar, and vinegar. Turn the blender on and add hot water, a teaspoon at a time, until the mixture is smooth and creamy. (You will not need more than 3 teaspoons of water.)

3 Grill or broil the chicken, turning once or twice. Total cooking time will be 6 to 8 minutes for breasts, 10 to 12 minutes for thighs. Meanwhile, peel the cucumber (if it is waxed), slice it in half the long way, and scoop out the seeds with a spoon. Cut it into 1/2-inch dice and combine in a bowl with the sauce. When the chicken is done, toss it with the sauce and cucumber. Taste and adjust seasoning if necessary, then serve hot or cold, garnished with the cilantro.

With MINIMAL Effort

Asian Chicken Salad with Greens: To make this into a larger salad, wash and dry 6 cups salad greens. Double the quantities for the dressing. After blending, remove half of the mixture and combine with the cucumber and chicken as above; chill. To the remaining dressing in the blender, add about 1/3 cup hot water, and blend until well combined. Toss the dressing with the greens, top with the chicken and cucumber, garnish, and serve.

ADD minced bell pepper (preferably red or yellow), celery, and/or zucchini to the mix.

GARNISH with basil (Thai basil is especially good), mint, or minced scallions in place of or in addition to the cilantro.

Cucumber Salad with Scallops
A One-Dish Meal

WORK TIME	20 minutes
PREP TIME	1 hour
CAN BE	easily multiplied
MAKES	4 servings

SOMETIMES A SIMPLE SALAD features such powerful flavors that by adding a couple of straightforward ingredients a whole meal appears as if by magic. Here, the starting place is a Southeast Asian–style cucumber salad, with a dressing made from lime juice, lemongrass, fish sauce (called *nam pla* in Thailand and *nuoc mam* in Vietnam), and a few other strong seasonings.

This dressing commingles perfectly with the natural juices of the cucumbers, which are drawn out by salting, a process that takes some time but almost no effort. If you slice cucumbers before salting and squeeze them afterward, you wind up with ultracrisp slices that contain little remaining liquid. For a salad like this one, I salt the seeded halves *before* slicing them, thereby removing some but not all of their liquid. The result is firm but still quite moist cukes that continue to weep and exude their liquid after slicing. This transforms a dressing that is already juicy—because it contains no oil, it has none of the body of a creamy vinai-grette—into one that is quite thin. This consistency has its advantages.

When you place the cucumbers on top of a bed of salad greens, their dressing moistens the greens instantly. And by topping them with grilled scallops—or other fish or meat—you create an easy one-dish meal whose flavor really jumps off the plate. It looks lovely, too, especially if your cucumbers are good enough to leave unpeeled. And—although not by design, I assure you—this salad is extremely low in fat.

If some of these ingredients are new to you, relax: You can find them in any city and in most decent suburban and even rural supermarkets. Although fish sauce may be an acquired taste, the only ingredient here that requires what might be an unfamiliar technique is whole lemon-grass, which is usually sold by the stalk, looks like a scallion, and is easily handled (see photographs, page 11). Sometimes supermarkets sell young lemongrass in packages; you can simply mince them with no prior preparation.

4 medium cucumbers, at least
  2 pounds

Salt

2 tablespoons nam pla (fish sauce)

Juice of 2 limes

1 small garlic clove, very finely
  minced

Crushed red pepper flakes or
  finely minced fresh chiles

1 tablespoon minced lemongrass
  (photographs, page 11)

½ teaspoon sugar

6 cups mixed salad greens

1 to 1½ pounds sea scallops

1 tablespoon neutral oil,
  such as canola or grapeseed

⅛ teaspoon cayenne pepper

½ cup chopped mint, cilantro,
  basil, or a combination

2 teaspoons dark sesame oil

1 Peel the cucumbers if they have been waxed, then trim their ends and cut them in half the long way. Scoop out the seeds with an ordinary teaspoon. Sprinkle each half with about ¼ teaspoon salt, then place them all in a colander. Let drain for about 30 minutes. Rinse lightly and drain again. Cut into ⅛- to ¼-inch-thick slices and place in a bowl.

2 Mix together the fish sauce, lime juice, garlic, red pepper flakes to taste, lemongrass, and sugar. Thin with a tablespoon of water. Taste and add more of any flavoring you wish. Toss the dressing with the cucumbers and set aside while you proceed with the recipe.

3 Place the greens on a large platter. Put a large nonstick skillet over high heat. Toss the scallops with the oil, then sprinkle them with salt and the cayenne. When the skillet begins to smoke, add the scallops, one at a time and without crowding, until they are all in the pan. Cook for about 2 minutes on the first side, turning as they brown; depending on their size, cook for 1 to 3 minutes on the second side. (Scallops are best when their interior is slightly underdone; cut into one to check it.)

4 Toss the cucumbers with most of the herbs and spoon them and all of their juices over the greens. Top with the scallops. Drizzle with the sesame oil and top with the remaining herbs. Serve immediately.

With MINIMAL Effort

Cucumber Salad with Shrimp: The easy way, and it's a good one, is simply to treat the shrimp exactly as you do the scallops; take about 1½ pounds shrimp (unpeeled are fine if you're willing to let your family or guests use their fingers at the table) and cook exactly as you do the scallops; shrimp are done when pink all over. Alternatively, peel the shrimp and marinate them for about 30 minutes in a mixture of 1 teaspoon minced garlic, 1 tablespoon coarse salt, ½ teaspoon cayenne, 1 teaspoon paprika, 2 tablespoons olive oil, and 2 teaspoons freshly squeezed lemon juice. Then cook and serve the shrimp as you would the scallops.

Cucumber Salad with Chicken: Marinate 1 to 1½ pounds boneless, skinless chicken breasts in a mixture of 2 tablespoons nam pla or soy sauce and 2 tablespoons lime juice while the cucumbers drain. Grill or broil the chicken until it is done, about 3 minutes per side. Cut into strips and serve as you would the scallops.

> **TOSS** a cup of washed, dried, and roughly chopped watercress, arugula, or spinach into the cucumbers before dressing.
>
> **ADD** a cup of peeled and minced apple, jicama, or minced bell pepper—preferably red or yellow, or a combination—to the cucumbers.
>
> **SLICE** a medium onion thinly, and separate it into rings. Salt the rings along with the cucumbers; their flavor will mellow considerably.
>
> **INCREASE** the amount of herbs to one cup.
>
> **TOSS** a cup of bean sprouts into the salad.

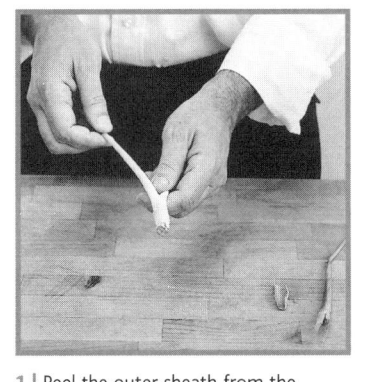

1 | Peel the outer sheath from the lemongrass stalk, as you would the outer layer of a scallion.

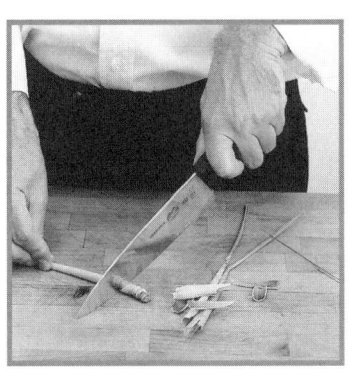

2 | Trim the top of the lemongrass.

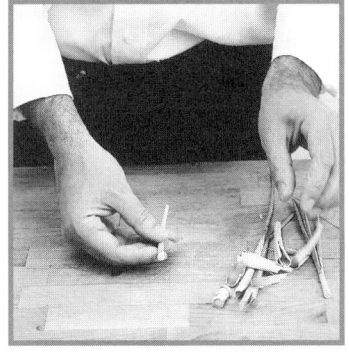

3 | Continue to peel off layers, until you expose the tender inner core.

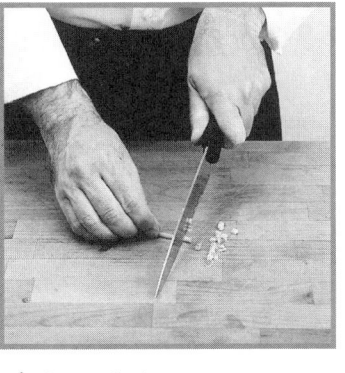

4 | Mince as finely as you can.

Minty Broiled Shrimp Salad

WORK TIME	20 minutes
PREP TIME	20 minutes
CAN BE	easily multiplied
MAKES	4 to 6 servings

THE JUICES THAT FOODS exude as they're cooking are often lost in the shuffle, especially when that shuffle is grilling. One time I produced this dish, however, it rained so hard I was forced to resort to the oven broiler. It was then I remembered why broiled shrimp are so desirable: You get to savor the delicious juices, the essences, produced by the shrimp themselves. (This is also true of shrimp that are sautéed or roasted or, for that matter, are steamed in aluminum foil or poached in a stew.)

I usually serve spicy grilled shrimp on skewers, which is how I cook them, but the presence of the newfound liquid and the time of year cried for a bed of greens. Not wanting to completely overwhelm delicately flavored greens with the powerfully spiced shrimp, I used a mixture of arugula, lettuce, and a high proportion of mint, dressed with olive oil and lemon juice.

There are many different directions in which you can take this dish. You can grill the shrimp instead of broiling them, and forget the salad; their lively flavor and lovely color—contributed by the paprika—make them a great starter or finger food.

There are two things about shrimp that are worth remembering: One is that almost all shrimp are frozen before sale (when I say "almost all," I mean literally about 95 percent; it's difficult, but not impossible, to find fresh shrimp). So, unless you're in a hurry, you might as well buy them frozen and defrost them yourself; this will guarantee you that they are defrosted just before you cook them, therefore retaining peak quality.

Secondly, you should know that there are no universal standards for shrimp size, which means that small shrimp of seventy or more to the pound are frequently labeled "medium," as are those twice that size. Learn to judge shrimp size by the number per pound, as retailers do. Shrimp labeled "16/20," for example, contain sixteen to twenty per pound; those labeled "U-20" require fewer (Under) twenty to make a pound. Shrimp from fifteen to about thirty per pound usually give the best combination of flavor, ease (peeling tiny shrimp is a nuisance), and value (really big shrimp usually cost more than ten dollars a pound).

Finally, there is, as always, the question of deveining; I don't. You can, if you like, or if you think one of your guests will be offended if you do not. But it's a thankless task, and there isn't one person in a hundred who could blind-taste the difference between shrimp that have and have not been deveined.

2 pounds shrimp in the 15-to-30-per-pound range, peeled (and deveined if you like)	1 teaspoon paprika
	4 tablespoons olive oil
1 teaspoon minced garlic or more to taste	2 tablespoons plus 2 teaspoons fresh lemon juice
1 teaspoon salt	30 to 40 mint leaves
½ teaspoon cayenne pepper, or to taste	6 cups arugula and/or other greens

1 Preheat the broiler, and adjust the rack so that it is as close to the heat source as possible. Place a large ovenproof skillet or thick-bottomed roasting pan on the stove over low heat.

2 Combine the shrimp with the garlic, salt, cayenne, paprika, half the olive oil, and the 2 teaspoons lemon juice; stir to blend. Turn the heat under the skillet to high.

3 When the skillet smokes, toss in the shrimp. Shake the pan once or twice to distribute them evenly, then immediately place the skillet in the broiler.

4 Mince about one-third of the mint. Tear the remaining leaves and toss them with the arugula. Stir the remaining olive oil and lemon juice together in a bowl.

5 The shrimp are done when opaque; this will only take about 3 or 4 minutes. Use a slotted spoon to transfer the shrimp to a plate; it's fine if they cool for a moment. Add the shrimp juices to the olive oil–lemon juice mixture and stir. Dress the greens with this mixture and toss (if the greens seem dry, add a little more olive oil, lemon juice, or both). Place the greens on a platter and arrange the shrimp on top of or around them; garnish the shrimp with the minced mint.

With MINIMAL Effort

Spicy Chicken Salad: This is better with boneless chicken thighs than breasts, but you can use either. Marinate and cook 1-inch chunks as you would the shrimp; they will take about the same amount of time. Remove the chicken, then place the pan over a burner; turn the heat to high and add ½ cup water. Stir and scrape to release any of the flavorful bits remaining in the pan (the chicken will not release as much liquid as the shrimp, which is why this step is necessary). When the liquid is reduced to a couple of tablespoons, combine it with the olive oil–lemon mixture and proceed as above.

USE a combination of mint, cilantro, parsley, basil, and/or other aromatic herbs in place of mint alone. In fact, the herb component of this salad is infinitely variable. Use what you like, in any amounts and combinations you prefer.

SUBSTITUTE sherry vinegar for lemon juice and add a teaspoon of cumin along with the paprika. Use chopped parsley in place of mint.

USE peanut oil in place of olive oil, lime juice in place of lemon juice, and cilantro in place of mint. Add a tablespoon or two of soy sauce or fish sauce (nam pla or nuoc mam) to the salad before tossing it.

Soups

Lemongrass-Ginger Soup
with Mushrooms

Not-My-Grandma's Chicken Soup

WORK TIME	15 minutes
PREP TIME	30 minutes
CAN BE	prepared in advance; easily multiplied
MAKES	4 servings

ALMOST EVERY AMERICAN who was not raised in an Asian household flavors basic soup in pretty much the same way: with onions, carrots, celery, perhaps parsley or dill. There is nothing wrong with these essentially European flavors—in fact they have taken soup making quite a long way—but there is an entirely different set of flavors that can turn an ordinary simple soup into what for many people is an unusual tasting experience.

This is a Thai-flavored soup, and it begins, as do most European soups, with chicken stock. You can use canned stock if you like, because the added ingredients here are so strong that all you're really looking for from the base is a certain amount of body (of course good stock has better body than canned stock, but we all do what we can).

The ingredients here will seem exotic to many home cooks, but I've found them all in my far-from-exceptional suburban supermarket, and if you don't have luck in yours, try any Asian market, where they are as common as carrots, celery, and onions. You don't need oyster mushrooms, by the way—fresh shiitakes or even white button mushrooms are just as good.

6 cups good chicken stock

3 lemongrass stalks

4 nickel-sized slices fresh ginger

3 to 4 small hot chiles, minced, optional

2 tablespoons nam pla (fish sauce), or to taste

6 to 8 ounces roughly chopped oyster mushrooms

2 teaspoons minced lime leaves or lime zest

Juice of 1 lime

¼ cup minced cilantro leaves

1 Heat the stock over medium heat. Trim two of the lemongrass stalks of their toughest outer layers, then bruise them with the back of a knife; cut them into sections and add them to the stock with the ginger and about one-fourth of the minced chiles. Simmer for about 15 minutes, longer if you have the time. (You can prepare the recipe in advance up to this point; cover and refrigerate for up to 2 days before proceeding.)

2 Peel all of the hard layers off the remaining stalk of lemongrass and mince its tender inner core (see page 11).

3 When you're just about ready to eat the soup, remove the lemongrass and ginger. Add 1 tablespoon of the nam pla and the chopped mushrooms. Taste the broth and add more chiles if you like, as well as some salt if necessary. In the bottom of each of four warmed bowls, sprinkle a little chile, lime leaves or zest, lime juice, cilantro, and minced lemongrass.

4 Ladle the soup into the bowls and add a teaspoon of nam pla to each bowl. Serve piping hot.

With MINIMAL Effort

Lemongrass-Ginger Soup with Chicken: Just add about 2 cups cubed boneless, skinless chicken during the last 10 minutes of cooking (it's easier to remove the ginger and lemongrass stalks before adding the meat).

Lemongrass-Ginger Soup with Shrimp: Peel about 1 pound shrimp; devein if you like, and cut them into bite-sized chunks (small shrimp may be left whole). Add to the stock during the last 5 minutes of cooking (it's easier to remove the ginger and lemongrass stalks before adding the shrimp).

As a basic soup, this will take a variety of additions easily. Some ideas:

COOKED noodles, especially rice or bean-thread noodles

COOKED vegetables, cut into small bits—asparagus, broccoli, watercress, and cabbage are especially good

RAW vegetables, such as bean sprouts or snow peas, added just a minute or two before the end of cooking

CUBED soft or firm tofu, added just a minute or two before the end of cooking

Egg Drop Soup and Stracciatella
The Chinese-Italian Soup Connection

WORK TIME	15 minutes
PREP TIME	15 minutes
CAN BE	easily multiplied
MAKES	2 to 4 servings

THE EGG DROP SOUP, a cliché of American-Chinese restaurants for at least fifty years, has a less well-known Italian counterpart, called *stracciatella*. Each one demonstrates the ease with which a basic dish can be transformed in spirit, moving from one cuisine to the other almost as quickly as you can change your mind about which you prefer.

Both are based on a simple principle: eggs, when broken into, scramble or curdle in boiling water or stock. When you use eggs to thicken a sauce or stew, you keep the heat low in order to gain a smooth, creamy result. In egg drop soup, whether Chinese or Italian, you do just the opposite—keep the heat relatively high so the eggs cook in shreds, or curds. The result is a lightning-fast soup of substance.

Egg drop soup is best flavored with soy sauce, plenty of chopped scallions, and a bit of sesame oil. Stracciatella is flavored with freshly grated Parmesan cheese (the real thing, Parmigiano-Reggiano, is essential here for best flavor) and a suspicion of garlic; some chopped parsley is an untraditional but acceptable addition, at least for us heretical Americans.

Both these soups rely on stock—you cannot make them of water and expect them to taste like anything—but the results are pretty good even with canned stock.

4 cups chicken stock

4 eggs

1 tablespoon soy sauce, or to taste

Salt and freshly ground black pepper

½ cup chopped scallions, both white and green parts

1 teaspoon sesame oil, or to taste

1 Bring 3 cups of the stock to a boil over medium-high heat in a 6- to 8-cup saucepan. Beat the remaining stock with the eggs and soy sauce until well blended.

2 When the stock is boiling, adjust the heat so that it bubbles frequently but not furiously. Add the egg mixture in a steady stream, stirring all the while. Stir occasionally until the eggs gather together in small curds, 2 or 3 minutes.

3 Taste and add salt if necessary (or more soy sauce), then add plenty of pepper, the scallions, and the sesame oil. Taste again, adjust seasoning, and serve.

Stracciatella

4 cups chicken stock	**A tiny grating of fresh nutmeg**
4 eggs	**2 tablespoons minced parsley**
4 tablespoons freshly grated Parmesan cheese	**Salt and freshly ground black pepper**

1 Bring 3 cups of the stock to a boil over medium-high heat in a 6- to 8-cup saucepan. Beat the remaining stock with the eggs, cheese, nutmeg, and parsley until well blended.

2 When the stock is boiling, adjust the heat so that it bubbles frequently but not furiously. Add the egg mixture in a steady stream, stirring all the while. Stir occasionally until the eggs gather together in small curds, 2 or 3 minutes.

3 Taste and add salt and pepper to taste, then serve. Garnish with a little more Parmesan if you like.

With MINIMAL Effort

Stracciatella with Greens: Add 2 cups chopped collards, kale, spinach, or watercress, to the simmering stock *before* stirring in the eggs. Spinach will cook almost instantly; the others will take a few minutes to become tender. Proceed as above.

Both of these soups are quite filling, but to make them into a real one-pot meal:

ADD about 2 cups finely chopped boneless chicken or peeled shrimp to either soup just before the eggs; it'll only take a minute to cook.

ADD about 2 cups *cooked* thin egg noodles or rice to either soup. (If you use rice, add a couple tablespoons of lemon juice; you'll have Greek-diner egg-lemon soup.)

Garlic Soup with Shrimp

The Basics of Boiled Water

WORK TIME	30 minutes
PREP TIME	30 minutes
CAN BE	easily multiplied
MAKES	4 servings

MANY SOUPS HAVE extraordinarily simple origins, none more so than the peasant dish of southern France called *l'aigo boulido* (boiled water). At its most impoverished, this is no more than garlic simmered in water to give it flavor, with a few crusts of bread added for bulk. Simple as it is, boiled water is the perfect example of how an almost absurdly elementary preparation can be quickly and easily converted into one that is nearly grand; all it takes is a couple of quick techniques and a few common ingredients.

Begin the soup by gently cooking the garlic in some olive oil to add the complexity and color of the browning process. By browning the bread in the same oil, you increase its flavor immeasurably. Using stock in place of water is a no-brainer—and note that this is a great place for canned stock, because the garlic-scented oil will boost it to a higher level.

Although even after all of this tinkering the resulting soup remains on the meager side, it only requires one more ingredient to turn it into a meal. My choice here is almost always shrimp, for two reasons: They add great flavor of their own, and the shells can be used to make shrimp-shell stock, a freebie that isn't exploited nearly as often as it should be.

Making shrimp-shell stock is simple: Put shrimp shells in a pot, cover with water, bring to a boil, and simmer for about five minutes; strain. The liquid can be used in many shrimp dishes, or in place of fish stock in most recipes. You can accumulate shells and freeze them over a period of months if you like, and there's no need to defrost them before making the stock.

The amount of stock made by the pound or so of shrimp in this recipe isn't enough to complete the soup, but its volume can be increased with water or enhanced with chicken stock. If you have some of the latter, it's worth using, as the combined flavor of the shrimp and chicken stocks is really quite magnificent.

Finally, I must confess that I almost always double the amount of bread given in the recipe here, or at least make an extra slice or two for myself; I find the allure of bread crisped in garlic-scented oil irresistible.

¼ cup extra virgin olive oil	6 cups shrimp stock (see above),
8 to 16 medium-to-large garlic cloves, peeled	chicken stock, water, or a combination
Salt and freshly ground black pepper	1 to 1½ pounds shrimp, peeled
4 thick slices French or Italian bread	Minced parsley leaves for garnish, optional

1 Combine the olive oil and garlic in a deep skillet or broad saucepan, turn the heat to medium, and sprinkle lightly with salt and pepper to taste. Cook, turning the garlic cloves occasionally until they are tender and lightly browned all over, about 10 minutes; lower the heat if they seem to be browning too quickly. Remove the garlic with a slotted spoon.

2 Turn the heat to low and add the bread (in batches if necessary); cook on each side until nicely browned, a total of about 4 minutes. Remove the bread, add the stock, and raise the heat to medium-high.

3 When the stock is nearly boiling, add the shrimp and salt and pepper to taste. Cook until the shrimp are pink, about 4 minutes. Place a piece of bread and a portion of garlic in each of 4 bowls, then ladle in a portion of soup and shrimp. Sprinkle with the optional parsley and serve.

With MINIMAL Effort

Spicy Garlic Soup: To make the soup even more flavorful, brown a little spice in the oil after removing the bread and before adding the stock. I especially like a combination of cumin and paprika (about a teaspoon of each), which gives the soup a decidedly Spanish feeling. Curry powder, mild chili powder, a pinch of cayenne, or a few rosemary leaves are all possibilities, too; this is a good place to experiment.

Thai Garlic Soup: Add a minced fresh chile, or a few dried chiles, to the oil along with the garlic (discard dried chiles after cooking). Omit the bread; add 2 cups cooked rice to the soup along with the shrimp. Substitute cilantro for the parsley, and serve with wedges of lime.

Meaty Garlic Soup: Substitute 2 cups boneless chicken or pork, cut into ½-inch chunks, for the shrimp; cooking time will be about the same.

Carrot-Garlic Soup: Substitute 2 cups peeled carrots, cut into ½-inch chunks, for the shrimp; cooking time will be about 10 minutes.

Prosciutto Soup
Meaty Soup Without Stock

WORK TIME	30 minutes
PREP TIME	30 minutes
CAN BE	prepared in advance; easily multiplied
MAKES	4 servings

WHILE THERE IS SOME magic in cooking, it's difficult to make a silky soup without a sow's ear—or something like one. Water-based soups are great, but soups with character are best when made with meat stocks.

Of course you don't always have stock, and there are shortcuts that produce in-between soups. One of the easiest and most effective ways of making a potent soup quickly and without stock is to start with a small piece of prosciutto or other dry-cured ham, such as Smithfield. The long aging process this meat undergoes—almost always a year or more—ensures an intense flavor that is quickly transferred to anything in which it is cooked, including water. There are no other ingredients that will contribute as much taste and body to a soup with so little effort. Even fresh meat, for example, requires more quantity and longer simmering; and bacon and other smoked meats yield a strong but one-dimensional flavor.

One of the beauties of making a prosciutto-based soup is that regardless of the ingredients you choose to add, the procedure follows a series of small steps. Because each of these can be executed sequentially, there is almost no preparation time; while you render the ham, you chop the vegetables and add them one at a time. By the time you're done chopping, you've added all the ingredients except water. And if you bring the water to a boil before you begin chopping, you minimize cooking time, producing a thick, rich soup in less than thirty minutes.

The basic recipe here, though delicious, is on the meager side, the kind of soup people make either when times are hard or no one's been shopping lately: a small piece of meat, some common vegetables, a little pasta. But you can make it as elaborate as you like, and even convert it to a stew by doubling the amount of meat, vegetables, and pasta; the chopping time will be extended slightly, but the cooking time will remain more or less the same.

One last word: Do not omit the final drizzle of olive oil; its freshness really brings this soup to life. In fact, if you have a bottle of oil that you reserve for special uses, consider this one of them and break it out.

3 tablespoons extra virgin olive oil	½ pound greens, such as spinach or kale
¼ pound prosciutto, in 1 chunk or slice	¾ cup small pasta, such as orzo or small shells
4 garlic cloves	Salt and freshly ground black pepper
1 medium onion	

1 Set 6 cups water to boil. Put 2 tablespoons of the olive oil in the bottom of a medium saucepan and turn the heat to medium. Chop the prosciutto (remove the fat if you must, but remember that it has flavor) into ¼-inch or smaller cubes and add to the oil. Brown, stirring occasionally, for about 5 minutes, while you prepare the garlic, onion, and greens.

2 Peel the garlic and chop it roughly or leave it whole. Peel and chop the onion. Wash and chop the greens into bite-sized pieces.

3 When the prosciutto has browned, add the garlic and cook, stirring occasionally, until it begins to color, about 2 minutes. Add the onion and cook, stirring occasionally, until it becomes translucent, 2 or 3 minutes. Add the greens and stir, then add the 6 cups boiling water. (You can prepare the dish in advance up to this point. Cover and refrigerate for up to 2 days, then reheat before proceeding.) Stir in the pasta and a good sprinkling of salt and pepper; adjust the heat so the mixture simmers.

4 When the pasta is done, taste and add more salt and pepper if necessary. Drizzle with the remaining olive oil and serve.

With MINIMAL Effort

This soup is fair game for whatever you have around, and almost every ingredient can be swapped for something else. The only things that I consider essential are the prosciutto, olive oil, and, of course, water.

ADD more root vegetables: Thin-sliced carrots or chopped celery are the most obvious additions, but potatoes or turnips are also good as long as they're cut small enough to cook in 10 minutes or so.

VARY the greens: Shredded cabbage is perfect for this soup, and will cook as quickly as kale. Collard, mustard, or turnip greens are also appropriate. Some peas and/or corn work nicely, too, even if they come from the freezer.

SWAP any starch for the pasta: Rice or barley, each of which may take a few minutes longer than pasta, are the best choices.

USE tomatoes, either fresh, canned, or paste, to add color and flavor. To use tomato paste, just stir a couple of tablespoons into the sautéing vegetables before adding the water. Tomatoes should be added with the onions, so they have time to break up.

THIS is a perfect place to use leftovers—a bit of chopped chicken, or some vegetables from last night (rinse them with boiling water if they were sauced).

CONSIDER, too, the chopped-up rind of hard cheese, such as Parmesan, which will not only soften enough to become edible during cooking but will add great flavor to the soup.

Turkey Stock
Making Stock from Leftovers

WORK TIME	About 30 minutes
PREP TIME	About 2½ hours
CAN BE	prepared in advance; frozen; easily multiplied
MAKES	about 2 quarts

THERE ARE PLENTY OF WAYS to make stock, and one of them—*jus roti,* also known as brown stock, a staple of classic French cuisine—begins with roasted meat and vegetables. As it happens, almost every time you make a roast, whether it is one of turkey, chicken, or beef, you have roasted meat and bones left over. These can make the beginnings of a perfectly fine stock.

I'll use turkey as an example, since turkey is all about leftovers anyway. Most turkey meat finds its way into sandwiches, but many cooks make a turkey soup as well, tossing the bones with some of the leftover meat into a pot with water to cover, and simmering until the meat falls off the bones—a technique that produces quite decent results.

However, there's a nearly-as-simple method that allows you to produce dark, rich turkey stock in the turkey roasting pan. This broth has a broader range of uses than the throw-everything-in-the-pot variety; in fact, the result is very close to jus roti. To make brown stock, you brown (or, in culinary lingo, "caramelize") meat and vegetables, then simmer them with water. That's just what you do here: Take the leftover turkey, including bones, any meat you won't be using for sandwiches, and the meaty carcass, and place them in the same roasting pan you used for the turkey; you need not even wash it first. Throw it in the oven and brown it; add vegetables, then water. With far more time than work you'll have a strong, sweet, and meaty turkey stock—good enough to eat unadulterated as clear broth, and a perfect base for almost any other soup.

The process is easy, and there are only two things to remember: You must chop or break the carcass into a few pieces before adding it to the pan or you will need too much water to cover it. And, although precise measuring of vegetables is not essential, bear in mind that each has its own strong flavor, and an overabundance of one or all can throw the stock out of balance.

| Bones, leftover meat, and carcass from a 15-pound turkey | 1 large onion, peeled and quartered |
| 2 carrots, peeled and cut into chunks | 1 celery stalk, roughly chopped |

1 Preheat the oven to 450°F. Place the bones, meat, and chopped carcass in a large roasting pan and put in the oven. Roast, stirring occasionally, for about 1 hour, or until nicely browned. Don't worry if the meat sticks to the bottom of the pan.

2 Add the chopped vegetables and roast for about 30 minutes more, stirring once or twice.

3 Remove the roasting pan to the stovetop and place it over one or two burners, whichever is more convenient. Turn the heat to high and add water to barely cover the bones, about 8 to 10 cups; don't worry if some of the bones poke up out of the water. When the water boils, turn the heat down so that the liquid simmers.

4 Cook, stirring occasionally and scraping the bottom of the pan to loosen any bits of meat, for about 30 minutes. Cool, then strain. Refrigerate and skim off excess fat, then store for up to 3 days in the refrigerator (longer if you bring the stock to a boil every second day) or several months in the freezer.

With MINIMAL Effort

Roast Chicken Stock: Since a chicken carcass won't be as large, you'll have to either cut back on the water or add some fresh chicken; wings and/or legs are best. Proceed exactly as above.

There are dozens of additions you can make to the stock as it is cooking, or convert it into soup when it is done. Some quick ideas:

ADD a head of garlic, cut in half, to the roasting pan along with the other vegetables.

ADD a small handful of mushrooms, or mushroom trimmings, or reconstituted dried mushrooms to the roasting pan along with the other vegetables.

ADD stems and/or leaves of parsley or dill to the simmering stock; don't overdo it.

ADD chopped vegetables, leftover turkey, and noodles or rice to the broth to turn it into a full-fledged soup.

TO make tortellini in broth, gently simmer about 10 tortellini per serving in broth until tender; garnish with freshly grated Parmesan cheese. You can do the same with ravioli.

TO make mushroom-barley soup, add sliced fresh mushrooms, reconstituted dried mushrooms, and about $\frac{1}{2}$ cup barley per 4 cups of stock; cook until the barley is tender.

COOK chopped tomatoes (canned are fine), cooked beans, minced vegetables, and small pasta in the stock to make minestrone.

Pumpkin Soup
Creamy Soup Without Cream

WORK TIME	15 minutes
PREP TIME	40 minutes
CAN BE	prepared in advance; frozen; easily multiplied
MAKES	4 servings

TO MOST PEOPLE, pumpkin means pie, a limited role for a large vegetable that is nearly ubiquitous from Labor Day through Christmas. But soup based on pumpkin—or other winter squash such as acorn or butternut—is a minimalist's dream, a luxuriously creamy dish that requires only two major ingredients: a stove and a blender.

Despite its simplicity, this soup is so good it (or something very much like it) is served at swank restaurants all over the country; waiters proudly declare, "It's very creamy, but contains no cream at all." (I'll be the first to confess, however, that it is at least a little bit better with some cream—fresh or sour—added at the last minute.)

Putting the soup together is a snap: You combine peeled pumpkin or other winter squash with any good stock and simmer until the squash is soft—about thirty minutes. Then you puree in a blender and reheat, with or without seasonings or garnish. That's it. If time allows, cool the mixture before pureeing, for safety's sake.

If there is a challenge here, it lies in peeling the squash. The big mistake many people make is to attack it with a standard vegetable peeler; the usual result is an unpeeled pumpkin and a broken peeler. A quicker and more reliable method is to cut the squash up into wedges; then rest each section on a cutting board and use a sharp, heavy knife to cut away the peel. You'll wind up taking part of the flesh with it, but given the large size and small cost of winter squash, this is hardly a concern.

2 pounds peeled pumpkin or other winter squash (weighed after peeling; see above for peeling instructions)

4 to 5 cups chicken or other stock

Salt and freshly ground black pepper

1 Place the pumpkin or squash in a saucepan with stock to cover and a pinch of salt. Turn the heat to high and bring to a boil. Cover and adjust the heat so that the mixture simmers. Cook until the pumpkin or squash is very tender, about 30 minutes. If time allows, cool.

2 Place the mixture, in batches if necessary, in the container of a blender and puree until smooth. (The recipe can be prepared a day or two in advance up to this point; cool, place in a covered container, and refrigerate.) Reheat, adjust seasoning, and serve.

With MINIMAL Effort

Pumpkin and Apple Soup: This screams autumn: Add ½ teaspoon dried ginger or 1 teaspoon minced fresh ginger to the soup. Peel, core, and thinly slice 2 apples; cook them in 2 tablespoons butter until lightly browned, turning occasionally. Use the slices to garnish the soup.

Creamy-and-Chunky Pumpkin Soup: Measure about 1 cup of pumpkin or squash (you will almost always have extra), cut into ¼-inch dice, steam until tender, and stir into the soup about 2 minutes before removing from the heat.

Pumpkin and Mushroom Soup: Sauté about 1 cup sliced mushrooms—chanterelles are best, but shiitakes (discard the stems) or button mushrooms are good—in 2 tablespoons butter or extra virgin olive oil until they give up their liquid and begin to become crisp. Use to garnish the soup.

To make this basic soup more complex:

ADD a teaspoon of ground ginger (or 1 tablespoon finely minced fresh ginger) or a teaspoon of curry powder (and, if you have it, ½ teaspoon of turmeric) to the simmering soup.

ADD ½ teaspoon of cinnamon, ¼ teaspoon of allspice, and a small grating of nutmeg to the simmering soup.

GARNISH each bowl of soup with three or four grilled, sautéed, or roasted shrimp; or about ¼ cup crabmeat or lobster meat per serving.

GARNISH the soup with chopped chervil, chives, parsley, or dill.

STIR 2 tablespoons to 1 cup of crème fraîche, sweet cream, sour cream, or yogurt into the pureed soup as you are reheating it.

STIR about 1 cup of cooked long-grain rice into the pureed soup as you are reheating it.

Creamy Broccoli Soup
The Three-Two-One Formula

WORK TIME	15 minutes
PREP TIME	30 minutes (longer if you choose to chill the soup)
CAN BE	prepared in advance; frozen; easily multiplied
MAKES	4 servings

IT'S NOT OFTEN THAT YOU can apply a simple formula to a broad range of dishes, but when it comes to creamy vegetable soups—whether hot or cold—there is one that actually works. The soups have three basic ingredients, and their proportions form a pyramid: three parts liquid, two parts vegetable, one part dairy.

The pyramid's foundation is chicken stock (you can substitute vegetable stock or water, but the result will be somewhat less substantial).

One cup of milk or other dairy, two cups of broccoli, and three cups of stock combine to make a creamy vegetable soup.

The middle section is any vegetable, or combination of vegetables, that will puree nicely and produce good body and flavor. The peak is cream, or nearly any other liquid dairy product—milk, yogurt, or sour cream.

To make four servings, the three-two-one measurement is in cups, conveniently enough, because a total of six cups is the perfect amount of soup for four people. Aromatic vegetables, such as onions, carrots, or celery, which are almost always welcome additions, count as part of the vegetable portion, but seasonings like salt, pepper, herbs, spices, or garlic or shallots, are extras, and can be added pretty much to taste.

The procedure is nearly as straightforward as the formula: Simmer the vegetables in the stock until they're quite tender. Puree in a blender, in batches if necessary (make sure the blender lid is on securely to avoid scalding). Stir or blend in the dairy and seasonings. Then reheat gently (especially gently if you're using yogurt, which will curdle if it boils) or chill to serve cold.

There are a couple of shortcuts worth mentioning: Leftover vegetables are super candidates for this soup. Rinse off any remnants of dressing with hot water, then combine with stock and puree. Some vegetables— like winter squash—are so dense that they create their own creaminess, reducing the amount of dairy needed in the final step.

But this is a matter of judgment, perhaps best left until after you've experimented following the basic rules, which are:

Keep the proportions in line. If there are too many vegetables your blender won't be able to puree the mixture; too much liquid will cut the flavor of the vegetable and thin the soup; too much dairy will reduce the intensity of flavor and make it too rich.

Always cook the vegetables until very tender, but no more than that. Spinach is tender in a couple of minutes; potatoes, even cut into chunks, will require ten or fifteen. Almost nothing will take longer than that. Cover the pot while the vegetables cook to prevent too much of the stock from evaporating.

Seasonings that require cooking, like garlic and onions, should be added with the vegetables. Those that do not, like herbs and spices, are best added before pureeing the cold mixture so they retain their freshness. Generally speaking, cold soups require more seasoning than hot ones.

For that same reason, cookbooks will usually instruct you to oversalt soup you're planning to serve cold. I recommend, however, that you still salt only to taste; beyond that is risky.

There's obviously a difference in the amount of richness added to the soup by cream, sour cream, yogurt, and milk. So stir in the dairy gradually by hand after pureeing and adjust the consistency as you like.

2 cups broccoli florets and peeled stems (about ½ average head), cut into chunks

3 cups chicken stock

1 garlic clove, peeled and cut in half

1 cup milk, cream, or yogurt

Salt and freshly ground black pepper

1 Combine the broccoli and the stock in a saucepan and simmer, covered, until the broccoli is tender, about 10 minutes. During the last minute or so of cooking, add the garlic (this cooks the garlic just enough to remove its raw taste). If you're serving the soup cold, chill now (or refrigerate for up to 2 days, or freeze for up to a month before proceeding).

2 Puree in a blender, in batches if necessary, until very smooth. Stir in the milk, cream, or yogurt and reheat gently (or chill again); do not boil. Season to taste and serve.

Potato and Onion Soup

WORK TIME	15 minutes
PREP TIME	30 minutes (longer if you choose to chill the soup)
CAN BE	prepared in advance; frozen; easily multiplied
MAKES	4 servings

1 cup potato (about 1 large),
    peeled and cut into chunks

1 cup onion or leeks, peeled or
    trimmed, washed if necessary,
    and cut into chunks

3 cups chicken stock

1 cup milk or cream

Salt and freshly ground black
    pepper

Chopped parsley leaves or chives
    for garnish

1 Combine the potato, onion, and stock in a saucepan and simmer, covered, until the potato is tender, about 15 minutes. If you're serving the soup cold, chill now (or refrigerate for up to 2 days, or freeze for up to a month before proceeding).

2 Puree in a blender, in batches if necessary, until very smooth. Stir in the milk or cream and reheat gently (or chill again); do not boil. Season to taste, garnish with the parsley or chives, and serve.

With MINIMAL Effort

The possible combinations for creamy vegetable soups are literally infinite; here are ten suggestions:

BEET. Add some minced scallion or chive before pureeing. Puree with sour cream and garnish with chives and a teaspoon of sour cream per serving.

SPINACH. Start with 10 to 16 ounces leaves (remove thick stems). Cook quickly, adding a bit of garlic if you like.

TURNIP AND PARSNIP. Or turnip and potato. Cook with a small onion and some thyme.

RED PEPPER AND TOMATO. Peel and seed both before cooking. Puree with sour cream to thicken the mixture, which will be thin. Garnish with chervil (ideally) or parsley.

CARROT. Nice with a pinch of cayenne and a teaspoon or more of minced ginger, added after cooking.

CUCUMBER. Don't cook, but peel the cucumbers, cut them in half, and scoop out seeds before combining with stock. Use sour cream and plenty of fresh dill.

PEAS OR SNOW PEAS. Make sure to remove the strings from snow peas. Cook with thyme or mint.

CELERY OR FENNEL. Cook a few cloves of garlic along with the vegetable.

ARTICHOKE HEARTS. If you use canned hearts, simply puree with cold chicken stock; there's no need to cook.

TOMATILLOS OR GREEN TOMATOES. Season with chili powder, puree with sour cream, and garnish with a teaspoon of sour cream.

Clam Chowder

The Real Thing

WORK TIME	20 minutes
PREP TIME	30 minutes
CAN BE	prepared in advance; easily multiplied
MAKES	4 servings

CLAM CHOWDER TAKES MANY guises: It can be overwhelmed by bacon or other strong flavors or thickened with flour or loads of cream. The best clam chowder is a simple affair that has as its flavorful essence the juices of the clams themselves.

And as long as you begin with fresh clams these juices are easily extracted and reserved; the minced clam meat becomes a garnish. Some onion and garlic are welcome, although only the former, I think, is essential. Diced potatoes are a near-necessary addition, for the body they lend. And I confess that I like finishing the chowder with a little cream—or at least milk—for both color and a certain silkiness.

Of course, what is actually "essential" in clam chowder is debatable: Manhattanites, in theory at least, prefer theirs with tomatoes. New Englanders, we assume, like it with cream. There is also Rhode Island clam chowder, which in spirit at least is closest to the minimalist ideal: It contains clams, onion, celery, water, salt, and pepper.

The geographical preferences no longer matter, especially if you are making clam chowder at home. The base for any chowder is the same, and the additions or omissions are entirely up to you.

Just be sure to begin with the right clams. The first choice is littlenecks, the smaller the better. But in fact any hard-shell clam—larger ones are called cherrystones or quahogs—will do, because they're easy to clean and contain little if any sand in their interior. (Although the meat of the larger clams is tough, this is not a huge issue because it will be diced.) The cockles seen in some fish markets these days, which resemble small clams, are also good. Steamers contain so much sand that some will inevitably, find its way into your broth.

When buying hard-shell clams, remember that live ones have tightly closed shells; reject any whose shells are open or cracked. Those which do not open fully during steaming are perfectly fine; simply pry them open with a knife.

At least 3 dozen littleneck clams (3 pounds or more), or an equivalent amount of other clams	2 large potatoes (about 1 pound), peeled and cut into ¼-inch dice
1 medium onion, peeled and minced	Salt and freshly ground black pepper

1 Wash the clams well, scrubbing if necessary to remove external grit. Place them in a pot with ½ cup water and turn the heat to high. Steam, shaking the pot occasionally, until most of the clams are open, 7 to 10 minutes. Use a slotted spoon to remove the clams to a broad bowl; reserve the cooking liquid.

2 When the clams are cool enough to handle, shuck them over the bowl, catching every drop of their liquid; discard the shells. If any clams remain closed, use a thin-bladed knife to pry them open (it will be easy).

3 Chop the clams. Strain all the liquid through a sieve lined with a paper towel or a couple of layers of cheesecloth. Measure the liquid and add enough water to make 3½ cups. (You may prepare the dish in advance up to this point; refrigerate, covered, for up to a day before reheating.)

4 Combine the liquid with the onion and potatoes in a saucepan; cover and bring to a boil. Reduce to a simmer, still covered, and cook until the potatoes are tender, about 10 minutes. Stir in the clams, season to taste with salt and pepper, and serve.

With MINIMAL Effort

New England Clam Chowder: Add ½ cup or more of milk, cream, or half-and-half along with the chopped clams.

Manhattan Clam Chowder: Add 1 cup peeled, seeded, and diced tomatoes (canned are fine) to the steaming water.

Rhode Island Clam Chowder: Replace the potatoes with ½ cup minced celery.

SUBSTITUTE white wine for the water in the initial steaming.

ADD 3 crushed garlic cloves to the steaming water; discard them with the clam shells.

GARNISH the chowder with minced parsley or other herbs.

Cold Tomato Soup with Rosemary
But Not Gazpacho

WORK TIME	15 minutes
PREP TIME	15 minutes
CAN BE	prepared in advance; easily multiplied
MAKES	4 servings

IN MIDSUMMER, YOU OFTEN hear people say, "Give me a good tomato and I eat it like an apple." But no one actually does that, at least not more than a couple of times a summer.

That's because, unlike peaches—which can barely be improved upon—tomatoes are bursting with potential. The difference between consuming a tomato out of hand and slicing it, then sprinkling it with a pinch of salt and a few drops of olive oil, is the difference between a snack and a dish. And the great thing about tomatoes is that it takes so little to convert them from one to the other.

This soup is a great example, an almost instant starter that requires no cooking at all. It benefits from a period of chilling after being put together, but if you use ice cubes in place of chicken stock (or combine the two) you can even skip that.

Tomatoes should always be cored before using. With a paring knife, cut a cone-shaped wedge out of the stem end and remove it (see photographs, page 37). And in this instance, peeling and seeding the tomatoes are worth the effort as well. To do so, bring a pot of water to a boil. Meanwhile, cut a small X on the smooth (flower) end of each tomato. Drop them into the boiling water. In about thirty seconds, you'll see the skin begin to loosen. Immediately remove from the boiling water and plunge into a bowl of ice water. When they're cool, peel, then cut them in half through their equator. Squeeze and shake out the seeds. (You might consider doing this over a strainer and recombining the reserved juices with the pulp.)

2 slices good stale white bread, crusts removed

3 pounds ripe tomatoes, peeled, seeded, and roughly chopped

1 teaspoon fresh rosemary leaves

1 small garlic clove, peeled

1 cup chicken stock or ice cubes

Salt and freshly ground black pepper

Juice of 1 lemon or more

1 Soak the bread in cold water briefly; squeeze dry and combine in a blender with the tomatoes, rosemary, and garlic (you may have to do this in two batches). Add the ice cubes if using them. Turn on the machine and drizzle in the stock. Turn off the machine and pour the mixture into a bowl.

2 Season with salt and pepper to taste, then add lemon juice to taste. Chill and serve.

With MINIMAL Effort

USE fresh thyme (1 teaspoon), dill (1 tablespoon), basil (¼ cup), parsley (¼ cup), chervil (1 tablespoon), chives (¼ cup), or a mixture of herbs. Garnish with fresh herbs, too, if you like.

FINISH the dish with a sprinkling of top-quality extra virgin olive oil.

SUBSTITUTE a shallot or a small handful of chives for the garlic.

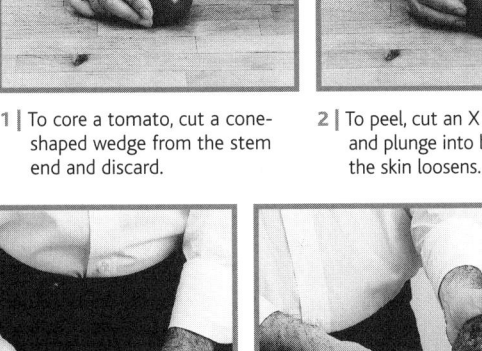
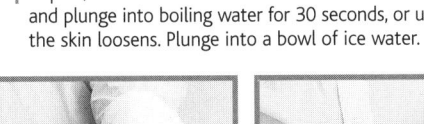

1 | To core a tomato, cut a cone-shaped wedge from the stem end and discard.

2 | To peel, cut an X in the bottom end of the tomato and plunge into boiling water for 30 seconds, or until the skin loosens. Plunge into a bowl of ice water.

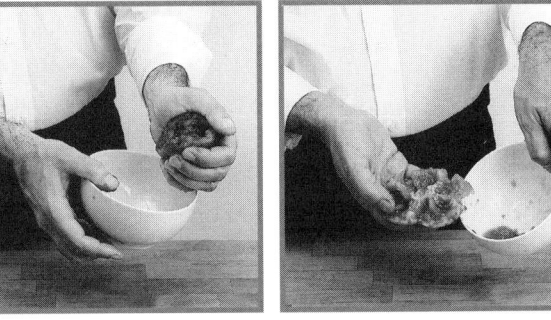

3 | The skin will easily slip off.

4 | Cut the tomato in half through its equator; squeeze and shake out the seeds.

5 | You'll be left with solid tomato flesh.

Tomato-Melon Gazpacho

WORK TIME	20 minutes, plus cooling time
PREP TIME	10 minutes
CAN BE	easily multiplied
MAKES	4 servings

I LIKE GAZPACHO, BUT THE ultimate minimalist version—take a few tomatoes, a red pepper, some onion, oil, and vinegar, and whiz it in a blender—doesn't cut it for me. I find this pulverized salad coarse, its raw flavor strong and altogether too lingering.

I have tried many variations to overcome the variations, most of them, in fact, traditional—roasting the vegetables first to reduce their rawness, using almonds, cucumbers, even grapes to lighten the flavor, letting the mixture sit to meld the flavors. None really did the trick for me.

Then a friend suggested that I abandon tradition entirely and combine tomatoes with another fruit of the season: cantaloupe. These, combined with basil and lemon—in place of vinegar—produce the mildest, most delicious, creamiest gazpacho I've ever tasted. With its bright orange color, it's also among the most beautiful.

4 tomatoes, about 1½ pounds	**10 basil leaves**
One 3-pound cantaloupe	**Salt and freshly ground black**
5 tablespoons olive oil	**pepper**
1½ cups of water _or_ 1 cup and	**Juice of a lemon**
½ cup ice cubes	

1 Core, peel and seed the tomatos (see page 37); cut the flesh into 1-inch chunks. Seed the melon and remove the flesh from the rind; cut into chunks. Place a tablespoon of olive oil in each of two 10- or 12-inch skillets and turn the heat under both to high (you can do this sequentially if you only have one skillet). Add the melon to one skillet and the tomatoes to the other and cook, stirring, until they become juicy, no longer than 2 minutes.

2 In a blender, puree the melon, tomato, water, and basil, along with some salt and pepper. Chill, then add lemon juice to taste and adjust seasoning. Serve.

Pasta

Linguine with Garlic and Oil
The Mother of All Pasta Sauces

WORK TIME	10 minutes
PREP TIME	20 minutes
CAN BE	easily multiplied
MAKES	4 servings

IF YOU HAVE A PANTRY, even a poorly stocked one, there is a good chance you can be eating this basic pasta dish in twenty minutes. If your pantry is well stocked—for example, if you have some olives, capers, chickpeas, dried chiles, and so on—you can be making any of several variations, also in less than half an hour. All of these dishes, which are based on olive oil and little more, make great late-night snacks, light dinners or lunches, and fine first courses.

This dish starts with olive oil—the best you can lay your hands on, since its flavor is the backbone of the preparation—and lightly colored garlic. The garlic is cooked slowly in the oil (it only takes ten minutes or so) with or without other flavorings or textures. That's the sauce. At its most basic, it is no more than oil, garlic, and salt. An easy variation adds a little chile and/or parsley. Next come anchovies, chickpeas, capers... almost anything you want. The overriding idea is: intense flavor derived from simplicity—true minimalism.

There's not much more to say. Keep the heat medium-low, because you want to avoid browning the garlic at all costs. (Well, not at all costs. If you brown the garlic, you'll have a different, more strongly flavored, kind of dish, but one that is still worth eating.)

| Salt | ½ cup extra virgin olive oil |
| 2 tablespoons minced garlic | 1 pound linguine, spaghetti, or other long, thin pasta |

1 Bring a large pot of water to a boil and salt it. Meanwhile, in a small skillet over medium-low heat, combine the garlic, oil, and a pinch of salt. Allow the garlic to simmer, shaking the pan occasionally, until it turns golden; do not allow it to become dark brown.

2 When the water boils, cook the pasta until it is tender but firm. When it is done, drain it, reserving a bit of the cooking water. Reheat the garlic and oil mixture briefly if necessary. Dress the pasta with the sauce, adding a little more oil or some of the cooking water if it seems dry.

With MINIMAL Effort

GARNISH with a good handful of chopped parsley. For 30 seconds' work, this makes an almost unbelievable difference.

ADD a couple of dried chiles to the oil along with the garlic. Discard before tossing with the pasta. Alternatively, sprinkle the pasta with crushed red pepper flakes or pass some at the table.

ADD 1 cup cooked, drained chickpeas to the garlic-oil mixture about a minute before tossing with the pasta.

ADD 1 to 2 tablespoons capers to the garlic-oil mixture about a minute before tossing with the pasta.

ADD ¼ to ½ cup minced pitted black olives (preferably imported) to the garlic-oil mixture about a minute before tossing with the pasta.

ADD a mixture of about 1 cup fresh herbs to the pasta when tossing it with the garlic-oil mixture. You probably will need more olive oil or some of the pasta-cooking water.

Pasta with Red Wine Sauce

WORK TIME	20 minutes
PREP TIME	30 minutes
MAKES	4 to 6 servings

FINISHING PASTA BY COOKING it for the final minute or two in stock is not all that uncommon. But simmering it in flavorful liquid for nearly all of its cooking time—almost as you would a risotto—is highly unusual. And when that liquid is red wine, the pasta is, well, unique.

This dish was created by Alessandro Giuntoli, a Tuscan who at the time of this writing is chef at Osteria del Circo, an Italian restaurant in midtown Manhattan. Sandro, as he's known, believes that it is "sort of" traditional, although he'd only heard of it in vague terms before going ahead and doing what he "thought was right."

The dish is in fact much better suited to home than restaurant cooking, because it must be prepared entirely at the last minute. It's simple enough, and there are aspects of it that are quite splendid: The pasta takes on a fruity acidity—smoothed by the last-minute addition of butter—and a beautiful mahogany glaze that's like nothing you've ever seen.

Sandro scents the dish with garlic, olive oil, and crushed red pepper, but the dominant flavor is unquestionably that of wine, so the kind you use is of some importance, although it need not be expensive. Try a decent Chianti Classico, a light wine from the Côtes-du-Rhône, or a good (red) Zinfandel. The other critical ingredient is the pasta: For the timing to be precise, Sandro insists that only spaghetti will work here. (Knowing that many Italians take pasta shapes far more seriously than I do, I experimented with a couple of other shapes, but in this instance I was forced to agree: Spaghetti produces the best texture.)

In any case, it's the technique that is most interesting. Sandro starts cooking the pasta and the sauce simultaneously, and as soon as the pasta begins to bend he drains and plunges it into the simmering red wine mixture. At first, the pasta absorbs a great deal of wine, but soon it is cooking in a small amount of bubbling liquid. As it cooks, he tastes, and the instant the pasta is done he stirs in the butter and serves it.

Salt and freshly ground black pepper	1 teaspoon red pepper flakes, or to taste
½ cup extra virgin olive oil	1 pound spaghetti
1 tablespoon minced garlic	1 bottle red wine, such as Chianti
	1 tablespoon butter

1 Bring a large pot of water to a boil and salt it. Place the oil, garlic, and red pepper in a large, deep skillet.

2 When the water boils, add the pasta; turn the heat under the skillet to high. Cook the pasta as usual, stirring. As soon as the garlic begins to brown, sprinkle it with salt and pepper to taste and add three-fourths of the bottle of wine (a little more than 2 cups); bring to a boil and maintain it there.

3 When the pasta begins to bend—after less than 5 minutes of cooking—drain it and add it to the wine mixture. Cook, stirring occasionally, adding wine a little at a time if the mixture threatens to dry out completely.

4 Taste the pasta frequently. When it is done—tender but with a little bite—stir in the butter and turn off the heat. When the butter glazes the pasta, serve it immediately.

With MINIMAL Effort

YOU can easily add another dimension to this dish by tossing in about a cup of chopped walnuts—pieces of about ¼ inch, no smaller—along with the butter.

A GARNISH of chopped parsley or basil will make the presentation more attractive and the flavor somewhat brighter.

Pasta with Sausage, without Tomatoes

WORK TIME	15 minutes
PREP TIME	30 minutes
CAN BE	easily multiplied
MAKES	4 to 6 servings

MOST OF US ASSOCIATE PASTA and sausage with a dense, heavy tomato sauce, the kind that is so Italian-American it is just about indigenous. Yet sausage can contribute to a relatively light, almost delicate pasta sauce, especially if it is used in small amounts.

In fact, sausage is the ideal meat to use in a quick pasta sauce, for a couple of reasons. First of all, it is preseasoned; different sausages contain different spices, but most "Italian" sausage contains at least salt, pepper, fennel seeds, and other seasonings in small amounts; hot sausage contains some form of red pepper as well. Secondly, if you buy bulk sausage, or sausage patties, or remove sausage from its casing, it cooks almost instantly.

These two facts mean that you can simmer sausage and extract its flavor into a light sauce within minutes. (You might say that this is another of those sauces that can be made in the time it takes to boil water for pasta, but in fact it's even faster than that, at least if your stove is as slow to bring water to a boil as mine is.) And because the sausage is intensely flavored, you don't need much; I use about a half-pound to make pasta for four people.

The technique is simple. It's easiest to start with bulk sausage or patties, because then there's no need to remove the meat from the casing. You crumble it into a little melted butter, which adds smoothness to the final sauce (you could even omit the butter if you prefer), add water or other liquid, and finish with grated Parmesan cheese.

Salt and freshly ground black pepper	½ cup water
1 tablespoon butter	1 pound ziti or other cut pasta
½ pound sweet or hot Italian sausage, removed from the casing if necessary	½ cup or more freshly grated Parmesan cheese

1 Bring a large pot of water to a boil for the pasta and salt it.

2 Place the butter in a medium skillet over medium-low heat. As it melts, crumble the sausage meat into it, making the bits quite small, ½ inch or less in size. Add the water and adjust the heat so that the mixture simmers gently.

3 Cook the pasta until it is tender but not at all mushy. Reserve about ½ cup of the pasta-cooking water.

4 Drain the pasta and dress with the sauce, adding some of the reserved cooking liquid if necessary. Taste and add salt and pepper as necessary. Toss with the Parmesan and serve.

With MINIMAL Effort

White Pasta with Sausage and Onions: Before adding the sausage, gently cook about a cup of minced onion in the butter until it is translucent. Proceed as above.

Red Pasta with Sausage: Still far lighter than the pasta with sausage you're expecting. Cut up, seed, and drain 5 to 6 plum tomatoes; they may be fresh or canned. Add them to the sauce along with the sausage.

ADD about a teaspoon of minced garlic, or a couple of tablespoons of minced shallots, to the butter as it melts.

TOSS in a handful of chopped parsley or basil at the last moment; or add about a teaspoon of fresh thyme leaves or minced fresh sage along with the sausage.

USE red wine as the cooking liquid; its astringency offsets the sweet richness of butter and meat beautifully.

Pasta with Meaty Bones

WORK TIME	20 minutes
PREP TIME	1 hour or more
CAN BE	prepared in advance (sauce only); frozen (sauce only); easily multiplied
MAKES	4 to 6 servings

A BASIC TOMATO SAUCE is (or at least should be) a part of every cook's repertoire, since it's among the most fundamental dressings for pasta. Typically, you make this sauce by coloring a little garlic or onion in oil, then adding crushed tomatoes—this is one instance where canned are as suitable as fresh—and cooking them over medium-high heat. When the mixture becomes "saucy," about twenty minutes later, it's done.

The variations on this theme are nearly infinite. One of my favorites, which requires considerably more time but almost no extra effort, adds the wonderful depth of flavor, silken texture, and satisfying chewiness of slow-cooked meat. Southern Italian in origin, it begins with bony meat (or meaty bones) and requires lengthy simmering. Otherwise, it's little different from basic tomato sauce.

You can use almost any meat you like here, but it's most wonderful with a single piece of meaty veal shank, the cut you'd use for osso buco. Whatever you use, the idea remains constant: Meat is a supporting player, not the star, so an eight- to twelve-ounce piece of veal shank provides enough meat, marrow, and gelatin to create a luxuriously rich sauce, sprinkled with chewy bits. Just cook until the meat falls off the bone, then chop it and return it to the sauce along with any marrow.

Simple as this is, there are a couple of fine points: For best flavor, brown the meat well before adding the tomatoes. And use a narrow pot, because you don't want the sauce to become too thick during the relatively long cooking period; it's worth partially covering the pot as well.

Finally, this sauce is rich enough without grated cheese. A better garnish is a large handful of coarsely chopped parsley or basil. Either freshens the sauce while adding color and flavor.

2 tablespoons olive oil	Salt and freshly ground black pepper
2 small dried hot red chiles, optional	One 28-ounce can whole plum tomatoes, with juice
1 piece meaty veal shank, ½ to 1 pound	1 pound ziti, penne, or other cut pasta
3 garlic cloves, peeled and roughly chopped	½ cup or more roughly chopped parsley or basil

1 Place the olive oil in a saucepan over medium heat. After a minute, add the optional chiles and cook for about 30 seconds. Add the veal shank and raise the heat to medium-high; cook, turning as necessary, until the meat is nicely browned, 10 minutes or more. When the meat is just about done, add the garlic and salt and pepper to taste.

2 When the garlic has softened a bit, crush the tomatoes and add them along with their juice. Turn the heat to medium-low to maintain a steady simmer. If you are using a broad pot, cover it partially. Cook, stirring occasionally, until the meat is tender and just about falling off the bone, at least 1 hour.

3 Bring a large pot of water to a boil and salt it. Cook the pasta until it is tender but firm. Remove the veal shank, scoop out any marrow, chop the meat coarsely, and return the meat to the sauce (discard the bone). Remove and discard the chiles.

4 Drain and sauce the pasta; sprinkle it with the herb, toss, and serve.

With MINIMAL Effort

Pasta with Ribs: This is one of the best ways to use a small amount of meat in a highly satisfying way. Substitute 6 to 8 meaty spareribs for the veal shank (you can even use a couple more). The cooking time may be a little shorter. Serve the pasta topped with sauce along with a couple of ribs on the side.

CARROTS make a nice addition to this sauce; add about a cup, cut into chunks, along with the tomatoes. Some chopped onion won't do any harm, either.

A BIT of smoked meat is really great in place of the fresh meat. Use a ham hock or a big piece of bacon.

YOU can use almost any bony meat you want here. Some of the best are: beef shin (it's the same cut as veal shank); oxtail, cut into sections; fresh ham hock; short ribs; veal ribs; or lamb shank.

Ziti with Butter, Sage, and Parmesan
Using Pasta Cooking Water in Sauces

WORK TIME	20 minutes
PREP TIME	30 minutes
CAN BE	easily multiplied
MAKES	4 to 6 servings

THE FLOUR-ENRICHED WATER IN which pasta has cooked is never going to be an essential component of fine cooking, and it seldom appears in recipes. Yet from its origins as a cost-free, effortless substitute for stock, olive oil, butter, cream, or other occasionally scarce or even precious ingredients, pasta-cooking water has become a convenient and zero-calorie addition to simple sauces.

As Americans become increasingly Italian in our cooking and eating of pasta—as we learn to improvise, make quick sauces, and use sauce as a complementary rather than dominating partner—water will rightly play a role. And the water need not come only from cooking pasta; if you're making a sauce with vegetables such as broccoli or asparagus, that strongly flavored cooking liquid is another natural choice for the sauce base.

Even water that gains the minimal flavor of pasta has attributes. When you compare a lightly creamy sauce like the one in this recipe to the highly flavorful and ever-popular Alfredo sauce of butter, cream, eggs, and cheese, the latter seems relatively heavy. Substituting water for much of the butter and all of the cream and eggs produces a sauce with a perfect balance of weight and flavor. The water lends a moist quality, not unlike that produced by tomatoes, as opposed to the slickness contributed by straight fat.

Water can form a part of vegetable- or even meat-based sauces, but it is ideal in those based on butter. Like many simple dressings, this one takes less time to prepare than the pasta itself. It also cuts back on butter enough to salve the guilty conscience, but not so much that the flavor entirely disappears. And finally, it provides an excuse to load up on Parmesan cheese, which not only adds its distinctive sharpness, but serves as a thickener.

1 pound ziti, penne, or other cut pasta	About 1 cup freshly grated Parmigiano-Reggiano
2 tablespoons butter	Salt and freshly ground black pepper
30 fresh sage leaves	

1 Bring a large pot of water to a boil and salt it. Cook the pasta until it is tender, but a little short of the point at which you want to eat it.

2 Meanwhile, place the butter in a skillet or saucepan large enough to hold the cooked pasta; turn the heat to medium and add the sage. Cook until the butter turns nut-brown and the sage shrivels, then turn the heat down to a minimum.

3 When the pasta is just about done, scoop out a cupful of the cooking water. Drain the pasta, immediately add it to the butter-sage mixture, and raise the heat to medium. Add ½ cup of the water and stir; the mixture will be loose and a little soupy. Cook for about 30 seconds, or until some of the water is absorbed and the pasta is perfectly done.

4 Stir in the cheese; the sauce will become creamy. Thin it with a little more water if necessary, season liberally with pepper and salt to taste, and serve immediately, passing more cheese at the table if you like.

With MINIMAL Effort

FRESH, fragrant sage is my herb of choice here, but substitutions abound. Try parsley, thyme, chervil, or other green herbs in its place.

COOK ¼ to ½ cup minced shallots or onions in the butter, just until they're translucent.

TOAST ½ cup bread crumbs or chopped nuts in the butter, just until they're lightly browned.

SUBSTITUTE extra virgin olive oil for some or all of the butter. The result will be good if not as creamy.

Linguine with Spinach
One-Pot Pasta and Greens

WORK TIME	15 minutes
PREP TIME	25 minutes
MAKES	4 to 6 servings

NOT LONG AGO, IT seemed that most cooks believed that the best pasta was topped with the most complex sauce imaginable. This led to improbable combinations such as penne with artichoke hearts, shrimp, goat cheese, pine nuts, sun-dried tomatoes, basil, cream, and Parmesan, and other dishes that not only betrayed tradition but were inedible.

The true nature of pasta is simplicity. I've long made a vegetable sauce by poaching greens such as spinach in the pasta water, then removing them and adding the pasta, a neat trick. But my friend Jack Bishop, author of *Vegetarian Italian Cooking,* mentioned that he'd gone one step further, cooking the greens right in with the pasta and adding seasonings at the last minute.

The method relies on the fact that there is a range of doneness between the moment when the pasta's last traces of chalkiness disappear and it begins to become mushy, and this range lasts for two or three minutes. If, just before the pasta is done, you add the greens, whose tough stems have been removed, greens and pasta will finish cooking at the same time.

While the pasta cooks, mix the seasonings in a warm bowl. When Jack first showed me this technique, we made this recipe, which contains olive oil, garlic, and hot peppers. The sauce is finished by the spinach and the moisture retained by it and the pasta itself. But this is only one of many possibilities, as I've discovered since.

When making this dish and others like it, you must adhere to the often ignored canon of allowing at least a gallon of water per pound of pasta, because you need a pot large enough to accommodate the greens, and because they cannot be allowed to slow down the cooking too much. And although there is no "correct" moment to add the vegetable, I suggest that you add tender greens such as spinach when the pasta is just about done, since the additional cooking time is only going to be another thirty seconds or so. Add tougher greens, such as kale or collards—or vegetables like broccoli florets—a minute or two before you judge the pasta to be finished, so that the greens have enough time to become tender.

Salt and freshly ground black pepper	1 pound linguine or other long pasta
1 medium garlic clove	1 pound spinach, washed, tough stems removed, roughly chopped
½ teaspoon red pepper flakes, or to taste, optional	
¼ cup plus 1 tablespoon extra virgin olive oil	

1 Bring a large pot of water to a boil and salt it. Meanwhile, mince the garlic as finely as possible and combine it in the bottom of a warm bowl with the red pepper and olive oil.

2 Add the pasta to the pot and cook until it is nearly done (test it for doneness by tasting). Plunge the spinach into the water and cook until it wilts, less than a minute. Drain quickly, allowing some water to cling to the pasta, and toss in the bowl with the garlic and olive oil mixture. Season with salt and pepper to taste and serve.

With MINIMAL Effort

One-Pot Pasta and Greens, Asian Style: Use Asian wheat noodles, and substitute ¼ cup peanut oil plus 1 tablespoon sesame oil for the olive oil. Add 1 tablespoon soy sauce to the hot pepper and garlic; garnish with 2 tablespoons lightly toasted sesame seeds.

TOSS the pasta with freshly grated Parmesan or pecorino cheese to taste.

ADD any of the following to the garlic-pepper-oil mixture, singly or in combination: about 15 kalamata or other olives, pitted and roughly chopped; about ¼ cup chopped sun-dried tomatoes packed in oil; about 2 tablespoons drained capers; about ½ cup toasted bread crumbs; about ¼ cup minced prosciutto or other dry-cured ham.

USE other greens; as long as they will cook quickly, they'll be fine. Try the chopped leaves of kale, collards, Swiss chard, turnip or mustard greens, or Chinese cabbage, or bite-sized florets of broccoli or cauliflower.

Spaghetti with Zucchini
Carbonara Without the Bacon

WORK TIME	20 minutes
PREP TIME	30 minutes
CAN BE	easily multiplied
MAKES	4 to 6 servings

THE INCREASING TENDENCY toward international food distribution has reduced the excitement associated with the first seasonal appearance of each individual vegetable and fruit. This has its advantages and disadvantages. No fruit or vegetable is as good as those from local sources, grown in season, but it's nice to have fresh vegetables year-round.

The dish described here—which has zucchini as its focus—is simply amazing when made in midsummer with tender, crisp squash, but it isn't half-bad even when made in midwinter with a limp vegetable that's traveled halfway around the world to get to your table.

Either way, it is an unusual use for zucchini, which is used to substitute for meat in a kind of vegetarian spaghetti carbonara. Carbonara—named for the Italian charcoal producers who worked for weeks on end in the woods and depended on long-keeping ingredients for cooking—was, for many Americans, among the first pasta dishes we ate that was not swimming in tomato sauce. Tossed with egg, crisp bacon or pancetta, and loads of Parmesan cheese, it was a revelation.

Made with zucchini, obviously, the dish becomes a little less fat-laden. But because the backbone of the sauce remains eggs and Parmesan, it is still quite rich—and quite delicious.

This is one of those pasta sauces that can be put together in just about the time it takes to bring a gallon of water to a boil. And although there is almost no technique involved, there are a few points worth making:

Be sure to cook the zucchini long enough to brown it a bit, which will enhance its flavor.

The eggs will cook fully from the heat of the pasta. If this makes you at all nervous, however, do the final tossing of eggs, cheese, and pasta in the cooking pot, over the lowest flame possible.

Use top-quality hard cheese here, since its flavor will dominate. Genuine Parmigiano-Reggiano is best, but a good hard pecorino is nice here, too.

Mint is the herb of choice, its distinctively fresh taste is the most unusual aspect of this preparation. But you can certainly substitute basil or parsley.

Salt and freshly ground black pepper	2 eggs
3 tablespoons olive oil	1 cup freshly grated Parmesan cheese
3 or 4 small zucchini (about 1 pound), washed, trimmed, and cut into slices ⅛ to ¼ inch thick	1 pound spaghetti, linguine, or other long pasta
	½ cup roughly chopped mint, parsley, or basil

1 Put a large pot of water to boil over high heat and salt it. Place the olive oil in a 10- or 12-inch skillet over medium-high heat. A minute later, add the zucchini; cook, stirring only occasionally, until very tender and lightly browned, 10 to 15 minutes. Season with a little salt and a lot of pepper.

2 Meanwhile, beat the eggs and ½ cup of the Parmesan together. Add the pasta to the boiling water and cook until it is tender but firm. When it is done, drain it and combine it immediately with the egg-cheese mixture, tossing until the egg appears cooked. Taste and add more salt and pepper if necessary.

3 Toss in the herb and serve immediately, passing the remaining Parmesan at the table.

With MINIMAL Effort

Spaghetti Carbonara: The classic. Substitute ½ to 1 cup chopped bacon (preferably from a slab) or pancetta for the zucchini. When crisp, remove with a slotted spoon and drain on paper towels. It's traditional, but not essential, to use some of the cooking fat in the sauce. Garnish with parsley (or not at all).

Fettuccine Alfredo: Omit the zucchini. Just toss the pasta (preferably fettuccine) with eggs, cheese, and enough heavy cream to bind the sauce. Best served as a small first course for 6 to 8.

Spaghetti with Fresh Tomato Sauce

WORK TIME	20 minutes
PREP TIME	20 minutes
CAN BE	easily multiplied
MAKES	4 to 6 servings

IF YOU'RE THE TYPE of person who believes that timing is everything, then this is the dish for you. You can only make it for part of the year, and you must seize the right moment to stop cooking the sauce—which happens to be a mere ten minutes or so after you begin.

This is the dish I immediately produce when good plum tomatoes make their first appearance. It has a thick creaminess that you can never duplicate with canned tomatoes, no matter how good they are. So the season is fairly short—where I live, just two or at the most three months a year.

The cooking itself is easy enough, but there is an ideal instant for serving this sauce: When the tomatoes soften and all of their juices are in the skillet, the sauce suddenly begins to thicken. At that moment, it is at its peak; another minute or two later, many of the juices have evaporated and, although the essence of the sauce is equally intense, it doesn't coat the pasta as well. If this happens, just add a little fresh olive oil or butter to the finished dish.

Fresh tomatoes should always be cored before using them; see page 37 for a description. Peeling is entirely optional here—if you object to little bits of skin in your sauce, it's worth the effort. (You can also fish out the skin as the sauce simmers; it automatically separates from the flesh.)

3 tablespoons butter or olive oil	½ cup freshly grated Parmigiano-Reggiano
1½ to 2 pounds fresh tomatoes (preferably plum), cored and roughly chopped	Salt and freshly ground black pepper
1 pound spaghetti, linguine, or other long pasta	

1 Bring a large pot of water to a boil and salt it. Place the butter or oil in an 8- or 10-inch skillet and turn the heat to medium. When the butter melts or the oil is hot, add the tomatoes and turn the heat to high.

2 Cook, stirring occasionally, until the tomatoes begin to juice up, then turn the heat to low and cook, stirring occasionally, until the sauce thickens.

3 Cook the pasta until it is tender but firm. Drain and toss with the tomatoes and cheese. Season with salt and pepper to taste, toss again, and serve immediately.

With MINIMAL Effort

ADD about a teaspoon of minced garlic to the butter or oil, just before the tomatoes. Garnish with minced parsley instead of Parmesan.

ADD about a tablespoon of minced shallot to the butter or oil.

COOK the tomatoes with a couple of branches of basil, remove them before serving, and stir about ½ cup or more of roughly chopped basil leaves into the pasta.

TOSS the pasta with about a cup of cubed (½ inch or less) mozzarella, preferably fresh.

ADD crushed red pepper flakes to taste along with the tomatoes.

Ziti with Chestnuts
and Mushroooms

Celebrating Fall

WORK TIME	30 minutes
PREP TIME	30 minutes
CAN BE	easily multiplied
MAKES	4 to 6 servings

WHEN CHESTNUTS WERE abundant, before the early-century blight that virtually wiped them out, most home cooks not only knew how to cook them but looked forward to the yearly windfall. When the fruit of a chestnut tree ripens, it covers the ground, and the chestnuts are there for the taking.

Of course whether you pick chestnuts or buy them, they are a pain in the neck (the fingers, actually) to peel. And it's likely that this work is what keeps chestnuts from being popular with home cooks these days. Because although they are all imported, chestnuts are neither rare nor especially expensive, usually under three dollars a pound.

The good news is that their complex, fragrant flavor is so powerfully distinctive that just a few chestnuts can have an enormous impact on a dish. Similarly, their texture is uniquely dense; again, a small amount is all that's needed to make its presence felt. So although it may take thirty seconds to a minute to process a single chestnut, if you only need a dozen or so for a dish the work amounts to about ten minutes. And in a creation like the one here, the time is well worth the effort.

Chestnuts and dried mushrooms have a wonderful affinity for one another. Their unusual flavors and textures seem distantly related; they are both meaty and complex, chewy but neither tough nor crunchy. With shallots and plenty of black pepper for bite, the combination makes a great pasta sauce.

There are many ways to peel chestnuts, which like most nuts have a hard outer shell and a soft inner skin. Removing them both is a three-step process. First, use a paring knife—a curved one with a sharp point makes this quick and easy—to cut a ring around the equator of each nut (although most cookbooks instruct you to cut an x on the side of the nut, in my experience that's not as effective).

Plunge the nuts into boiling water to cover for about three minutes, then turn off the heat, leaving the chestnuts in the water. Remove two or three at a time and, using the knife and your fingers, peel off both shell and skin; use a towel to protect your hands from the heat if necessary. If you're doing a large batch—say, twenty or more—you'll notice that as the water cools the skins become more difficult to remove. Bring the pot back to a boil and they'll begin to slip off again.

Although the exact count of chestnuts for this dish is not critical, I begin with fifteen, because there are usually a couple of rotten ones, or some whose inner skin refuses to come off. These must be discarded.

15 chestnuts

1 ounce dried mushrooms—
    porcini, shiitake, black trum-
    pets, morels, or an assortment

3 tablespoons butter or extra
    virgin olive oil

½ cup peeled and sliced
    shallots

Salt and freshly ground black
    pepper

1 pound ziti or other cut pasta

1 See photographs on the next page for cutting a ring around each chestnut. Place them in boiling water to cover and cook for 3 minutes. Remove them from the water, a few at a time, and peel while still hot. Meanwhile, soak the mushrooms in about 1½ cups very hot water.

2 Bring a large pot of water to a boil and salt it. Place half the butter or oil in a skillet, turn the heat to medium-high and, a minute later, add the shallots. Sprinkle lightly with salt to taste and cook, stirring, until softened, 3 to 5 minutes. Chop the chestnuts into ½- to ¼-inch chunks, then measure about 1 cup. Add them to the skillet, along with a little more salt.

3 Cook, stirring occasionally, until the chestnuts deepen in color, about 5 minutes. Remove the mushrooms from their soaking liquid; reserve and strain the liquid. Chop the mushrooms and add them to the skillet; cook, stirring, for a minute or two, then add the strained mushroom-soaking liquid. Turn the heat to low and season to taste with salt and lots of black pepper.

4 Cook the pasta until tender but not mushy. If the sauce is too thick, add a little of the pasta-cooking water to it when the pasta is nearly done. Stir in the remaining butter or oil, then drain the pasta and dress with the sauce. Serve immediately.

1 | Cut an O around the center of each chestnut.

2 | Boil for 3 minutes, then, while they're still hot, slip off the outer shell and inner peel.

With MINIMAL Effort

Ziti with Chestnuts and Fresh Mushrooms: You'll need about 8 ounces fresh mushrooms, trimmed and chopped (again, an assortment is best); 1 to 1½ cups chicken or other stock; and a few more minutes. Steps 1 and 2 remain the same; in Step 3, add the mushrooms before the chestnuts, and cook, stirring, until they become tender, about 5 minutes; then add the chestnuts and cook, stirring, another 5 minutes. Add 1 cup of the chicken stock and cook until the chestnuts are tender and the mixture "saucy," about 10 minutes, adding a little more stock if necessary.

COMBINE fresh and reconstituted dried mushrooms—first cook the fresh until soft, then add the dried. Proceed as in the variation above.

ADD a few sprigs of fresh thyme along with the shallots. Remove before serving, and sprinkle fresh thyme leaves as a garnish.

ADD diced (¼ inch or less) zucchini, peeled, seeded, and diced tomato, or red bell pepper—no more than a cup total—along with the chestnuts.

Pasta with Potatoes

WORK TIME	30 minutes
PREP TIME	60 minutes
CAN BE	prepared in advance; frozen; easily multiplied
MAKES	8 or more servings

PASTA WITH POTATOES IS about as unlikely a dish as I've ever come across, a soupy combination containing little more than the two main ingredients and canned tomatoes. Not only does the thought of it tweak the mind—doesn't this sound something like a bread sandwich?—but it counters a number of the conventions that have been drummed into our collective consciousness.

Chief among these is that the dish is at its best when the pasta is cooked until it is fat, juice-laden, and quite soft. Here, there is no need to seize the ideal moment at which the pasta is al dente; in fact you cook the pasta somewhat past that point, and it is even acceptable for it to sit for a while. Nor need you worry about the "correct" pasta shape; pasta with potatoes requires several different shapes, in varying quantities, preferably broken. Finally, not only may you serve pasta with potatoes as a leftover, it's just as good after sitting for a day.

Strange as it sounds, this heretical concoction is a traditional Neapolitan gem according to my friend Andrea Graziosi, who taught me the recipe. "It began, I suppose, as a simple way to use up the bits and pieces of dried pasta that accumulated during the week," says Andrea, who grew up in Naples and lives in Rome. "Now it's so popular that you can buy bags of mixed pasta all over Italy."

Few of us will need to make a special trip to find bits and pieces of pasta, since most pasta lovers have a few open boxes in their cabinets. (It's equally true that the dish is just as good, if somewhat less enchanting, if made with only one shape of pasta.) Another of the many assets of pasta with potatoes is that it's an entirely from-the-pantry dish; the chances are good you can produce it right now, without shopping at all. It's a warming, homey creation, great in cold weather, and suitable for informal entertaining. Just don't plan to impress anyone with your presentation; this is not gorgeous.

It's worth mentioning that pasta with potatoes is very kid-friendly, with much of the appeal of alphabet soup or even Chef Boyardee (although in my experience few children would ever rank a home-cooked dish as highly as canned pasta). For that reason, you might consider cooking it without chiles and passing crushed red pepper at the table, so adults can add some assertiveness to this somewhat bland dish while kids eat it as is.

There are no tricks involved, but be careful not to cook the dish too dry. If, at the last minute, the pasta has absorbed nearly all the liquid, stir in another cup or so of water and cook for a minute or two longer.

2 tablespoons olive oil	One 28-ounce can whole plum
About ½ cup minced pancetta or	tomatoes, not drained
bacon, optional	About 1½ pounds assorted
3 to 4 potatoes, (about 1½	leftover dried pasta
pounds), peeled and cut into	Salt and freshly ground black
bite-sized chunks	pepper
1 tablespoon chopped garlic	Several cups of water, kept at a
3 to 4 small dried hot red chiles	simmer in a pot or kettle
(or about 1 teaspoon crushed	
red pepper flakes), or to taste	

1 Place the olive oil in a large saucepan and turn the heat to medium. If you're using pancetta or bacon, add it to the oil and cook, stirring occasionally, until it becomes slightly crisp, about 10 minutes. (If you are omitting the meat, proceed to the next step.)

2 Add the potatoes, garlic, and chiles, and raise the heat to medium-high. Cook, stirring occasionally, until the potatoes begin to brown all over, about 10 minutes.

3 Add the tomatoes and their juice, along with 2 cups water, and bring to a boil. Turn the heat down to medium-low and cook, uncovered, stirring occasionally to break up the tomatoes and prevent sticking.

4 While the potatoes are cooking, break long pasta, such as spaghetti, into several lengths; place cut pasta, such as ziti, in a bag and smack it into pieces with the back of a pot or a hammer. After the potatoes have simmered for about 10 minutes, add the pasta and plenty of salt and pepper to the pot. Simmer, stirring and adding water as necessary—the mixture should remain thick and stewy, never dry.

5 When the potatoes and pasta are both quite tender—this will take 20 minutes or more—the dish is done. (It may be covered and refrigerated for a day or two, or put in a closed container and frozen for several weeks;

it's likely that you will need to add more liquid when you reheat it.) Check the seasoning and add some crushed red pepper flakes, black pepper, and/or salt if needed. Serve hot, in bowls.

With MINIMAL Effort

Pasta and Potato Soup: This dish is a stew, and like most stews it can readily be converted to soup: Add 2 to 4 cups water (or, even better, chicken stock) in Step 5. Heat and serve with a spoon.

AFTER the potatoes begin to brown, add 1 to 2 cups chopped onions and cook, stirring, until they soften before proceeding.

ADD small bits of cooked or raw meat—up to 2 cups—along with the potatoes.

ADD chunks of carrots and/or celery—up to 2 cups—along with the potatoes.

COOK a few stems of basil in the stew. Remove before serving, then garnish with plenty of chopped fresh basil.

SERVE with freshly grated pecorino or Parmesan cheese.

Penne with Butternut Squash

WORK TIME	30 minutes
PREP TIME	30 minutes
CAN BE	prepared in advance (sauce only); easily multiplied
MAKES	4 to 6 servings

GO TO CENTRAL OR NORTHERN Italy in autumn and you're sure to be offered tortelli or other pasta filled with zucca, a pumpkinlike vegetable whose flesh, like that of butternut or acorn squash, is dense, orange, and somewhat sweet. To make a pasta filling, zucca is cooked and pureed with nutmeg, eggs, and Parmesan cheese.

The resulting tortelli, normally bathed in butter and grated Parmesan, are unforgettably delicious. The rub is that making them is a serious project, beginning with making and rolling out fresh pasta dough and ending with cutting, stuffing, and sealing the individual tortelli.

Because preparing the stuffing is simplicity itself, however, the flavor and essential nature of pasta with zucca can be captured in a thirty-minute preparation that is admittedly a compromise, but a very good one. In this version, prepare the zucca—butternut squash is a near-perfect substitute—and thin it slightly so that the stuffing becomes a sauce. The result is inside out, and not as attractive as tortelli, but the flavor and texture are right there.

Pasta with butternut squash is not only interesting but practical. First off, winter squashes are incredibly cheap (usually less than fifty cents a pound, and often far less), nearly ubiquitous, and easy to store. Yet they are not particularly versatile (this is especially true of the nearly impossible-to-peel acorn squash). They can be baked, or pureed as a side dish or soup (page 28), but there isn't much beyond that. This dish provides another way to work them into the fall repertoire.

In addition, this recipe features nutmeg, a highly flavorful, generally enjoyed spice that doesn't make its way into savory foods often enough. The combination of squash and nutmeg is slightly pumpkin pie–like, which makes for a surprising pasta, but one that even most kids seem to enjoy.

Note that some butternut squash is sweeter than others, and there's no way to predict this by appearance. Since this sauce relies on sweetness for its character, if the squash seems a little bland as it cooks, add about a teaspoon of sugar. It will brighten the flavor considerably.

1 pound peeled and seeded
  butternut squash (start with a
  whole squash weighing about
  1½ pounds)
2 tablespoons butter or olive oil
Salt and freshly ground black
  pepper

1 pound penne or other cut pasta
⅛ teaspoon freshly grated
  nutmeg, or to taste
1 teaspoon sugar, optional
½ cup freshly grated Parmesan
  cheese

1 Cut the squash into chunks and place it in a food processor. Pulse the machine on and off until the squash appears grated. Alternatively, grate or chop the squash by hand. Set a large pot of salted water to boil for the pasta.

2 Place a large skillet over medium heat and add the butter or oil. A minute later, add the squash, salt and pepper to taste, and about ½ cup water. Cook over medium heat, stirring occasionally. Add water, about ¼ cup at a time, as the mixture dries out, but be careful not to make it soupy. When the squash begins to disintegrate, after about 10 or 15 minutes, begin cooking the pasta. While it cooks, season the squash with the nutmeg, sugar if necessary, and additional salt and pepper if needed.

3 When the pasta is tender, scoop out about ½ cup of the cooking liquid and reserve it, then drain the pasta. Toss the pasta in the skillet with the squash, adding the reserved pasta-cooking water if the mixture seems dry. Taste and add more of any seasonings you like, then toss with the Parmesan and serve.

With MINIMAL Effort

SUBSTITUTE 1 teaspoon minced garlic or 2 tablespoons minced shallot or onion for the nutmeg.

GARNISH with a handful of chopped fresh herbs—parsley is a natural, but basil or chervil would also be good. Or add a few leaves of minced sage in Step 2 (omit the nutmeg).

FINISH the dish with ½ cup of sweet cream, sour cream, or crème fraîche in place of the pasta-cooking water.

COOK about ½ pound of crumbled ground meat (beef, pork, chicken, or turkey) along with the squash.

Rice Noodles with Basil

WORK TIME	15 minutes
PREP TIME	40 minutes
CAN BE	easily multiplied
MAKES	4 servings

WHEREAS EUROPEAN COOKS RELY almost exclusively on wheat noodles, Asians use wheat and rice noodles with equal frequency—but not interchangeably. In fact, rice noodles look different, require different handling, and taste different than wheat pasta.

Three types of rice noodles, from left: thick rice stick, thin rice stick, and vermicelli.

For one thing, they're stark white. For another, they're best when soaked for a few minutes in hot water, then boiled just until their raw flavor disappears. (In fact, in a stir-fry like this one, you can get away with simply soaking the noodles, but I believe there's a little improvement in boiling the noodles for 30 seconds or so after soaking.) Finally, they're never really what you call al dente, but rather quite soft.

You might see fresh rice noodles from time to time, but for the most part they are sold dried, like most pasta, only in far fewer shapes, ranging from very thin to linguinelike to fettuccinelike; that's about it. The superthin ones (usually called vermicelli) are best for soups. The two thicker varieties, usually called rice sticks, are best for stir-fries like this one.

None of the other ingredients is especially unusual. Thai nam pla (called *nuoc mam* in Vietnamese and roughly translated as fish sauce) is used in place of salt or soy sauce in much of Southeast Asia—it's smelly, very salty, and delicious.

Substitute soy sauce if you like. Thai basil, which looks different from regular basil, can be found in many Asian markets; it's fabulously fragrant.

12 ounces rice sticks (see headnote)	Salt and freshly ground black pepper
2 tablespoons peanut or vegetable oil	2 tablespoons nam pla (fish sauce) or soy sauce, or to taste
1 tablespoon minced garlic	1 tablespoon lime juice, or to taste
1 teaspoon minced fresh hot chiles or crushed red pepper flakes, or to taste	½ cup roughly chopped Thai or other basil or mint
1 teaspoon sugar	

1 Soak the rice noodles in hot water to cover for 15 to 30 minutes, changing the water once or twice if possible. (If you change the water a couple of times the noodles will soften faster.) Meanwhile, bring a pot of water to a boil. When the noodles are soft, drain them, then immerse them in the boiling water for about 30 seconds. Drain and rinse in cold water.

2 Heat the oil in a deep skillet (preferably nonstick) over medium-high heat. Add the garlic and chiles and cook for about 30 seconds, stirring. Raise the heat to high, then add the noodles and sugar and toss to blend. Season with salt and pepper to taste.

3 When the noodles are hot, add the nam pla and lime juice. Taste and adjust seasoning as necessary, then stir in the basil or mint and serve.

With MINIMAL Effort

Pad Thai: It's not a far cry from this dish to the ever-popular pad Thai, which takes a little more effort, but not much. In Step 2, add about 1 cup medium shrimp, peeled; stir for a minute, then add 2 lightly beaten eggs. Let set for a few seconds, then scramble the eggs. Add the noodles, sugar, salt, pepper, nam pla, and lime juice as above. Garnish with about a cup of mung bean sprouts, ½ cup chopped salted peanuts, and basil (or cilantro). Serve with lime quarters.

BEFORE adding the garlic, quickly stir-fry about 1 cup of ground or chopped pork, beef, chicken, or turkey until the color is gone. Proceed as above.

BEFORE adding the garlic, stir-fry 1 to 2 cups of tender shredded vegetables, such as leeks, cabbage, Chinese cabbage (like bok choy), celery, bean sprouts, sliced mushrooms, or a combination. Proceed as above.

ADD about a tablespoon of curry powder to the oil along with the garlic. Add more to taste if necessary. Proceed as above.

Parmesan Cups with Orzo Risotto

WORK TIME	15 minutes
PREP TIME	30 minutes
CAN BE	easily multiplied
MAKES	4 servings

I'VE LONG THOUGHT THAT the flexibility of real Parmesan—the kind that comes from Italy, not the green cardboard can—made it the single cheese whose presence in my refrigerator is essential. Several times a week I grate it over pasta, into soup, or onto bread, and it has become a near-requisite ingredient for most egg dishes. It's nibbled at daily, if not by the cook then by those passing through the kitchen. And, years ago, I learned that even the rind (since it is no more than super-dry cheese, it's perfectly edible) can be enjoyable: Cut into small cubes and integrated into a risotto or soup, it becomes delicious morsels of chewy saltiness.

A couple of years ago, on a trip to central Italy—where true Parmigiano-Reggiano is made—I learned one more use for the cheese. A cook in a trattoria was taking handfuls of the grated stuff, sprinkling them in a skillet, and forming melted cheese pancakes. While they were still warm, he draped them over the back of a cup, to form crisp, edible, single-ingredient containers. He filled these with a mixture of zucchini, eggplant, and tomatoes, and sent them out as a first course.

I found the idea intriguing, but not all that easy to duplicate at home, where my skillet seemed always too hot or too cool, the pancakes too thick or too thin. But when I took the task seriously and set about figuring out the most reliable way to produce these Parmesan cups, it turned out to be fairly straightforward. Thanks to the miracle of the nonstick surface, just place four rounds of grated cheese on a baking sheet and, five minutes later, they're done.

There are a couple of tricks to this, both easily mastered. First of all, you must be careful not to grate the cheese too finely; you don't want the same powdery consistency you might prefer on pasta. One of the larger holes of a box grater works well, and so does the steel blade of the food processor, which produces small, even pellets of cheese.

Baking the cheese disks doesn't present much of a problem, and it's easy enough to tell when they're done because the edges begin to brown.

But removing them from the baking sheet can be tricky: Make sure to allow the rounds to cool slightly so that they can firm up a bit—thirty to sixty seconds is right for me, but if your baking sheet retains more heat it might take a little longer—and then use the thinnest spatula you have to gently lift them off the baking sheet. Drape the soft mass over a narrow glass, and shape gently; the cups will be ready to fill in a few minutes. Although they're best when fresh, they will retain both shape and flavor for a couple of hours.

2 cups good chicken or other stock

1 cup orzo (rice-shaped pasta)

1 cup freshly grated Parmesan cheese (about ¼ pound)

Salt and freshly ground black pepper

½ cup minced parsley leaves

1 Preheat the oven to 350° F.

2 Bring the stock to a boil in a 6- to 8-cup saucepan; stir in the orzo, cover, and turn the heat to medium-low. Set a timer for 15 minutes.

3 Use a ¼-cup measure to make 4 rounds of Parmesan on a nonstick baking sheet. Smooth the rounds into thin pancakes, 5 or 6 inches across; the thickness need not be perfectly uniform. Place the baking sheet in the oven.

4 The Parmesan rounds are done when the centers darken slightly and the edges begin to brown, about 5 to 6 minutes. Remove the baking sheet from the oven and let it stand for about a minute, then carefully lift each of the rounds and drape it over the bottom of a narrow cup or glass to form a cup shape. Let dry for about 5 minutes.

Gently lift the cooked Parmesan disk from the baking sheet and drape it over a cup or glass to form a bowl.

5 The orzo is done when it is tender and all the liquid has been absorbed in about 15 minutes. Season it with pepper and very little salt, then stir in the parsley. Spoon a portion of orzo into each of the Parmesan cups and serve.

With MINIMAL Effort

Cheese cups can be made with almost any hard cheese, or a combination of cheeses. Manchego, pecorino, and other sheep's milk cheeses are especially good. As for fillings, try:

STEAMED and chopped spinach (other than a grating of pepper, no seasoning is necessary)

BLAND beef stew or other stewed meat

RATATOUILLE or other stewed vegetables

Fish and Shellfish

Emma's Cod and Potatoes

WORK TIME	20 minutes
PREP TIME	1 hour or less
CAN BE	prepared in advance; frozen; easily multiplied
MAKES	4 servings

WHEN MY YOUNGER DAUGHTER, Emma, was small, it sometimes seemed as if her main passion in life was potatoes, especially crispy ones. It didn't matter how they were cooked—as home fries, french fries, or roasted—as long as they had that external crunch and internal mealiness, she was happy.

For one special occasion, I produced potatoes Anna, in which potatoes are thin-sliced, drenched in butter, and roasted until golden—the ultimate in crisp potato dishes. This was a fatal error, because potatoes Anna are a pain to make; they contain about a week's allotment of butter, and they were forever in demand thereafter.

So I set about not only shortcutting the process, making it a little less artery-clogging while creating something approaching an entire meal. I cut back on the butter (when attacks of conscience strike I substitute olive oil) and enlisted the aid of the broiler in speeding the browning process. I figured that it would be just as easy to broil something on top of the potatoes during the last few minutes of cooking and, after a few tries, I found a thick fillet of fish to be ideal. The result is this simple weeknight dish that I now make routinely, and one that even seems to impress the occasional guest.

Cooking time is determined by thickness, both of the potato slices and the fish. If you have a mandoline (or a sharp knife and good cutting skills), aim for slicing the potatoes about an eighth of an inch thick—this will allow them to cook through and begin to brown within forty minutes or so. The cod or other fish should be about an inch thick; during the eight or so minutes it takes to cook through, the tops of the exposed potatoes will gain a fine crust, while the fish browns lightly.

| 4 to 5 medium potatoes, 2 pounds or more | Salt and freshly ground black pepper |
| 6 tablespoons extra virgin olive oil or melted butter | 1½ pounds cod or other fillets, about 1 inch thick (skinned), in 2 or more pieces |

1 Preheat the oven to 400° F. Peel the potatoes and cut them into slices about ⅛ inch thick (a mandoline comes in handy here). Toss the potatoes in an 8 × 11-inch or similar size baking pan with 4 tablespoons of the oil or butter. Season the potatoes liberally with salt and pepper, spread them evenly, and place the pan in the oven.

2 Cook for about 40 minutes, checking once or twice, until the potatoes are tender when pierced with a thin-bladed knife and have begun to brown on top. Turn on the broiler and adjust the rack so that it is 4 to 6 inches from the heat source.

3 Top the potatoes with the fish, drizzle with the remaining oil or butter, and sprinkle with some more salt and pepper. Broil until the fish is done, 6 to 10 minutes depending on its thickness (a thin-bladed knife will pass through it easily). If at any point the top of the potatoes begins to burn, move the pan a couple of inches farther away from the heat source.

With MINIMAL Effort

TOSS 1 teaspoon or more of minced garlic with the potatoes.

MIX up to ½ cup chopped parsley, dill, basil, or chervil, or smaller amounts (1 or 2 teaspoons) of stronger herbs like thyme or rosemary with the potatoes.

SEASON the potatoes with a tablespoon or so of curry, chili powder, or paprika, or a few pinches of cayenne or crushed red pepper flakes.

TOP the fish with thin-sliced tomatoes and drizzle them with olive oil or dot them with butter before broiling.

ADD other vegetables to the potatoes—a cup or more of chopped spinach, for example—but be aware that their moisture may keep the potatoes from browning well.

Roast Cod with Tangerine Sauce

WORK TIME	30 minutes
PREP TIME	30 minutes
CAN BE	easily multiplied
MAKES	4 servings

NEARLY EVERYONE LIKES the taste of tangerine, yet it remains rare in cooking, probably because it is easily overwhelmed by other foods. Other citrus flavors are more powerful, of course: A tablespoon of lemon or lime juice added at the end of cooking makes its presence felt, but a similar amount of tangerine juice is lost instantly.

To have an impact, a significant quantity of tangerine juice must be used. But you cannot just use a cup of the stuff to finish a dish; it's simply too thin. My goal in making a sauce that smacked of tangerine, then, was not only to preserve the fresh and distinctive flavor of the fruit but to create something that would have substance.

I reduced some stock and stirred in the juice to provide much-needed body (this is essentially how you make the sauce for the classic duck à l'orange). But reducing and thickening the stock made the sauce taste more of stock than tangerine. So I eliminated the stock altogether, and simply reduced the tangerine juice. The resulting liquid had some body, but still not enough. A little butter, however, took care of that; olive oil worked nearly as well.

Another problem remained: Cooking tangerine juice flattens out the flavor, removing all the high notes. By stirring in the fresh, uncooked zest of the tangerines, however, the brightness was restored.

Finally, there was the notion of complexity. Sweetness, however appealing, is not enough on its own. There is some acidity in tangerine juice, but the sauce tasted one-dimensional. Lemon or lime juice confused matters, but I found that a few pinches of cayenne—along with some salt—did the trick.

The sauce remains delicate, best suited to a piece of fish, and a mild-flavored one at that. It's equally good with chicken and—while it doesn't stand out as much—it is not bad with duck or pork. With any of these, serve white rice; the juices of the fish or meat mingle with the tangerine sauce in a way that makes the rice heavenly.

4 to 5 large tangerines, at least 1½ pounds	Salt
1 tablespoon olive oil	Cayenne pepper
1½ pounds cod or other mild white fish	2 tablespoons butter or olive oil

1 Preheat the oven to 500° F; if you have a baking stone, use it. Finely grate the zest of the tangerines, avoiding grating any of the bitter white part (you should be able to get away with one swipe per section of skin on a good grater, rather than rubbing over and over). Set the zest aside. Juice the tangerines and measure 1¼ cups of the juice. Set the juice in a small saucepan over medium-high heat, bring to a boil, and reduce, stirring occasionally, to about ½ cup; this will take at least 10 minutes.

2 Place a large, ovenproof skillet, preferably nonstick, over high heat and add the oil. If necessary, cut the cod into serving pieces so that it will fit in the skillet comfortably. When the oil smokes, pour out any excess (you only need a film of oil). Add the fish and put the skillet in the oven; set a timer for 6 minutes.

3 When the timer goes off, check the fish; it is done when it offers no resistance to a thin-bladed knife and is opaque, or nearly so, throughout. Unless it is unusually thick, it will be done in no more than 8 minutes.

4 While the fish is cooking, season the tangerine sauce with salt and cayenne to taste—it should have something of a bite. Whisk in the butter or oil, a little at a time, until the sauce is smooth and thick; taste and adjust seasoning, then add the grated zest; cook another 15 seconds. Serve the fish napped with the sauce.

With MINIMAL Effort

Roast Chicken with Tangerine Sauce: Use bone-in or boneless breasts, and broil them. For bone-in, set the rack 4 to 6 inches from the heat source, sprinkle the breasts (4 halves for 4 people) with salt and pepper, and rub with olive oil or butter. Broil, turning frequently, until nicely browned and cooked through, 10 to 15 minutes. For boneless, set the rack 4 inches or closer to the heat source; sprinkle the breasts (4 halves for 4 people) with salt and pepper, and rub with olive oil or butter. Broil without turning until cooked through, about 6 minutes.

ADD a teaspoon of coriander seeds to the sauce as it reduces. These add a mysterious if mild flavor and a tiny bit of crunch.

DIFFERENT HERBS change the character of the sauce in different ways, even when added as a simple garnish. A tablespoon or two of minced dill accentuates the sweetness of the tangerine; a quarter-cup of chopped parsley leaves offsets it with bitterness; and a couple of tablespoons of chopped cilantro leaves (especially if there are coriander seeds in the sauce) makes the entire preparation seem exotic.

Cod Cakes with Ginger and Scallions

Fish Cakes with Flavor

WORK TIME	30 minutes
PREP TIME	1 hour
CAN BE	prepared in advance; frozen; easily multiplied
MAKES	4 servings

BETWEEN YOUR FAVORITE restaurant crabcake and a box of frozen fish sticks lies a world of crisp, easily produced fish cakes that make for great weeknight eating. In addition to fish, they all have two elements in common: something to "bind" the cake as it cooks, and a fair amount of seasoning.

Most fish cakes are bound by eggs, cream, mayonnaise, flour, or bread crumbs, or a combination of these, and seasoned with mustard, parsley, scallions, and like flavorings. These are fine ingredients, but all together, they may remind you of the salmon croquettes from your high school cafeteria.

Yet it's easy to improve both binding and flavoring while simultaneously simplifying the process. My favorite way to hold fish cakes together is to mix the flaked meat with mashed potatoes, in a proportion of about three parts fish to one part potato. Starchy, baking potatoes are best for this, and they add both flavor and substance without fat—unless you mash the potatoes with butter and cream.

If you begin with a mild fish, such as cod, the flavorings can be as adventuresome as you like. My preferred combination is a hefty dose of ginger and cilantro, spiked with a bit of hot red pepper. The result is a zingy cake that needs nothing more than a squeeze of lime.

Fish-cake recipes usually recommend shaping and refrigerating the cakes for an hour or more. This is not a bad idea—it firms up the cake without changing its delicate nature, allowing it to withstand the rigors of pan-frying—but this step isn't always necessary, because a good fish cake can gain a perfectly crisp, golden crust with the aid of a moderately hot, carefully watched broiler. Although this cuts the amount of fat used in cooking the cakes, it's not the primary goal; I'm more interested in keeping the cakes intact with a minimum of time and work, and in reducing the amount of spattering on my stovetop.

Of course, you can assemble these cakes with leftover fish and leftover mashed potatoes (even those made with butter and cream), and this is especially easy if you can think far enough ahead to prepare extras of each for preceding meals. (While the three-to-one proportion is ideal, you can make these cakes with one part fish to one part potato, although the taste will be different.) Worth thinking about, too, is boiling the potatoes and poaching the fish hours or even a day or two in advance; with this out of the way, the cakes can be assembled and broiled in about twenty minutes.

1 baking potato, about ½ pound	½ cup minced cilantro leaves plus more for garnish
1½ pounds fillet of cod or other mild, delicate white fish	1 fresh or dried hot red chile, minced, or ¼ teaspoon cayenne pepper, or to taste
Salt and freshly ground black pepper	2 teaspoons peanut or vegetable oil
1 tablespoon peeled and minced fresh ginger	Lime wedges

1 Boil the potato in salted water to cover until it is tender but not mushy, 30 to 40 minutes.

2 Meanwhile, place the fish in a skillet that can later be covered. Add water to cover, salt the water, and bring to a boil over high heat. Cover, turn off the heat, and set a timer for 10 minutes. Use a slotted spoon to remove the fish to a bowl.

3 When the potato is done, peel it and mash it with the fish. Add the ginger and cilantro along with some salt and pepper to taste, and work the mixture with your hands until it is well blended. Shape into 8 equal burger-shaped patties.

4 Preheat the broiler and set the rack about 4 inches from the heat source. Brush the patties on both sides with the oil, then place on a nonstick baking sheet. Broil carefully until nicely browned on top, then turn and brown on the other side. Sprinkle with more cilantro and serve hot, with lime wedges.

With MINIMAL Effort

Pan-fried Fish Cakes: Increase the oil to $1/3$ cup, or more if necessary. Heat oil in a large skillet (the oil should be to a depth of about $1/16$ inch) over medium-high heat. When it is hot (a pinch of the fish mixture will sizzle immediately), add the cakes. Cook, turning once, until brown on both sides, about 10 minutes total.

> **SUBSTITUTE** minced garlic, shallot, scallion, or onion for the ginger, and parsley or other herb(s) for the cilantro.
>
> **SEASON** with a grating of nutmeg or a teaspoon or more of curry powder (in place of the seasonings in the original recipe).
>
> **ADD** $1/4$ cup or more sour cream and a little butter to the potato as you mash it.
>
> **ADD** minced yellow or red bell pepper to the mix.
>
> **SERVE** with Mayonnaise (page 216), Worcestershire sauce, tartar sauce, or any other condiment.

Flounder Poached in Broth
An Easy Way to Cook Thin Fish Fillets

WORK TIME	15 minutes
PREP TIME	15 minutes
MAKES	4 servings

THIN FISH FILLETS CAN BE tricky to prepare, mostly because they fall apart the instant they're overcooked. But the fact that quarter-inch-thick fillets of flounder, sole, and other flatfish take so little time to cook can be an advantage.

By poaching them in barely hot liquid, you slow the cooking and gain control. By flavoring the liquid first with a quick-cooking aromatic vegetable, you create a dish that only needs bread or rice to become a meal. Unlike with broiling or sautéing, the fish never dries out.

The traditional liquid for poaching fish is court bouillon, a stock made from scratch using fish bones, onions, carrots, and celery enhanced with white wine and herbs. Assuming you don't have any court bouillon on hand—and who does?—my poaching liquid of choice is chicken stock. The usually insipid canned variety is fine, because you're going to add flavor to it, and quickly.

This recipe takes just fifteen minutes from start to finish. While the stock comes to a boil and reduces slightly in volume, clean and chop some leeks, adding them to the liquid as they're ready. A couple of minutes later, season the broth and add the fillets. The subsequent cooking time depends largely on your equipment. If you have an electric stove, simply turn the heat off; the element will remain warm enough to cook the fish. You may need a low flame with a gas stove, but it should be the minimum. A heavy-duty pan may retain enough heat to make even that unnecessary.

2 cups chicken stock (or one 14-
    or 15-ounce can)
Three 1-inch-thick leeks
	1½ pounds flounder or other
	    thin fish fillets
	Salt and freshly ground black
	    pepper

1 Place the stock in a large skillet that can be covered and turn the heat to high. Let it boil and reduce by about half while you prepare the leeks. Trim the leeks of the root and green end; cut the white part in half the long way and rinse thoroughly. Chop each half into ⅛- to ¼-inch-thick semicircles, adding them to the boiling broth as you cut them.

2 When all the leeks are added, cook for another minute. Add salt and pepper to taste and stir, then add the fish. Cover and turn off the heat, or keep the heat at an absolute minimum. Uncover and check the fish after 3 minutes; it is done when a thin-bladed knife encounters no resistance. Continue to check every minute until the fish is done.

3 Serve the fish with the leeks and some broth spooned over it; top all with a sprinkling of coarse salt.

With MINIMAL Effort

USE any aromatic vegetable you like in place of the leeks, alone or in combination: shallots, onions, scallions, garlic, celery, or carrots (cut carrots into very small pieces, or shred them on a grater or in a food processor so they'll cook quickly).

ADD herbs, especially parsley, chervil, or dill, alone or in combination.

ADD spices, alone or in combination. For example, a North African–style combination of a few coriander seeds, a small piece of cinnamon, and a little cumin is easily assembled and appealing. Or add a tablespoon of curry powder to the broth.

YOU can also use this technique for thicker fillets, like red snapper, sea bass, or cod. After you cover the skillet, keep the heat on low and, after about six minutes, check the fish every minute. When a thin-bladed knife encounters no resistance, the fish is done; when it begins to flake, it's overdone—but only slightly, and it will still be juicy.

Sparkling Cider-Poached Fish

WORK TIME	15 minutes
PREP TIME	15 minutes
CAN BE	easily multiplied
MAKES	4 servings

IT ALWAYS SURPRISES ME when I change one basic ingredient in a familiar recipe and find something so strikingly different that it becomes more than a variation. While experimenting with poaching fish steaks in white wine with shallots, butter, and mushrooms, the dish reminded me of a chicken preparation I'd seen in Brittany. Although the chicken was browned in unconscionable amounts of butter by our standards then poached—also with shallots and butter—in the local dry cider and finished with a hefty dose of cream, it was the flavor of the cider that made the finished dish so memorable.

Once I'd thought about this, I performed a simple conversion and marriage: I mixed together a little butter, some chopped shallots, and mushrooms, splashed in a dose of hard cider (the dry, sparkling kind from France or England, sold nearly everywhere you can buy beer and wine), and brought the mixture to a boil. I added a piece of filleted haddock—you could just as easily use cod, monkfish, halibut, red snapper, or any other white-fleshed fish—and poached the dish in a hot oven. The cider provided a distinctively sour fruitiness, not at all like white wine, and the completed dish had complementary textures: crunchy shallots, meaty mushrooms (I used portobellos), and tender fish.

This creation does not even need a garnish, since you can simply spoon the mushroom-shallot mixture over the fish to keep it from being too naked. And although the sauce was on the thin side, I decided its clean flavors worked so perfectly that it wasn't worth the addition of flour, cornstarch, or cream to give it more body.

In fact, after experimenting for a while, I realized the lone improvement I could make was to add more butter. Although I stopped at four tablespoons—half a stick—I realized that there really was almost no upper limit as far as my taste buds were concerned, but the dish is awfully nice when made on the lean side, too.

1 teaspoon butter, or more (see headnote)

½ cup sliced or minced shallots

1 cup roughly chopped portobello or other mushrooms

1½ pounds any white-fleshed fillet of fish, such as cod or red snapper, about 1 inch thick, in 1 or 2 pieces

Salt and freshly ground black pepper

1 cup dry sparkling cider

1 Preheat the oven to 500° F. Smear the bottom of an ovenproof skillet with the butter; sprinkle the shallots and mushrooms around the sides of the skillet. Season the fish with salt and pepper to taste and lay it in the center of the skillet. Pour the cider around the fish.

2 Bring to a boil on top of the stove, then transfer to the oven. Bake for about 8 minutes; it's highly unlikely the fish will need more time than this unless it is very thick (or you like it very well done). Baste with the pan juices and serve.

With MINIMAL Effort

SUBSTITUTE any aromatic vegetable, or a combination, for the shallots: onion, leek, carrot (cut very small), celery, fennel, scallions.

USE a mixture of mushrooms, or fresh mushrooms combined with reconstituted dried mushrooms. A little of the strained mushroom-soaking liquid added to the poaching liquid is nice, too.

YOU can enhance the apple flavor and enrich the sauce by adding chopped peeled apples to the mix. Even better, although a little more work is involved, is to peel, core, and slice some apples, then sauté them in butter until tender and lightly browned. Spoon a little over each portion of fish.

A TEASPOON of thyme leaves added to the poaching liquid is great; also good are parsley (a small handful of stalks), chervil (a small bunch), or dill (a few stalks). Garnish with chopped fresh leaves of the same herb.

SOME seeds are good in the poaching liquid, too—try caraway, coriander, or fennel

Grilled Fish
The Mediterranean Way

WORK TIME	15 minutes
PREP TIME	30 minutes
MAKES	4 servings

COOKS WITH ACCESS TO perfectly fresh fish make an absolute fetish of simplicity, largely because the subtle flavor of the fish is easily lost, especially if it is one of the delicate, white-fleshed varieties. It doesn't matter much where you go or who you talk to: When fishermen, chefs, or home cooks are proud of their fish, they don't fuss with it.

One extremely simple preparation, common throughout the Mediterranean, is fish grilled on a bed of fennel stalks. The technique, undoubtedly as old as grilling itself, solves a couple of problems at once: It seasons the fish subtly and without effort, and it helps prevent the fish from sticking to the grill and falling apart. In fact, this method allows you to grill even relatively delicate fillets like cod, usually among the most challenging because of their tendency to fall apart as they near doneness.

This is one of those recipes in which the shopping may take you longer than the cooking. You must start with a perfectly fresh piece of fish, of course. Moreover, fennel stalks—or those from dill, which are nearly as good—are almost always discarded by grocers. When you buy a bulb of fennel, you're buying the bottom, trimmed of its long stalks; when you buy a bunch of dill, you're buying the feathery tops, trimmed of the stalks that support them. Because this recipe requires some of those stalks, you will probably have to speak directly to a produce manager, visit a farm stand or a friend's garden, or simply get lucky.

I like this dish best made with halibut. It's worth spending the few minutes it takes to convert a single halibut steak into fillets. A good fishmonger will do this for you, but it's as easy as removing the skin from a piece of chicken. Just use a sharp, thin-bladed knife and cut straight down, following the outline of the bone; a halibut steak will produce four fillets. If you buy a one-and-a-half-inch-thick piece of fish, each fillet will be the perfect serving size. Alternatively, use striped bass (preferably skin-on and scaled), monkfish, cod (also best with the skin on), or any other fillet with some substance. Do not attempt to grill flatfish such as flounder or sole.

The preparation is just one step: Lay the fennel on the grill, lay the fish on the fennel, and cook. I finish the fish with a tiny sprinkling of fennel

1 | Use a boning or other sharp thin-bladed knife to cut around the bone and inside the skin of each of the four sections of the steak.

2 | Remove each of the four fillets.

seeds, decorate it with lemon slices, and moisten it with a little lemon juice and olive oil. For an absolutely minimalist preparation, consider all of this optional. Given the simplicity of this dish, it's also best to keep side dishes modest—I like it with no more than bread and salad.

4 to 6 fennel or dill stalks (see headnote), each at least 6 inches long

Four 6-ounce halibut fillets (see headnote) or 1½ pounds any white-fleshed fish fillet, such as striped bass, monkfish, or cod

Salt and cayenne pepper

1 teaspoon fennel or dill seeds

1 lemon

2 teaspoons extra virgin olive oil

1 Preheat a charcoal or gas grill (for broiling instructions, see the variation below); the fire should be quite hot, and the grill rack about 4 inches from the heat source.

2 When the grill is ready, make a bed of the fennel or dill stalks. Sprinkle the fish lightly with salt and cayenne to taste and lay it (skin side down, if there is a skin side) directly onto the fennel or dill. Close the grill if possible and cook, without turning, until the fish is done—it will be just about opaque all the way through, and offer no resistance to a thin-bladed knife—about 10 minutes.

3 While the fish is cooking, mince or grind the fennel or dill seeds. Cut about 1 inch off each end of the lemon and juice those pieces; slice the remaining lemon as thinly as you can.

4 When the fish is done, remove it from the grill, leaving as much of the stalks behind as possible (some of the burned fronds will adhere to the fish; this is fine). Sprinkle the fish with the fennel or dill seeds, then decorate it with the lemon slices. Drizzle with the lemon juice and olive oil and serve.

With MINIMAL Effort

Broiled Fish on Fennel or Dill: Preheat the broiler and place the rack as close to the heat source as possible. Put about ½ inch of water in the bottom of a roasting pan and lay the fennel or dill stalks in it. Sprinkle the fish lightly with salt and pepper and lay it (skin side down, if there is a skin side) directly onto the fennel or dill. Broil until the fish is lightly browned on top and opaque throughout, about 10 minutes. (If at any time the fish is browning too quickly, move the broiler rack down a notch.) Finish as above.

Grilled or Broiled Fish on Fennel or Dill with Butter Sauce: You can take this dish to another level by making a simple butter sauce to serve with it: In a small saucepan, cook 2 tablespoons minced shallot with ⅓ cup each white wine and white wine vinegar, along with a little salt and pepper, until the liquid is almost evaporated. Over the lowest possible heat, stir in ½ to 1 stick of butter, a bit at a time, adding the next bit only when each has been absorbed, until the sauce is smooth and creamy. Serve immediately.

Striped Bass with Mushrooms
Cooking Fish on One Side

WORK TIME	20 minutes
PREP TIME	30 minutes
MAKES	4 servings

SEVERAL TIMES I'VE SAT AT lunch with friends and colleagues and heard them wonder, when presented with a nicely crisped piece of fish, "How do they get such a fabulous crust on there?" The fish isn't fried, nor is it breaded; it's just perfectly browned. The detectives among them notice that the fish is only perfectly browned on one side, and that's the key. In fact, it is cooked on one side only—or nearly so.

Most fish is so moist that it is difficult to brown it; the surface of the flesh must dry out before it browns and, because fish cooks so quickly, the interior is usually done long before this happens. That's why fish is often coated before cooking; the coating browns much more rapidly than the fish itself.

If, however, you brown only one side of the fillet, that side develops a crisp crust, and the center remains moist. In restaurants, where this technique is common, the cooking is completed by flipping the fish for the last minute or so of cooking, which is sufficient (it is then presented crisp side up, and few people ever notice that the downward-facing side is relatively pale). This technique will work at home, too; however, the results are not only nicely cooked fish but a messy stovetop and a lingering aroma. Restaurants solve these problems with powerful exhaust fans and a crew of night cleaners.

Most home cooks need a different solution, and here it is: Preheat your oven to the absolute maximum before beginning to cook (even 600° F is not too hot). If you have a baking stone, place it in a cold oven before preheating. Start the fish on top of the stove, and immediately move it to the oven; it will brown beautifully on the bottom, eliminate the need for turning, and remain moist within (as long, of course, as it isn't overcooked).

This technique works equally well with fish that retains its skin and that which has had its skin removed. If the skin is on, it becomes irresistibly crisp and delicious (especially when sprinkled with a little coarse salt). If removed, the flesh becomes crisp, even tough, a nice contrast to the remaining part of the fish, which remains moist and tender.

Even with this technique, a too-thin piece of fish will overcook in the time it takes to brown one side, so don't try this with a fillet of flounder, or even a thin piece of cod. It's best performed with fillets of a near-uniform thickness of about one inch: thicker pieces of cod—for example, center cuts of striped bass or salmon, or a thick piece of sea bass. All of these have edible, delicious skin, so see if you can get a piece that has not had the skin removed—just make sure it has been scaled.

3 tablespoons olive oil

2 tablespoons minced shallot

1 pound mushrooms, preferably a mixture (such as shiitake, crimini, and button), trimmed, rinsed, and sliced

Salt and freshly ground black pepper

1½ to 2 pounds 1-inch-thick fillet of striped bass or other fish, in 1 or 2 pieces, preferably with the skin on

1 teaspoon vinegar

Minced parsley for garnish

1 Preheat the oven to its maximum, at least 500° F; if you have a baking stone, use it. Place 2 tablespoons of the oil in a large skillet and turn the heat to medium. Add the shallots and cook, stirring, until they soften, about 3 minutes. Add the mushrooms and raise the heat to medium-high. Cook, stirring occasionally, until the mushrooms give up their liquid and become tender, about 10 minutes. Season to taste with salt and pepper and keep warm.

2 Meanwhile, heat an ovenproof skillet over high heat. Add the remaining 1 tablespoon oil; when it smokes, add the fish, skin side down. Season the fish with salt and pepper and transfer to the oven; set the timer for 6 minutes.

3 Stir the vinegar into the mushrooms; taste and adjust seasoning. Check the fish when the timer goes off; it is done when the interior is opaque and a thin-bladed knife passes through it with little resistance. Serve the fish, skin (or crisp) side up, on a bed of the mushrooms. Drizzle with the fish pan juices and garnish with the parsley.

With MINIMAL Effort

Note that this fish cooking technique is independent of the sauce, which means you can omit the mushroom-shallot mixture entirely and serve the fish with a wide variety of accompaniments, including:

FIG RELISH (page 222)

CUMIN-TOMATO RELISH (page 218)

PAN-GRILLED TOMATO SALSA (page 219)

PARSLEY-VINEGAR SAUCE (page 206)

RED PEPPER PUREE (page 226)

VINAIGRETTE, or any of its variations (pages 208–210)

MAYONNAISE, or any of its variations (pages 216–217)

NEARLY any sauce or salsa you like, or something as simple as a squeeze of lemon, a pat of butter, or a drizzle of good vinegar.

Grilled Tuna with Mesclun Stuffing

WORK TIME	20 minutes
PREP TIME	45 minutes, or longer if you have it
CAN BE	easily multiplied
MAKES	4 servings

A FEW YEARS AGO, around Memorial Day, a friend and I were about to grill a two-inch slab of tuna. The grill was fired up, we made a quick marinade and were washing some greens for a salad. In a flash of inspiration, we decided to combine everything in one dish.

We carefully cut a pocket in the tuna—just as if we'd been stuffing a pork chop—drenched the salad greens in the tuna marinade, and crammed them in there. We closed the pocket with a couple of toothpicks and let the tuna marinate for a while longer. Then we grilled it.

When the tuna was done, we sliced it, exposing lovely rare slices lined with a vein of dressed, barely warm salad. I've made this easy and rather impressive dish several times a year ever since.

Of course I've hardly made it the same way twice; once the idea had stuck I couldn't help but play with it. The concept works just as well with a thick slab of sirloin as it does with tuna. (Which isn't surprising. Like sirloin, tuna is red, tender, flavorful, and better rare than well done. The major differences are that tuna is more tender and lower in fat.) The method isn't bad with swordfish or salmon, either, but since both are better closer to fully cooked than rare, the greens tend to wilt.

When you buy tuna for this dish, make sure to get a slice that is *at least* 1½ inches thick; you need a substantial piece for stuffing. As with all tuna, the skin should be removed. Try to find dark-red yellowfin (or bluefin if you're lucky), rather than the paler albacore.

Juice of 3 limes

¼ cup high-quality soy sauce

5 tablespoons extra virgin olive oil

2 tablespoons water

1 teaspoon dark sesame oil, optional

½ teaspoon coarsely ground black pepper

2 cups mesclun, arugula, or other greens, washed, dried, and torn into bits

1 tuna steak (about 1½ pounds), no less than 1½ inches thick

Salt and freshly ground black pepper

1 Start a charcoal or wood fire, or preheat a gas grill or broiler. Combine the first 6 ingredients in a bowl or the container of a blender and whisk or blend until emulsified. Soak the greens in this mixture while you prepare the tuna.

2 See the photographs below for making a pocket in the tuna. Be careful not to cut through the top, bottom, or opposite edge of the tuna, and try to keep the entry point relatively small.

3 Drain the greens of excess marinade and cram them into the pocket; you can overstuff the tuna (it won't shrink, nor will the greens expand) as long as you don't tear the tuna. If you've kept the pocket opening small, seal it with a toothpick; if it's more than an inch or two wide, use a couple of skewers. Marinate the tuna in the remaining soy mixture until the grill is hot, or up to an hour at room temperature or several hours, refrigerated.

4 Grill the tuna, turning once, about 6 minutes per inch of thickness (if the steak is 1½ inches thick, for example, turn it after about 4 minutes and cook 4 or 5 minutes more). Cut into ½-inch-thick slices and serve.

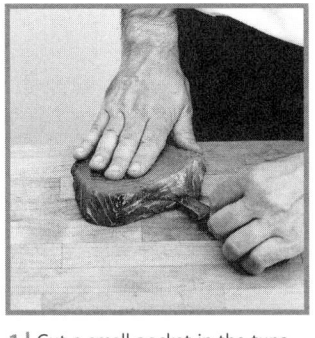

1 | Cut a small pocket in the tuna.   2 | Fill the pocket with greens, but avoid tearing the tuna.

With MINIMAL Effort

USE this stuffing and marinade with swordfish, salmon, lamb, or beef.

STUFF the steaks with pureed roasted garlic; roasted red peppers (or Red Pepper Puree, page 226); about 1 cup chopped fresh herbs; thick pesto; or a mixture of lightly cooked onions, red peppers, and chiles.

SUBSTITUTE any vinaigrette (pages 208–210) for the soy dressing.

Spice-Rubbed Salmon

WORK TIME	15 minutes
PREP TIME	30 minutes
CAN BE	prepared in advance; easily multiplied
MAKES	4 servings

THE FLAVOR OF SALMON IS DISTINCTIVE but chameleonlike, showing itself differently depending on its surroundings. Chef Katy Sparks once demonstrated to me how you can exploit the fickle nature of salmon by varying a few seasonings.

One day Katy and I put some salmon fillets through their paces, flavoring them with rosemary, fennel, and orange; a powder made of porcini and pumpkin seeds; and a variation on the French classic *quatre épices* (four spices). The beauty of Katy's minimalist but infinitely variable system is that the technique remains the same regardless of the herbs or spices used in the coating.

First, season the salmon with salt and pepper and prepare the herb or spice mix, which you firmly press into the top (nonskin side) of the fish. Then, in a well-heated, well-oiled pan (a nonstick surface helps, but is not essential if the pan is hot enough), sear the fillets, coated side down. Within a minute, the flavorings brown beautifully and adhere perfectly, after which the fillets are turned and finished in the oven.

With uniformly sized fillets, the cooking time can be gauged precisely, resulting in the kind of lovely individual pieces of salmon served in restaurants. For four servings, buy one and a half pounds of skinned salmon fillet, taken from the thick (not the tail) end of the fish. Cut across the fillet to make four pieces of equal size.

Although the technique is about as straightforward as can be, allowing the fillets to sit for a while after coating will encourage the fragrant seasonings to permeate the flesh of the fish; try fifteen minutes or so at room temperature, or a couple of hours in the refrigerator.

Four 6-ounce skinned salmon fillets	1 tablespoon minced fresh rosemary
Salt and freshly ground black pepper	1 tablespoon minced orange zest
1 tablespoon fennel seeds	2 tablespoons olive oil or butter

1 Season the fillets on both sides with salt and pepper to taste. Grind the fennel seeds coarsely in a coffee or spice grinder, and mix them with the rosemary and orange zest. Press this mixture into the top (nonskin side) of each fillet. Let sit, refrigerated and covered, for up to 24 hours.

2 When you're ready to cook, preheat the oven to 450° F. Preheat a large nonstick skillet over medium-high heat for 3 or 4 minutes. Add the oil or butter and, when it shimmers, place the fillets, coated side down, in the pan. Cook about 1 minute, or until the spice mixture forms a nicely browned crust.

3 Turn the fillets and cook about a minute more, then transfer to the oven. Cook about 4 minutes for rare salmon, 5 to 6 minutes for medium-rare, and 8 minutes for well done.

With MINIMAL Effort

Seed-Rubbed Salmon: Combine 2 tablespoons raw, shelled pumpkin seeds (pepitas) and 2 tablespoons (roughly) dried porcini pieces in a coffee or spice grinder and grind to a coarse powder. Press some of the mixture into the top (nonskin side) of each of the fillets and cook as above.

Spice-Rubbed Salmon: Combine 1 tablespoon coriander seeds or ground coriander, 1/4 teaspoon whole or ground cloves, 1 1/2 teaspoons cumin seeds or ground cumin, and 1 teaspoon freshly grated nutmeg (grind all together if necessary). Press some of the mixture into the top (nonskin side) of each of the fillets and cook as above.

THIS technique will work with nearly any spice, herb, or other rub you can think of. Try curry powder; minced lemon zest and parsley; minced lime zest and cilantro; or ground nuts and shallots.

SUBSTITUTE whole or clarified butter, peanut oil, or a neutral oil such as grapeseed or canola for the olive oil.

Salmon Burgers

WORK TIME	20 minutes
PREP TIME	20 minutes
CAN BE	prepared in advance (up until cooking); frozen (before cooking); easily multiplied
MAKES	4 servings

THERE WERE SEVERAL REASONS I wanted to create a salmon burger. I knew it would taste good, which is reason enough, and I figured it would not necessarily be accompanied by ketchup, another plus. Then there's the fact that salmon is more than widely available; it's practically ubiquitous and, when on sale, not much more expensive than ground meat.

The challenge, however, was not just to create a salmon burger but a minimalist salmon burger. And here's what I discovered: If you finely grind part of the salmon, it will act as glue for the rest of it, which could be coarsely chopped and therefore retain its moisture during cooking. Coarse bread crumbs keep the mixture from becoming as densely packed as bad meat loaf. And a few simple seasonings help produce a delicious burger in not much more time than it takes to make one from ground round.

The process is simple as long as you have a food processor. A portion of the salmon is finely ground, almost pureed; the machine takes care of that in about thirty seconds. Then the rest of the fish is chopped, by pulsing the machine on and off a few times. The only other trick is to avoid overcooking; this burger, which can be sautéed, broiled, or grilled, is best when the center remains pink (or is it orange?)—two or three minutes per side does the trick.

And the two-step grinding process means that those flavorings that you want finely minced, like garlic or ginger, can go in with the first batch of salmon; those that should be left coarse, like onion or fresh herbs, can go in with the second batch.

1½ pounds skinless, boneless salmon

2 teaspoons Dijon mustard

2 shallots, peeled and cut into chunks

½ cup coarse bread crumbs

1 tablespoon capers, drained

Salt and freshly ground black pepper

2 tablespoons butter or olive oil

Lemon wedges

Tabasco sauce

1 Cut the salmon into large chunks and put about a quarter of it into the container of a food processor, along with the mustard. Turn the machine on and let it run—stopping to scrape down the sides if necessary—until the mixture has become pasty.

2 Add the shallots and the remaining salmon and pulse the machine on and off until the fish is chopped and well combined with the puree. No piece should be larger than 1/4 inch or so in diameter, but be careful not to make the mixture too fine.

3 Scrape the mixture into a bowl and, by hand, stir in the bread crumbs, capers, and some salt and pepper. Shape into 4 burgers. (You can cover and refrigerate the burgers for a few hours at this point if you like.)

4 Place the butter or oil in a 12-inch nonstick skillet and turn the heat to medium-high. When the butter foam subsides or the oil is hot, cook the burgers for 2 to 3 minutes per side, turning once. Alternatively, you can grill them; let them firm up on the first side, cooking for about 4 minutes, before turning them over and finishing the cooking for just another minute or two. On no account should the burgers be overcooked. Serve the burgers on a bed of greens, or buns, or simply plates, with lemon wedges and Tabasco or any dressing you like.

With MINIMAL Effort

THE mustard, shallots, and capers can be considered optional, so you can combine them or omit them as you like when experimenting.

USE *any* fresh herbs, such as parsley, chervil, dill, or cilantro. Add 2 tablespoons or more with the second batch of salmon.

USE a combination of soy sauce (about a tablespoon), sesame oil (a teaspoon), and ginger (a teaspoon, added with the first batch of salmon). Use peanut oil for sautéing if you have it.

ADD a small clove of garlic along with the first batch of salmon. (Don't overdo it, because the garlic will remain nearly raw and strong-tasting.)

ADD 1/4 cup onions or scallions in addition to or instead of the shallots.

ADD spice mixtures such as curry or chili powder to the mixture—a teaspoon to a tablespoon, depending on your preference.

ADD red or yellow bell pepper (about 1/2 cup), cored, seeded, and roughly chopped, with the second batch of salmon.

ADD 1/4 cup or more lightly toasted pignoli nuts or about a tablespoon of sesame seeds along with the bread crumbs.

Gravlax

Curing Salmon, Fast and Easy

WORK TIME	15 minutes
PREP TIME	24 hours
CAN BE	prepared in advance; frozen; easily multiplied
MAKES	at least 12 servings

THE INTENSE ORANGE COLOR, meltingly tender texture, and wonderful flavor of gravlax gives it an allure shared by few fish preparations—not bad for a dish whose name means "buried salmon" in Swedish. The curing process intensifies the color, tenderizes the texture, and enhances the flavor.

Although most chefs jazz up gravlax with sauces and side dishes, it is brilliant on its own, or with just a few drops of lemon or mild vinegar. And the rankest kitchen novice can make it at home.

I make gravlax inexpensively, with almost no effort, and in quantities suitable for a single dinner party or a couple of family meals and snacks. I buy a single fillet (or even half a fillet) at the supermarket, cover it with salt, sugar, and dill, wrap it up—no weights—and serve it the next day.

Salmon for gravlax should be as fresh as possible, but this in no way eliminates supermarket fish; most supermarkets receive deliveries of popular fish like salmon three times a week, and farm-raised salmon is often harvested and shipped on the same day. Once you buy it keep it cold, and keep both your hands and your work surface impeccably clean.

Since you don't eat the skin of cured salmon, it need not be scaled. But you should check the fillet for pin bones, the long bones that run down the center of the fillet; these are not removed by the routine filleting process. Press your finger down the center of the flesh and you will feel them; remove them, one at a time, with a needle-nose pliers or similar tool.

It's worth noting that the timing for gravlax is imprecise; the longer it sits, the drier and more strong-flavored it will become. So if you're ready for dinner just twenty-four hours after beginning the cure, by all means serve the gravlax; similarly, if you want to hold the cure for an extra twelve or twenty-four hours, feel free. Alternatively, you can rinse off the cure when the gravlax is done and keep it for a couple of days before serving. In any case, you must treat finished gravlax as a fresh product. Keep it well wrapped and refrigerated, and use it within a few days. Freezing is a safe option, but will dry the salmon out to some extent.

1 cup salt	One 2- to 3-pound fillet of
2 cups sugar	salmon, pin bones
1 bunch dill, stems and all, chopped	removed

1 Mix together the salt, sugar, and dill. Place the salmon, skin side down, on a large sheet of plastic wrap. Cover the flesh side of the salmon with the salt mixture, making sure to coat it completely (there will be lots of salt mix; just pile it in there).

2 Wrap the fish well. If the air temperature is below 70 degrees and it is not too inconvenient, let it rest outside the refrigerator for about 6 hours, then refrigerate for 18 to 24 hours more. Otherwise, refrigerate immediately for about 36 hours.

3 Unwrap the salmon and rinse off the cure. Dry, then slice on the bias (see photograph). Serve plain, or with lemon wedges, crème fraîche, sour cream, or a light vinaigrette.

| Use a sharp knife and hold it at a very slight angle to cut thin slices from the salmon fillet.

With MINIMAL Effort

Low-Salt Gravlax: Use ½ cup salt and ¼ cup sugar. Combine a couple of chopped bay leaves, ¼ cup shallots, and 1 teaspoon cracked black pepper with the dill. Refrigerate for 48 hours and proceed as above.

Citrus Gravlax: Use 1 cup each salt and sugar, combined with the grated zests of 2 oranges, 2 lemons, 2 limes, and 2 grapefruit; 2 tablespoons juniper berries; 1 tablespoon cracked coriander seeds; and 1 bunch dill, stems and all. Marinate for 12 to 24 hours.

Lobster Boiled, then Grilled or Broiled

WORK TIME	30 minutes
PREP TIME	30 minutes
CAN BE	prepared in advance; easily multiplied
MAKES	4 to 8 servings

MANY BELIEVE THAT THE simplest method of cooking a lobster—boiling it in, or steaming it above, salted water—is the best. And if you don't have lobsters often, or you have the perfect lobster, it's tough to argue with that position.

I believe, however, that part of this attitude stems from the fact that the easiest way to kill a lobster (and since lobsters should always be purchased live—or cooked—they all have to be killed somehow) is to plop it into a pot of water, cover it, and pray that the lobster isn't strong enough to push the cover off. The alternative, inserting a knife into the lobster's head, does not have universal appeal—to say the least.

Unfortunately, most people believe that an unwillingness to perform surgery means that they're stuck with plain boiled lobster forever. Not so. There is a way to "parboil" lobster that will then allow you to grill or broil it without overcooking. The technique is easy, foolproof, and evidently humane.

What you do is cook the lobster just long enough to kill it. The meat remains uncooked, meaning that you can cut it up without having a squirming creature on your cutting board, and without cooking it through twice. During broiling or grilling, you can baste it with any number of combinations, and the results are quite exciting, especially if you're used to plain boiled lobster. A simple vinaigrette is good with cold or hot lobster, but try any of the sauce variations here.

Salt and freshly ground black pepper

Four 1¼- to 1½-pound live lobsters

¾ cup Basic Vinaigrette (page 208)

1 Start the charcoal grill if you're using it. Bring a large pot of water to a boil and salt it. Plunge the lobsters into the water (one or two at a time if necessary) and cook just until they turn red, about 2 minutes. Remove the lobsters and plunge them into an ice-water bath to stop the cooking. (You can do this several hours in advance and refrigerate the lobsters until you're ready to proceed.) Split the tails down the middle of their soft sides so they will lie flat.

2 Preheat the broiler if you're using it. With either broiler or grill, adjust the rack so that there will be about 3 inches between the lobsters and the heating source. Broil or grill the lobsters with their flesh side facing the heat until they are hot and their shells just begin to char, about 10 minutes. Sprinkle with salt and pepper and serve hot, warm, at room temperature, or cold, with the vinaigrette.

1 | After parboiling, insert a sturdy knife into the crossmarks just behind the lobster's head.

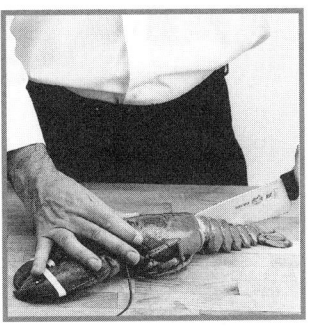

2 | Cut straight down through the body. The lobster is ready for grilling or broiling.

With MINIMAL Effort

SERVE the lobsters with melted butter.

MAKE ginger or garlic butter: Melt a stick of butter and add 1 tablespoon minced fresh ginger or garlic; cook gently for about 2 minutes.

ROAST the lobsters: Step 1 remains the same, but in Step 2, place them, flesh side up, in a 500° F oven. Roast for about 15 minutes. Baste with vinaigrette or with any other sauce while they cook.

USE any of the vinaigrette variations on pages 209–210 as a sauce.

Mussels, Asian Style

WORK TIME	15 minutes
PREP TIME	25 minutes
CAN BE	easily multiplied
MAKES	4 servings

THE MOST TYPICAL STEAMED-MUSSEL preparations contain parsley, garlic, and white wine, with the occasional addition of tomatoes and herbs.

There are, however, other directions in which you can prepare mussels, and they're no more effort than the familiar ones. Generally, there are two easy changes to make: First, use distinctive Asian seasonings such as ginger, soy, or curry powder. And second, omit the cooking liquid.

I never understood why cooks add wine when steaming mussels. The mollusk generates so much good-tasting broth of its own during cooking that additional liquid is superfluous. By relying only on the mussels' natural juices, you can add fewer seasonings (and less of each) and still produce a flavorful sauce that is less watery than most.

When cleaning mussels, discard any with broken shells. If the mussels have beards—the hairy vegetative growth that is attached to the shell—trim them off. Those mussels that remain closed after the majority have been steamed open can be pried open with a knife (a butter knife works fine) at the table.

When you finish mussels with soy, the sauce becomes a lovely shade of mahogany; with curry, it's stunningly yellow. Either way, these are mussel dishes that are better served with rice for sopping up the juices than with bread.

2 tablespoons peanut or canola oil

¼ cup roughly chopped scallions

1 tablespoon roughly chopped fresh ginger

2 cloves garlic, lightly smashed

4 pounds mussels, well washed

1 tablespoon soy sauce

1 Put the oil in a saucepan large enough to hold all the mussels and turn the heat to medium. A minute later, add the scallions, ginger, and garlic and cook, stirring occasionally, for about 1 minute.

2 Add the mussels, turn the heat to high, and cover the pot. Cook, shaking the pot occasionally, until they all (or nearly all) open, about 10 minutes. Turn off the heat.

3 Scoop the mussels into a serving bowl. Add the soy sauce to the liquid, then pass it through a fine strainer (or a coarse one lined with cheesecloth). Pour the liquid over the clams and serve.

With MINIMAL Effort

Steamed Mussels with Curry: Substitute butter for the oil. Substitute shallots for the scallions, and omit the ginger and garlic. When the shallots are soft, sprinkle them with 1 teaspoon curry powder and cook, stirring, another 30 seconds. Cook and finish as in main recipe, substituting the juice of 1 lime for the soy sauce.

Steamed Mussels with Fennel: Use olive oil. In place of the scallions and ginger, use 2 or 3 fennel stalks, roughly chopped, and 1 tablespoon fennel or anise seeds; add ¼ cup Pernod or other anise-flavored liqueur if you have it. Omit the soy sauce and finish with a squeeze of lemon.

Thai Steamed Mussels: Use peanut oil. Add 1 lemongrass stalk (see page 11), roughly chopped; 1 dried hot red chile; and 2 lime leaves to the scallions, ginger, and garlic. Substitute nam pla (fish sauce) for the soy sauce.

Steamed Clams with Soy: Any mussel recipe will work for steamers, which are also known as soft-shell clams. But steamers must be rinsed after shucking to remove all traces of sand, and you don't want to dilute these delicious broths by dipping clams into them one after the other. The solution is to substitute littlenecks—small hard-shell clams, the kind served on the half shell and used for pasta with clam sauce—for the mussels. These contain no sand at all, but because their shells are heavier, use 1½ to 2 pounds of littlenecks to replace each pound of mussels. Proceed exactly as above.

Paella, Fast and Easy

WORK TIME	10 minutes
PREP TIME	30 minutes
CAN BE	easily multiplied
MAKES	4 main-course or 8 side-dish servings

ALTHOUGH YOU WOULDN'T know it from the massive meat-and-shellfish dish served in restaurants, paella has simple roots. And, as is the case with many peasant dishes gone ritzy, the soul of paella is quite comfortable back in the home kitchen. Indeed, a simple rice-and-shrimp dish is as much a "real" paella as the twenty-five-dollar-a-plate version offered at Spanish restaurants.

The word *paella* comes not from a fancy combination of rice, seafood, sausage, and meat, but from *paellera,* a large pan that looks like a flat wok. And the only ingredient common to every traditional paella is rice—which makes sense, since the dish originated in Valencia, Spain's great rice-growing region.

Some people argue that a true paella must contain only meat or seafood, never both, that a true paella can be prepared only in a paellera, or that true paella must be cooked outdoors over wood. Perhaps they're all right. What's clear to me is that you can produce a fabulous rice dish I call paella in just over half an hour, which makes it a great option for weeknights.

There are some techniques to consider and ingredients to gather for this mini-paella. I don't have a paellera, and I'm not about to buy one, so I use a cast-iron skillet. Although I'm a great fan of nonstick cookware, here it is counterproductive, since one of the great joys of paella is the crust of rice that forms on the bottom. To encourage the formation of the crust, I finish the paella in an oven that's as hot as I can get it, usually on a baking stone.

The rice must be medium-grain, and since Spanish rice is not easy to find, I generally use Arborio, now sold everywhere. To save money, you could substitute an American or Asian short-grain rice, sold in most Asian markets and many supermarkets. Saffron-laced chicken stock makes the best liquid, although you can substitute a simple stock made from shrimp shells if you like (water is a desperate but acceptable alternative here).

Half of this recipe would produce an appropriate amount for a side dish for four; use an 8-inch skillet for best results.

4 cups chicken stock (see headnote)	2 cups medium-grain rice
Pinch saffron, optional	Salt and freshly ground black pepper
3 tablespoons olive oil	2 cups raw peeled shrimp, cut into ½-inch chunks
1 medium onion, peeled and minced	Minced parsley for garnish

1 Preheat the oven to 500° F, or as near that temperature as you can get it. Warm the stock in a saucepan along with the saffron if you're using it. Place an ovenproof 10- or 12-inch skillet over medium-high heat and add the oil. A minute later, add the onion and cook, stirring occasionally, until translucent, about 5 minutes.

2 Add the rice and cook, stirring occasionally, until glossy, just a minute or two. Season liberally with salt and pepper and add the warmed stock, taking care to avoid the rising steam. Stir in the shrimp and transfer the skillet to the oven.

3 Bake about 25 minutes until all the liquid is absorbed and the rice is dry on top. Garnish with parsley and serve immediately.

With MINIMAL Effort

Shrimp is my first choice for this dish, but the alternatives are numerous; as long as the pieces are less than ½ inch thick, anything will cook through in the time it takes for the liquid to evaporate. And you can combine them at will. Try:

SAUSAGE, cut into bits (especially chorizo)

PEAS and or other vegetables, cut up if necessary

SCALLOPS, treated exactly like the shrimp

BONELESS pork or chicken, cut into ½-inch cubes or smaller

TOFU, stirred into the rice during the last 5 minutes of baking

CLAMS and/or mussels, well scrubbed, placed on top of the rice when you put the pan in the oven

Shrimp with Lemongrass
A Fast Thai-Style Shrimp Dish

WORK TIME	15 minutes
PREP TIME	15 minutes
CAN BE	easily multiplied
MAKES	4 servings

SHRIMP IS A PERFECT WEEKNIGHT FOOD, not only because it cooks so quickly—usually in less than five minutes—but because it marries well with so many different flavors. One of the best pairings is shrimp and citrus, which includes not only lemon and lime but lemongrass, so named because of its haunting fragrance and subtle but unmistakable flavor.

Lemongrass, once considered exotic, is becoming increasingly easy to find. It is sold in almost every Asian market and even in many supermarkets. Lemongrass is easy to use; it does, however, require what may be an unfamiliar preparation. (See photographs, page 11.)

Lemongrass does not really tenderize with cooking, so if the core is on the tough side, you must take care to mince it finely. When minced, each stalk will produce about a tablespoon or even less of usable lemongrass. But since preparation time is fast, and lemongrass is cheap—I've paid as little as a dime per stalk—this hardly matters. Fresh lemongrass is green rather than brown, and its exterior sheath is moist and fresh-looking rather than dry. And lemongrass can be kept in the refrigerator for a very long time, although it gradually becomes tougher and tougher.

You can add minced lemongrass to any stir-fry, but its essence is most pronounced if you hold off until near the end of cooking before adding it. Teamed with lime zest (or, even better, lime leaves—also available at most Asian markets) and fish sauce, it will give a distinctively Southeast Asian flavor to the dish.

If fresh and quite tender, minced lemongrass can be used as a condiment. Sprinkle it with some minced fresh ginger on top of a piece of sautéed or steamed fish.

Since most lemongrass comes from Southeast Asia, and since it is not highly perishable, truly fresh specimens are rare. One solution is to grow it yourself. Pop a stalk unceremoniously into a pot of soil, set it in a sunny spot, it will multiply; a stalk planted outdoors in the spring will produce fifty or more by autumn.

2 tablespoons peanut or canola oil	½ cup chicken, fish, or shrimp stock, or water (if necessary)
1½ pounds shrimp, peeled	2 tablespoons nam pla or nuoc mam (fish sauce)
1 tablespoon minced lemongrass (see photographs, page 11)	Freshly ground black pepper
1 teaspoon minced garlic	
1 teaspoon minced lime zest or lime leaves	

1 Put the oil in a 10- or 12-inch skillet and turn the heat to medium-high; a minute later, add the shrimp.

2 Cook, undisturbed, until the bottoms of the shrimp turn pink, about 2 minutes. Stir in the lemongrass, garlic, and lime zest or leaves. If the mixture is dry, add the stock or water, then the fish sauce and plenty of black pepper. Serve immediately, with white rice.

With MINIMAL Effort

MADE with soy sauce in place of fish sauce, the stir-fry will taste more familiar.

SUBSTITUTE scallops for the shrimp. Cooking time will be just about the same. (Do not overcook the scallops; they should remain translucent in the middle.)

SUBSTITUTE boneless chicken, turkey, or pork, cut into ½-inch to 1-inch chunks, for the shrimp. Cooking time will be somewhat longer; 6 to 8 minutes total.

Shrimp in Yellow Curry
A Thai-Style Curry

WORK TIME	25 minutes
PREP TIME	25 minutes
CAN BE	prepared in advance; easily multiplied
MAKES	4 servings

THE RESTAURANTS AND FLAVORS we think of as originating in Thailand might best be thought of as coming from Bangkok, just as the cuisines of Paris and Rome are amalgams of the regional cuisines of their respective countries. Only when American cooks become as intensely curious about the cooking of Thailand as that of France and Italy will regional differences become apparent.

In the meantime, there are a number of ingredients, as well as a couple of overriding principles, that can serve to define Thai cooking. Many Thai dishes are not unlike what we call curries, since they may contain curry powder and are often based on a combination of herbs and aromatic vegetables rather than dried spices. A typical dish might feature a mixture of garlic, shallots, chiles, lime leaf, sugar, and galangal or ginger.

Note that this intense combination features three basic flavors—sweet, sour, and salty. Chiles, which provide heat (not exactly a flavor), are also ubiquitous, but their quantity is easily and frequently varied according to taste.

Herbs are used to freshen dishes, but the trinity of sweet, salty (in the form of nam pla, or fish sauce, and salt), and sour (lime in several forms, and also tamarind) is all-important, and ideally well balanced. Rice is served at most meals, and turns a curry like this one into a meal. Sticky rice is best if you have it, but ordinary white rice, preferably short-grain, is just fine.

Although canned coconut milk is ridiculously convenient, making coconut milk at home is easy, and contains no preservatives: Combine 2 cups water and 2 cups dried unsweetened shredded or grated coconut in a blender. Use a towel to hold the lid on tight and turn the switch on and off a few times quickly to get the mixture going. Then blend for about 30 seconds. Let rest for 10 minutes. Pour the milk through a strainer. This will be fairly thick. If you need more milk, just pour additional water through the coconut, up to another cup or two. Press the coconut to extract as much liquid as possible. Use immediately or freeze indefinitely.

2 tablespoons peanut or vegetable oil	1 cup fresh or canned coconut milk (see headnote)
1 cup minced onion	1½ to 2 pounds medium-to-large shrimp, peeled
1 tablespoon minced garlic	
1 tablespoon minced fresh ginger	Salt and freshly ground black pepper
1 teaspoon minced fresh hot chiles, or crushed red pepper flakes, or to taste	2 tablespoons nam pla (fish sauce), or to taste
1 tablespoon curry powder, or to taste	¼ cup chopped cilantro or mint leaves

1 Place the oil in a large, deep skillet and turn the heat to medium. Add the onion, garlic, ginger, and chiles and cook, stirring frequently, until the vegetables are tender and the mixture pasty. Add the curry powder and cook, stirring, another minute.

2 Add the coconut milk and raise the heat to medium-high. Cook, stirring only occasionally, until the mixture is reduced by about half. (If you want to cook the dish a few hours in advance, now is the time to stop. Finishing it will take only 5 or 10 minutes, and is best done just before serving.)

3 Add the shrimp, a few pinches of salt, and a little black pepper and cook, stirring frequently, until the shrimp release their liquid (the mixture will become quite moist again) and turn pink, 5 to 10 minutes. Add 1 tablespoon nam pla, stir, then taste and add the rest if necessary. Garnish with cilantro and serve with white or sticky rice.

With MINIMAL Effort

SUBSTITUTE boneless chicken or pork, cut into cubes no bigger than 1 inch across, for the shrimp. Increase cooking time slightly.

SUBSTITUTE scallops for the shrimp; cooking time will remain the same.

USE firm tofu in place of the shrimp; cooking time will remain the same.

USE skinned, bone-in chicken in place of the shrimp. Cover the skillet, and cook over low heat, stirring every few minutes, until the meat is done. Cooking time will increase significantly, to about 20 to 30 minutes after adding the meat.

Stuffing the Scallop

WORK TIME	20 minutes
PREP TIME	20 minutes
CAN BE	prepared in advance; easily multiplied
MAKES	4 servings

A LOGICAL CANDIDATE FOR THE kitchen minimalism is the sea scallop, which is one of the most perfect of nature's convenience foods, because almost nothing cooks faster. This is especially true if you opt to heat the mollusk until it remains rare in the center, as do most scallop admirers. (Shuckers separate the scallop's meat from its guts soon after capture, which makes scallops the safest shellfish to eat undercooked or even raw.)

Sea scallops are also large enough to stuff, not with bread crumbs or other fish, as is common with clams or lobsters, but with herbs, garlic, and other flavorings. As long as a scallop is a good inch across and roughly three-quarters of an inch thick, you can make an equatorial slit in it and fill it with any number of stuffings.

As the scallop cooks, the sauce—which will barely warm—will thin and drizzle out a bit from the center. The result is not only more colorful than merely garnishing the cooked scallops, but more flavorful, because as the herb past warms it infuses the meat with flavor. Although these may be grilled or broiled, I sauté them in order to allow the stuffing juices to mingle with those of the mollusks themselves; this liquid makes the scallops perfect to serve over raw or cooked greens.

A word about buying scallops: Many are dipped in a chemical solution to prolong their shelf life. Not coincidentally, this soaking causes them to absorb water, which increases their weight and—water being cheaper than scallops—decreases their value. Furthermore, the added water makes browning more difficult. You can recognize processed scallops by their stark white color; in addition, they are usually swimming in liquid. Buy dry, beige (or slightly pink or orange) scallops from a reliable fishmonger and you won't have a problem.

Many cooks remove the tough little hinge present on one side of most scallops before cooking. But when you're stuffing scallops, leave it on and cut from the side directly opposite. The hinge will then serve the purpose of holding the scallop together, and can be removed at the table or eaten; it's slightly tough, but not unpleasant.

20 large fresh basil leaves	3 tablespoons extra virgin olive oil
1 small garlic clove, peeled	
½ teaspoon coarse salt	1¼ to 1½ pounds large sea scallops of fairly uniform size
¼ teaspoon freshly ground black pepper	

1 Mince the basil, garlic, salt, and pepper together until very fine, almost a puree (use a small food processor if you like). Mix in a small bowl with 1 tablespoon of the olive oil to produce a thick paste.

2 Cut most but not all of the way through the equator of each scallop, then smear a bit of the basil mixture on the exposed center; close the scallop. (See photographs.)

3 Place a large nonstick skillet over high heat for a minute; add the remaining oil, then the scallops, one at a time. As each scallop browns— it should take no longer than 1 or 2 minutes—turn it and brown the other side. Serve hot, drizzled with the pan juices.

1 | Remove the tough, stark white hinge from the outside of scallops simply by pulling it off.

2 | Cut the scallop through its equator, leaving one edge intact to hold it together.

With MINIMAL Effort

Sautéed Scallops with Herb Paste: You can substitute prepared pesto for the basil mixture above. Alternatively, substitute parsley, cilantro, or dill for the basil in the original recipe.

Stuffed Scallops with Greens: When the scallops are done, place them on a bed of greens (about 6 cups is right for this amount of scallops). Turn the heat under the skillet to low and add 3 tablespoons fresh lemon juice.

Cook, stirring, for about 10 seconds, then pour the pan juices over the scallops and greens and serve, drizzled with more olive oil if you like.

Sautéed Scallops Stuffed with Peanut Sauce: Cream 2 tablespoons chunky natural peanut butter with ¼ teaspoon minced garlic; minced fresh chiles or cayenne to taste; 1 teaspoon sugar; and sufficient soy sauce to make a thin paste. Use this paste as you would the basil paste, above, and use peanut oil to sauté the scallops. When the scallops are done, place them on a bed of lightly steamed or sautéed bitter greens, such as dandelions or mustard. Turn the heat under the skillet to low and add 3 tablespoons lime juice. Cook, stirring, for about 10 seconds, then pour the pan juices over the scallops and greens and serve, drizzled with a little more peanut oil if you like.

Poultry

Honey-Orange Roast Chicken
Perfectly Browned Roast Chicken

WORK TIME	30 minutes
PREP TIME	60 minutes
MAKES	4 servings

SOMEHOW ROASTING A CHICKEN has become a daunting task, like making a dress or tuning up the car. In fact few dishes are simpler: Put the chicken in a hot oven and make sure it doesn't overcook. If you start with a good chicken—that's really the hard part—and use an instant-read thermometer to check for doneness, the process is a no-brainer.

Roast chicken is even better if you baste it with flavorful liquid while it's in the oven. Contrary to conventional "wisdom," this does nothing to keep the bird moist—the bird remains moist by itself as long as it isn't overcooked. It does, however, add flavor to the skin and create a ready-made sauce that can be spooned over the chicken when you serve it.

If you add some sugar or other sweetener to the basting liquid, the bird turns a dark mahogany color. As it heats, the sugar caramelizes, becoming thicker and stickier, and it turns the chicken skin crisp and gorgeous. The result is not overly sweet, either, because caramelized sugars have a bitter, complex component.

For maximum flavor I prefer honey to sugar, and I combine it with orange juice and cumin, which add acidity and even more complexity. The result is aromatic and enticing. The sauce is perfect spooned over rice or sopped up with some crusty bread.

There is a certain boldness of spirit you need to roast a bird this way. After twenty minutes of cooking, you will be certain that the skin is going to burn in spots, but have faith. Rotate the chicken back to front in the oven, continue to baste, and the skin will become uniformly dark brown. If you're convinced that scorching is an issue, lower the heat by 25 to 50 degrees.

As I mentioned earlier, the most challenging part of the process is buying a good chicken. I prefer kosher chickens. But nearly any premium chicken, such as D'Artagnan or Bell & Evans, is preferable to the least-expensive mass-produced birds, which are soft and nearly tasteless.

Finally, there is the question of doneness. The USDA recommends roasting chicken to an internal temperature of 180 degrees, even though its own literature acknowledges that foodborne bacteria are killed at 160 degrees, and even though no sauce can rescue a chicken cooked to that temperature. I remove chicken from the oven when an instant-read thermometer inserted into the thickest part of the thigh reads 155 degrees; any traces of pinkness disappear during the few minutes I let it sit before carving. If this procedure makes you nervous, cook the chicken a little longer; but I see no good reason to cook it beyond 165 degrees.

1/2 cup orange juice, preferably freshly squeezed	Salt and freshly ground black pepper
1/2 cup honey	3-pound chicken, giblets and excess fat removed
1 tablespoon ground cumin	

1 Preheat the oven to 400° F. To ease cleanup, use a nonstick roasting pan, or line a roasting pan with a double layer of aluminum foil. Combine the orange juice, honey, cumin, salt, and pepper in a blender or a bowl and blend or whisk until smooth. Place the chicken in the roasting pan and spoon all but 1/4 cup of the liquid over it, making sure to get some of the liquid on the legs and thighs.

2 Place the chicken in the oven, legs first. Roast 10 minutes, then spoon the accumulated juices from the bottom of the pan back over the chicken. Reverse the pan back to front, and return to the oven. Repeat 4 times, basting every 10 minutes and switching the pan position each time. If the chicken appears to be browning too quickly, lower the heat a bit (but see the headnote). If the pan dries out (unlikely but possible with an extremely lean bird), use the reserved liquid and, if necessary, some additional orange juice or water.

3 After 50 minutes of roasting, insert an instant-read thermometer into the bird's thigh; when it reads 155 to 165 degrees, remove the chicken from the oven and baste one final time. Let rest 5 minutes before carving and serving.

With MINIMAL Effort

Soy-Roasted Chicken: Replace the orange juice with 1/4 cup soy sauce; add 1 teaspoon minced garlic, 1 teaspoon peeled and grated or minced fresh ginger or 1/2 teaspoon ground ginger, and 1/4 cup minced scallions to the liquid; omit the cumin.

Herb-Roasted Chicken: Mix together ¼ cup extra virgin olive oil and 2 tablespoons chopped parsley, chervil, basil, or dill. Baste the chicken with this mixture as it roasts. Garnish with more chopped herbs.

Lemon-Roasted Chicken: Brush the chicken with olive oil before roasting; cut a lemon in half and put it in the chicken's cavity. Roast, more or less undisturbed, until done; squeeze the juice from the cooked lemon over the chicken and carve.

SUBSTITUTE paprika for the cumin.

ADD minced garlic to the basting mixture.

ADD some whole cumin seeds to the mixture.

ADD a tablespoon of vinegar or lemon juice to the mixture.

Chicken Under a Brick

WORK TIME	15 minutes
PREP TIME	45 minutes (longer with optional marinating time)
CAN BE	prepared in advance (and served at room temperature)
MAKES	4 servings

THERE ARE ALWAYS DIFFICULTIES in cooking chicken so that the skin crunches and the interior stays moist: It burns on the grill, spatters on the stove, becomes too greasy in a deep-fryer. But there is a foolproof and less messy technique for making chicken crisp and juicy.

You need two ovenproof skillets, or a skillet and a couple of bricks or rocks. Begin with a split chicken (any supermarket butcher will split one for you, or you can do it yourself with a heavy knife; see page 114), marinate it if you have the time, then blast it, skin side down, in a skillet on top of the stove.

At that point weight it with another skillet, clean or foil-wrapped rocks, bricks, or what-have-you. The weight serves two purposes: It partially covers the chicken, which helps it retain moisture, and it ensures that the flesh of the chicken remains in contact with the skillet, which enables it to brown. The dish is called *pollo al mattone* in Italian (a *mattone* is a heavy tile).

Once covered, the chicken is transferred to a very hot oven to finish cooking. Handling the hot, heavy pan takes two hands. I've been making chicken under a brick for years, and believe that it is the simplest and best method for producing crisp, delicious skin, and wonderfully moist meat. As a bonus, much of the chicken's own moisture remains at the bottom of the pan; it makes a perfect natural sauce.

1 whole 3- to 4-pound chicken, trimmed of excess fat, rinsed, dried, and split, backbone removed (see photographs, page 114)

1 tablespoon fresh minced rosemary, or 1 teaspoon dried rosemary

Salt and freshly ground black pepper

1 tablespoon coarsely chopped garlic

2 tablespoons extra virgin olive oil

2 sprigs fresh rosemary, if available

1 lemon, cut into quarters

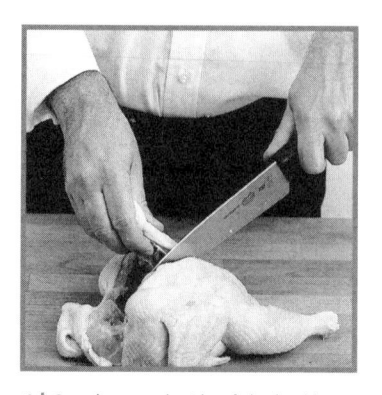

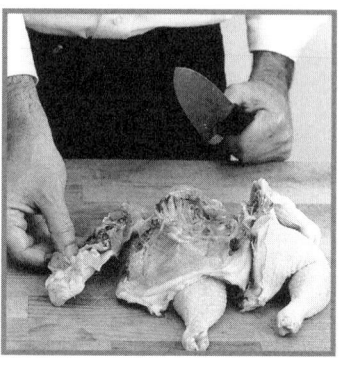

1 | Cut along each side of the backbone with a sharp, sturdy knife.

2 | Remove the backbone from the chicken.

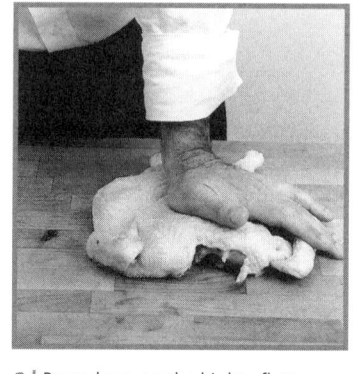

3 | Press down on the bird to flatten completely.

1 Place the chicken on a cutting board, skin side down, and press down as hard as you can with your hands to make it as flat as possible. Mix together the rosemary leaves, salt, garlic, and 1 tablespoon of the olive oil and rub this all over the chicken. Tuck some of the mixture under the skin as well. If time permits, cover and marinate in the refrigerator for up to a day (even 20 minutes of marinating is helpful).

2 When you are ready to cook, preheat the oven to 500° F. Preheat an ovenproof 12-inch skillet (preferably nonstick) over medium-high heat for about 3 minutes. Press the rosemary sprigs into the skin side of the chicken. Put the remaining olive oil in the pan and wait about 30 seconds for it to heat up.

3 Place the chicken in the skillet, skin side down, along with any remaining pieces of rosemary and garlic; weight it with another skillet or one or two bricks or rocks, wrapped in aluminum foil. The basic idea is to flatten the chicken by applying a fair amount of weight evenly over its surface.

4 Cook over medium-high to high heat for 5 minutes, then transfer to the oven. Roast for 15 minutes. Remove from the oven and remove the weights; turn the chicken over (it will now be skin side up) and roast 10 minutes more, or until done (large chickens may take an additional 5 minutes or so). Serve hot or at room temperature, with lemon wedges.

With MINIMAL Effort

USE different herbs in the place of rosemary; sage, savory, and tarragon are all perfect; Russians use paprika. Or try a light dusting of cinnamon, ginger, and/or other "sweet" spices.

USE minced shallot instead of garlic.

VARY the acidic ingredient: balsamic, sherry vinegar, or lime juice can all pinch-hit for the lemon, depending upon the other flavors.

USE clarified butter or neutral oil such as canola or corn in place of the olive oil.

LEAVE European flavors behind entirely and make the dish Asian, using peanut oil and a mixture of minced garlic, ginger, and scallions. Finish the dish with lime quarters and minced cilantro, or a drizzle of soy sauce and sesame oil.

Chicken with Riesling

WORK TIME	30 minutes
PREP TIME	90 minutes
CAN BE	prepared in advance; easily multiplied
MAKES	4 to 6 servings

WHEN WINE IS ADDED TO simmering chicken, it's most often dry and white. The common exception to this rule is the classic French dish *coq au vin,* in which the wine is dry and red. Yet a quick twist of these rules creates a chicken dish so distinctive that it should be in everyone's repertoire. The key is a slightly sweet white wine whose fruity complexity—at its best both subtle and well defined—adds a layer of flavor that no dry white wine ever could.

My chicken with Riesling has its roots in the classic Alsatian *poulet au Riesling,* which usually contains cream, bacon, and several other ingredients. This recipe contains no more than loads of sliced onion cooked in a small lump of butter along with the chicken and wine, a quartet that produces a dish of sublime tenderness, creaminess, and depth of flavor.

Whenever you cook with few ingredients the quality of each individual component gains importance. Plain yellow onions are fine, any decent butter or oil will do, and of course a good chicken is essential. But the wine plays such a major role here that it's worth buying the right one. Finding a good off-dry white is not difficult, as long as you know what you're looking for. Almost any German wine made with Riesling (the grape name will be on the label) will do, except for those labeled *trocken,* which means dry (since dry German wines are unusual, avoiding them is not a major challenge). The best German wines are labeled *Qualitätswein mit Prädikat* (quality wine with distinction) and any of these with the words *kabinett* or *spätlese* are likely candidates. Not quite as fine, but certainly good enough, are *QBA* wines. Any decent wine shop will have a good selection of both of these kinds of wines.

Although the cooking time for chicken with Riesling is not short, it is largely unattended, and the dish can be made well in advance. In fact, as with many meat-and-liquid preparations, this may be more delicious on the second day. And this is a preparation that you can take in many directions, as you'll see from the variations on page 117.

2 tablespoons butter or neutral
  oil, such as canola

4 medium-to-large onions (about
  1½ pounds), peeled and sliced

Salt and freshly ground black
  pepper

1½ to 2 cups off-dry Riesling

One 3- to 4-pound chicken,
  preferably kosher or free-range,
  cut into 8 or 10 serving pieces.
  (See photographs, pages
  117–118.)

1 Place the butter in a skillet large enough to hold the chicken and turn the heat to medium. Add the onions, a large pinch of salt, and some pepper and cook, stirring occasionally, until the onions soften completely and begin to melt into a soft mass, about 20 minutes.

2 Add 1½ cups of the wine and let it bubble away for a minute, then tuck the chicken pieces among the onions; sprinkle the chicken with salt and pepper. Turn the heat to low and cover the pan.

3 Cook, turning the chicken pieces once or twice, for 40 to 60 minutes, or until the chicken is very tender (the meat on the drumsticks will begin to loosen from the bone). If the dish appears to be drying out at any point, add the remaining wine.

4 Serve the chicken with crusty bread or white rice or another grain, spooning the onions and their liquid over all.

With MINIMAL Effort

COOK the onions an additional 10 minutes or so before adding the wine until they darken in color and become even softer.

WHILE the onions are cooking, brown the chicken by placing it, skin side up, in a 500°F oven for about 20 minutes. When you add the chicken to the onions, include some of its juice.

TUCK a couple of bay leaves and/or a few sprigs of thyme in among the onions after they've begun to soften.

SAUTÉ about ¼ pound of bacon or salt pork cut into ½-inch chunks in the pan before adding the onions.

COOK about ½ pound of sliced mushrooms (or an ounce or two of dried porcini mushrooms, reconstituted) along with the onions.

COOK 1 tablespoon or more of chopped garlic with the onions.

AFTER cooking, puree the onions and their liquid in a blender for a creamlike sauce; use it to top the chicken.

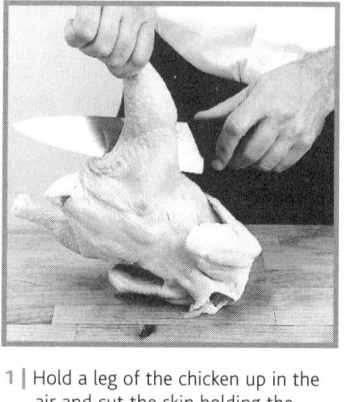

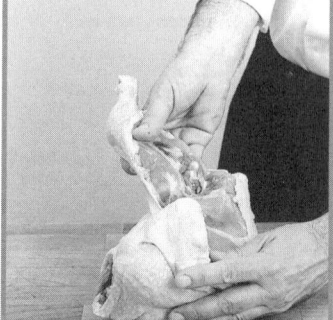

1 | Hold a leg of the chicken up in the air and cut the skin holding the thigh to the body.

2 | Break the joint.

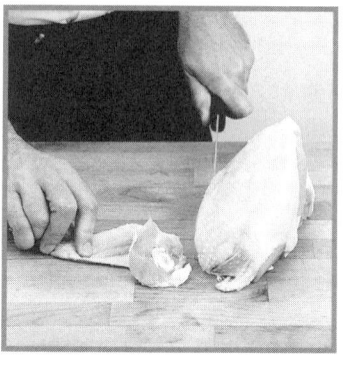

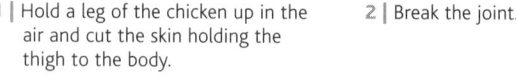

3 | Cut through the joint to separate leg from body.

4 | Cut along each side of the backbone with a sharp, sturdy knife.

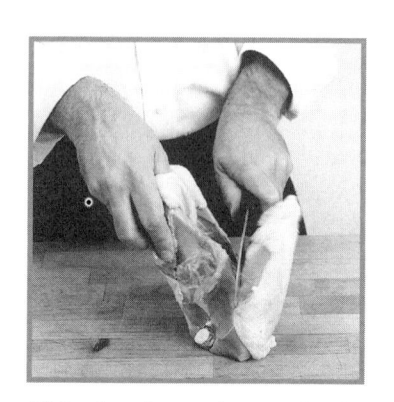

5 | Cut down between breast and back.

6 | Pull the breast and back apart.

7 | Cut back away from breast.

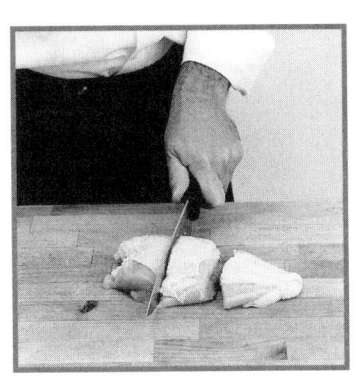

8 | Cut across the breast to make three more-or-less equal size pieces.

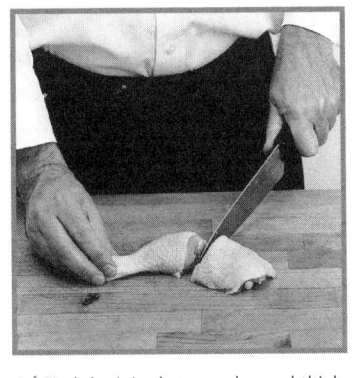

9 | Find the joint between leg and thigh and cut through it.

10 | Cut off and discard the wing tip. Cut between the two remaining wing sections.

11| The breast, one leg, and one wing.

Chicken with Rice

The Ultimate in Basics

WORK TIME	15 minutes
PREP TIME	30 minutes
CAN BE	cooked in advance; easily multiplied
MAKES	4 servings

YOU CAN MAKE A BIG DEAL OUT of chicken with rice—at its zenith, it becomes something grand—but it is also a dish that takes well to shortcuts. For fast weeknight meals, I strip chicken and rice to its bare essentials: oil, onion, chicken, and rice. Stock makes the best cooking liquid, but water works almost as well, because as it simmers with the chicken they combine to produce a flavorful broth.

To make the dish as quickly as possible, begin by boiling water and sautéing the onion at the same time; that way, when it's time to add the rice and the chicken to the skillet, the water is ready to go and the dish takes just another twenty minutes to complete. To reduce greasiness, remove the skin from the chicken before cooking it; in a moist dish such as this, the skin is not especially appetizing anyway.

To add the yellow color that traditionally comes from saffron, many restaurants use turmeric or annatto oil, a dark red oil made by gently heating achiote seeds. Although either of these is acceptable, nothing adds the same exotic flavor and depth of color as a tiny pinch of saffron, so try to stick with that. When buying saffron, steer clear of the tiny vials that contain a few threads; go to a reputable specialty store or mail-order house and buy either a gram, which will cost you under ten dollars and contain about five hundred threads, or a quarter of an ounce, which will cost about forty dollars and last several years.

3 tablespoons olive oil	1½ cups white rice
2 medium onions (about 8 ounces) peeled and sliced	Pinch saffron, optional
Salt and freshly ground black pepper	Freshly minced parsley or cilantro for garnish
1 chicken, cut into serving pieces	Lemon or lime wedges

1 Set 3 cups water to boil in a kettle or covered saucepan. Place the olive oil in a large skillet that can later be covered and turn the heat to medium-high. Add the onions and a sprinkling of salt and pepper to taste. Cook, stirring occasionally, until the onions soften and become translucent, 5 to 10 minutes. Meanwhile, remove the skin from the chicken.

2 Add the rice to the onions and stir until each grain of rice glistens; sprinkle with the saffron and stir again. Nestle the chicken pieces in the rice, add a little more salt and pepper, and pour in the boiling water. Turn the heat to medium-low and cover.

3 Cook for 20 minutes until all the water is absorbed and the chicken is cooked through. (You can keep this warm over a very low flame for another 15 minutes, and it will retain its heat for 15 minutes beyond that, and still be good warm rather than hot.) Garnish with parsley and serve with lemon or lime wedges.

With MINIMAL Effort

USE any stock instead of water for richer flavor.

SUBSTITUTE pearled barley for the rice.

IF you would like crisp-skinned chicken, sauté or roast it separately and combine it with the rice at the last minute.

ADD sausage or shellfish such as shrimp along with the chicken.

ADD strips of red bell pepper, or pitted olives, capers, chopped tomatoes, and/or shelled peas to the skillet along with the onions.

Chicken with Vinegar

WORK TIME	30 minutes
PREP TIME	40 minutes
MAKES	4 servings

CHICKEN WITH VINEGAR IS ONE OF many great poultry dishes from the area around Lyons, a region whose famous *poulet de Bresse* is considered by many to be the best chicken in the world. The story is that the dish was first popularized at La Mère Brazier, one of the Lyonnaise restaurants known as *les bonnes mères. Les bonnes mères* are not as numerous as they once were, but those that remain continue two traditions: They are run by women, and they are a step up from bistros in ambience, service, and presentation of food.

Chef Paul Bocuse worked at La Mère Brazier in his youth and learned how to prepare chicken with vinegar there. Some years later, he showed considerable audacity by putting what is essentially a peasant dish on the menu of a Michelin three-star restaurant. He insisted that it was neither how much work nor the cost of ingredients that determined the worthiness of a dish, but how it tasted. Bravo.

The stamp of Bocuse not only legitimized chicken with vinegar, but increased its popularity. He taught the dish to a generation of his students, one of whom taught it to me. The variations are numerous but don't matter all that much; the strong—almost piercing—and singular flavor of vinegar is so dominant that it matters little whether you use shallots or garlic, thyme or tarragon, or little seasoning at all.

Chicken with vinegar remains incredibly good, whether prepared with utter abandon (as taught by Bocuse, whose recipe I give as a variation below) or with contemporary restraint. In the original version, vinegar combines with chicken juices and what is by today's standards an embarrassment of butter to make a silken sauce—an interesting marriage of sharp flavors and soothing textures, and an elegant if simple dish worthy of serving to anyone.

I greatly reduce the overall quantity of fat, and rely primarily on olive oil. While it is undeniable that some of the wonderful texture is lost in the translation, so is the guilt.

One technical note: Most wine vinegar sold in the United States, even the high-quality brands, have an acidity level of seven percent; many French vinegars are just five percent acidity. So when using strong vinegar, it's best to cut it with some water, as I do here.

2 tablespoons olive oil	¼ cup minced shallots or
One 3-pound chicken, cut up for	scallions
sautéing	1 cup good red wine vinegar
Salt and freshly ground black	1 tablespoon butter, optional
pepper	

1 Preheat the oven to 450° F. Set a large skillet—preferably with steep sides to minimize spattering—over medium-high heat. Add the oil and wait a minute. When it is good and hot, place the chicken in the skillet, skin side down. Cook undisturbed for about 5 minutes, or until the chicken is nicely browned. Turn and cook 3 minutes on the other side. Season with salt and pepper to taste.

2 Place the chicken in the oven. Cook 15 to 20 minutes, or until it is just about done (the juices will run clear, and there will be just the barest trace of pink near the bone). Remove the chicken to an ovenproof platter and place the platter in the oven; turn off the oven and leave the door slightly ajar.

3 Pour most but not all of the cooking juices out of the skillet. Place the skillet over medium-high heat and add the shallots; sprinkle them with a little salt and pepper and cook, stirring, until they are tender, about 2 minutes. Add the vinegar and raise the heat to high. Cook for a minute or two, or until the powerful smell has subsided somewhat. Add ½ cup water and cook for another 2 minutes, stirring, until the mixture is slightly reduced and somewhat thickened. Stir in the optional butter.

4 Return the chicken and any accumulated juices to the skillet and turn the chicken in the sauce. Serve immediately.

With MINIMAL Effort

Paul Bocuse's Poulet au Vinaigre: In Step 1, brown the chicken in 7 tablespoons butter. In Step 3, add 3 tablespoons butter to the reduced vinegar sauce.

SUBSTITUTE chopped garlic or onion for the shallots.

ADD an herb to the chicken as it's browning: a sprig of tarragon (or a big pinch of dried tarragon), a few thyme sprigs (or a teaspoon of dried thyme), or 5 or 6 bay leaves.

USE Champagne, rice, or white wine vinegar.

ADD about 2 tablespoons of capers to the vinegar as it reduces.

STIR a tablespoon or more of Dijon mustard into the sauce just before serving.

Spicy Chicken with Lemongrass and Lime

Thai Braised Chicken

WORK TIME	25 minutes
PREP TIME	45 minutes
CAN BE	prepared in advance; easily multiplied
MAKES	4 servings

UPON FIRST CONSIDERATION IT MAY seem absurd, even insulting, to attempt to reduce an entire cuisine to a few flavors, but with just a handful of Thai ingredients—nearly all of which are available in most supermarkets—you can duplicate or even improve upon many of the dishes found in your typical neighborhood Thai restaurant. There are a few ingredients that will be unfamiliar to most American cooks, but there are no complicated techniques involved in either preparing or cooking.

A sweeping approach such as this one is, of course, overly simplistic. Thailand, like Italy, is a country of many regional cuisines. There are areas that feature cumin, cloves, cinnamon, nutmeg, and other spices we associate with India; those where an abundance of chiles makes the food fiercely hot; and still others that rely heavily on fresh green peppercorns. The country's geography (it contains farmland, jungle, and a long coastline, and it shares borders with China, Laos, Burma, Cambodia, and Malaysia), and its history (there are hundreds of thousands of ethnic immigrants, not only from neighboring countries but from Vietnam, India, Indonesia, and elsewhere) ensure that there is no one Thai cuisine.

Almost all Thai cooking has an intensity of flavor resulting from a strong combination of sweet, sour, and salty. Chiles, which provide heat (not exactly a flavor), are also ubiquitous, but their quantity is easily and frequently varied according to taste. Herbs are used to freshen dishes, and among the most important of these are lemongrass and lime, both of which are slightly sour but also wonderfully floral. Integrate them into your cooking and you will open a new world. (For more about lemongrass, see page 11.)

2 tablespoons peanut or vegetable oil	2 lemongrass stalks
½ cup minced shallots	One 3-pound chicken, cut into serving pieces (see photographs on pages 118–119)
1 tablespoon minced garlic	
1 tablespoon minced galangal or ginger	
1 teaspoon minced fresh hot chiles or crushed red pepper flakes, or to taste	Salt and freshly ground black pepper
	1 tablespoon minced lime leaves or zest
1 teaspoon turmeric	2 tablespoons nam pla (fish sauce)
1 teaspoon ground dried cilantro	¼ cup minced fresh cilantro leaves
1 teaspoon sugar	

1 Place the oil in a large, deep skillet and turn the heat to medium. Add the shallots, garlic, galangal, and chiles and cook, stirring frequently, until the vegetables are tender and the mixture pasty. Add the turmeric, cilantro, and sugar and cook, stirring, for another minute. Trim the lemongrass stalks of their toughest outer layers, then bruise them with the back of a knife; cut them into sections and add them to the mixture along with 1 cup water.

2 Add the chicken and turn it once or twice in the sauce, then nestle it in the sauce; season with a little salt and pepper to taste. Turn the heat to low and cover the skillet. Cook, turning once or twice, until the chicken is cooked through, 20 to 30 minutes. (You can prepare the recipe in advance up to this point; cover and refrigerate for up to a day, and reheat before proceeding.)

3 Uncover the skillet and raise the heat to medium-high; turn the chicken skin side down. Let most (but not all) of the liquid evaporate and brown the chicken just a little on the bottom. Stir in the lime leaves or zest and nam pla; taste and adjust seasoning as necessary, then garnish and serve, with white rice.

With MINIMAL Effort

This same preparation is used with many different foods in both Thailand and Vietnam, and most of them not only adapt perfectly to this recipe but are faster to prepare.

USE boneless chicken, cut into chunks. Cook only about 5 minutes after adding the chicken and bringing the liquid back to a boil. Or leave boneless breasts or thighs whole; cooking time will be about 10 minutes for breasts to 15 minutes for thighs.

USE whole shrimp or scallops, or a combination. Cooking time will be about 5 minutes from the time the liquid returns to a boil.

USE chunks of boneless pork or bone-in pork such as lean pork chops. Boneless pork will cook in about 10 minutes (from the time the liquid returns to a boil), bone-in in about 20 minutes.

USE chunks of firm tofu, which will cook through in 3 to 5 minutes.

USE vegetables in the dish: quartered peeled onions, roughly chopped bell pepper, or chunks of zucchini; add them along with the shallots and other seasonings.

Deviled Chicken Thighs

WORK TIME	15 minutes
PREP TIME	20 minutes
CAN BE	prepared in advance; easily multiplied
MAKES	4 servings

PREPARED MUSTARD IS ABOUT as underappreciated as a staple could be. After all, it's all-natural (or pretty much so), completely fat-free, ridiculously low in calories, and notably high in flavor. Despite these marked assets, its main role in most households is as a condiment for meat and, perhaps, an occasional ingredient in vinaigrette. In this chicken dish, however—essentially broiled chicken smeared with a spicy mustard paste—it plays a leading role.

In cooking, the term "deviled" has several different meanings—some inexplicable—but it most sensibly implies a preparation featuring a sharp flavor, most often derived from mustard, vinegar, cayenne or other chiles. You don't need vinegar here, because there is plenty of acidity in Dijon mustard. Nor, strictly speaking, do you need cayenne (and I omit it when serving this to kids); the taste is quite strong without it.

If you coat chicken before cooking, you simply cannot get a crisp skin. Broiling coated chicken almost ensures a quick burn, and baking guarantees sogginess. So broil the chicken, skin side up, until it's crisp. (This has another advantage: You can prepare the coating *after* beginning to cook the chicken, which cuts down on preparation time.) Then turn it over, flavor the underside, and let that cook for a few minutes. After coating the top, return the chicken to the broiler for a final browning; the result is skin that's crisp but not burned.

You can make this dish with chicken breasts if you prefer, but I recommend that you start with bone-in breasts and follow the same procedure. If you want to use boneless, skinless breasts (forget about crispness, of course) smear the meat all over with the mustard mixture, then broil for just about six minutes, turning two or three times to prevent burning.

8 chicken thighs, or a mixture of thighs and drumsticks	⅓ cup minced shallots, onions, or scallions
Salt and freshly ground black pepper	¼ teaspoon cayenne pepper or Tabasco sauce, or to taste
⅓ cup Dijon mustard	Minced parsley for garnish, optional

1 Preheat the broiler to its maximum, and set the rack about 4 inches from the heat. Season the chicken on both sides and place it in a pan, skin side up. Broil, watching carefully, until the skin is golden brown, about 5 minutes.

2 Meanwhile, combine the mustard, shallots, and cayenne. (If you have a small food processor, just throw them in there and pulse the machine on and off a few times.)

3 When the chicken has browned, remove it from the oven and turn it. Spread just a teaspoon or so of the mustard mixture on the underside of the chicken and broil about 5 minutes. Turn the chicken and spread the remaining mixture on the skin side. Broil until the mustard begins to brown.

4 At this point, the chicken may be done (there will be only the barest trace of pink near the bone, and an instant-read thermometer inserted into the meat will read 160 degrees). If it is not, turn off the broiler and let the chicken remain in the oven for another 5 minutes or so. Garnish with the optional parsley and serve.

With MINIMAL Effort

FOR extra crunch, combine the mustard and shallots with about 1 cup bread crumbs. Be especially careful in broiling, for the bread crumbs will burn very soon after they brown.

FOR extra flavor, combine the mustard and shallots with about ½ cup chopped parsley (or basil, cilantro, dill, or chervil). Proceed as above.

YOU can use the same coating with pork or veal chops; they should be at least 1 inch thick. Cooking time will be about the same.

Chicken Curry in a Hurry

WORK TIME	15 minutes
PREP TIME	15 minutes
CAN BE	easily multiplied
MAKES	4 servings

IF YOU'RE A CURRY AFICIONADO, you know that there is no spice called curry powder. In fact, curry is a spice blend, containing as few as four or five or as many as ten different spices, of which cumin, turmeric, coriander, cardamom, ginger, fenugreek, and black pepper occur most frequently.

You can, of course, mix your own curry, but preblended curry powder is one of the original convenience foods, a venerable spice rub that can boost the flavor of almost anything. I like to use it in tandem with a twentieth-century convenience food, the boneless, skinless chicken breast. Even a breast from a good chicken is about as bland as meat can get, and one from the supermarket is not much more flavorful than unsauced pasta.

Hit it with a little curry, though, and the flavor comes alive. In this dish, I season both onions and chicken breast with the spice, and finish the dish with yogurt or sour cream. The concept is hardly original (chicken in curried cream sauce was once a standard in English as well as French restaurants), but I've streamlined the process so that it takes no more than fifteen minutes. (This means you must begin cooking white rice, the natural accompaniment, before even chopping the onion.)

Select a good curry powder (supermarket varieties are acceptable but not exciting). If you like shopping by mail, you might choose from among the mixtures offered by Penzey's, a reliable Wisconsin-based spice house (800–741–7787; fax 262–679–7878); their vindaloo powder is sweet and not too hot. In the supermarket, look for the Sun brand of Madras curry powder.

You'll have to choose between yogurt and sour cream, each of which has advantages. Yogurt is lower in fat, and adds more tang to the dish; but it must be handled carefully and never allowed to boil or the sauce will curdle. High-fat sour cream not only can take more abuse during cooking, it produces a sauce that is creamy beyond compare. It's a can't-lose decision, really, and you'll probably want to try both.

1 tablespoon canola, corn, or other neutral oil

1 medium onion, peeled and sliced

Salt and freshly ground black pepper

1½ teaspoons curry powder, or to taste

1 pound boneless, skinless chicken breasts, in 4 pieces

1 cup sour cream

Minced cilantro or parsley leaves for garnish

1 Place the oil in a large skillet and turn the heat to medium-high. A minute later, add the onion. Sprinkle with some salt and pepper and cook, stirring occasionally, until translucent, about 5 minutes. Turn the heat to medium, sprinkle with about half the curry powder and continue to cook for a minute or two.

2 Meanwhile, season the chicken with salt and pepper to taste and sprinkle it with the remaining curry powder. Move the onion to one side of the skillet and add the chicken in one layer. Cook for about 2 minutes per side; remove to a plate.

3 Add the sour cream and stir constantly over medium-low heat until the mixture is nice and thick. Return the chicken to the skillet and cook for 2 more minutes, turning once. Garnish and serve with plenty of white rice.

With MINIMAL Effort

Chicken Curry with Yogurt: Because yogurt will curdle if it boils, some extra care must be taken here: In Step 3, turn the heat to very low and wait a minute before adding the yogurt. Stir the yogurt into the onion and cook, stirring constantly and over low heat, until the yogurt is hot. Return the chicken to the skillet and cook for 2 more minutes, turning once. At no point should the sauce boil.

ADD nuts (slivered almonds are best), raisins, and/or dried coconut pieces to the onion as it cooks.

ADD a couple of dried hot red chiles, or crushed red pepper flakes to taste, along with the onion; add more at the end of cooking if you like.

SUBSTITUTE peeled shrimp, or thin-sliced beef or pork, for the chicken; in each case, cooking time will be marginally shorter.

Chicken with Coconut and Lime

WORK TIME	10 minutes
PREP TIME	20 minutes
CAN BE	easily multiplied
MAKES	4 servings

ONE OF MY FAVORITE DISHES during a visit to Bangkok was a hastily served (and even more hastily eaten) chicken dish with a creamy but spicy lime sauce. At first I thought the rich texture had come from a pan reduction or even a béchamel-like sauce, but I detected the faint taste of coconut and realized it was little more than coconut milk spiked with lime.

Coconut milk is a standard ingredient throughout Southeast Asia. It isn't the watery liquid from the inside of a coconut, but a thick cream obtained by pressing hot water through grated coconut meat. It's sold in cans in every Asian food store and many supermarkets in the U.S., at about a dollar for thirteen ounces. But coconut milk is easy to make yourself, and because you only need a small quantity for this recipe it may make sense to do so (see page 104 for details).

In Thailand, the sauce was flavored with fresh lime leaves; since these are difficult to find here, I use lime zest, which is a decent substitute. The addition of fresh lime juice at the end of cooking also gives the dish a final hit of brightness. Nam pla—the fish sauce that serves as a replacement for salt in many Southeast Asian dishes—would add authenticity but isn't essential here.

Then there's the cooking method. You might grill this chicken, but unless you had the grill going for other reasons I wouldn't bother; it won't add significant flavor during the short cooking time and, besides, the sauce is the real star here. Broiling the boneless breasts without turning allows them to brown nicely on top while they cook without toughening.

2 limes	Salt and ground cayenne pepper
1 to 1½ pounds boneless, skinless chicken breasts, in 4 pieces	1 teaspoon nam pla (fish sauce), optional
½ cup canned or fresh coconut milk	4 minced scallions for garnish
	¼ cup minced cilantro for garnish

1 Remove the zest from the limes, either with a zester or a vegetable peeler (if you use a peeler, scrape off the white inside of the zest with a paring knife). Mince the zest and juice the limes. Marinate the chicken in half the lime juice while you preheat the broiler; adjust the rack so that it is about 4 inches from the heat source. (You may grill the chicken if you prefer.)

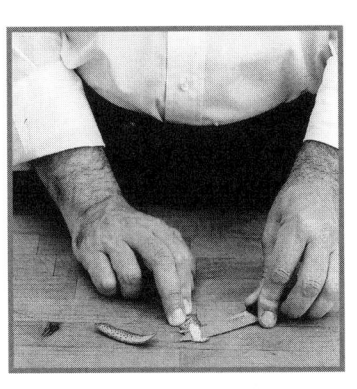

| Remove the zest with a vegetable peeler, then use a paring knife to scrape off as much of the inner white pith as you can.

2 Warm the coconut milk over low heat; season it with salt (hold off on salt if you use the nam pla) and a pinch of cayenne. Add the lime zest.

3 Put the chicken, smooth (skin) side up, on an ungreased baking sheet lined with aluminum foil and place in the broiler. Add half the remaining lime juice to the coconut milk mixture.

4 When the chicken is nicely browned on top, about 6 minutes later, it is done (make a small cut in the thickest part and peek inside if you want to be sure). Transfer it to a warm platter. Add the nam pla, if you're using it, to the coconut milk; taste and adjust seasoning as necessary. Spoon a little of the sauce over and around the breasts, then garnish with the scallions and cilantro and sprinkle with the remaining lime juice. Serve with white rice, passing the remaining sauce.

With MINIMAL Effort

This same sauce can be used with many different foods:

GRILLED or broiled shrimp or scallops, with the cooking time reduced by a minute or two;

BONELESS pork cutlets, treated like the chicken, with the cooking time increased by a couple of minutes (turn it once during cooking);

ALMOST any white-fleshed fillet of fish, especially firmer ones such as grouper, red snapper, or monkfish.

You can also make changes to the sauce:

ADD a pinch or more of cayenne, or a teaspoon of curry powder.

ADD a tablespoon of minced shallot to the coconut milk as it warms.

Chicken with Sweet-and-Sour Sherry Sauce

WORK TIME	20 minutes
PREP TIME	20 minutes
CAN BE	prepared in advance (sauce only); easily multiplied
MAKES	4 servings

CHICKEN BREASTS ARE SO BLAND that they demand *something*—a spice rub, a salsa, or a strong reduction sauce. Reduction sauces (see page 211) are made by boiling solids in liquids, concentrating the juice until little more than an essence remains. The simplest and most common example involves splashing some water into a skillet after you've roasted or sautéed meat or vegetables in it. The water gathers up the remaining bits, all of which have been nicely browned, and absorbs their flavor. As the quantity of water reduces, the flavor becomes more concentrated and the water is transformed into a sauce.

But if you start with strong-tasting solids and add a variety of bold liquids, reducing each one to a syrupy consistency, you end up with an intense and complex reduction sauce. The process can involve exoteric ingredients and procedures, or it can be quite straightforward. I learned the one here from Stephen Kalt, chef-owner at Spartina, a restaurant in Manhattan's Tribeca neighborhood.

It's direct, quick, and easy, especially considering that the result is a dark, complex sauce that can be used in many ways. Stephen began with mushrooms and shallots, then built a *gastrique*—a combination of intense sweet-and-sour flavors, in this case honey and vinegar. The sauce gains nuttiness from the sherry and body from the stock.

For added elegance, you can strain the sauce before serving it, as Stephen does in his restaurant. Because the mushroom-and-shallot mixture that forms the solid base of the sauce does not give up all of its flavor during this brief cooking—in fact, the mushrooms are chewy and sweet when the sauce is done—I like to spoon the sauce over the chicken.

It's worth noting that this sauce may be prepared well in advance. You can keep it warm over low heat for up to an hour, stirring it occasionally, or refrigerate it for a day or two, reheating it (thin with stock or water if necessary) just before adding the teaspoon of olive oil and serving.

1 tablespoon plus 1 teaspoon olive oil

½ cup oyster or shiitake mushrooms, trimmed and roughly chopped (discard the shiitake stems or reserve them for stock)

¼ cup sliced shallots

2 teaspoons honey

2 tablespoons sherry vinegar or good-quality wine vinegar

⅓ cup dry Fino or Oloroso sherry (do not use "cream" sherry)

1 cup meat, chicken, or vegetable stock

4 pieces boneless, skinless chicken breasts, 1 to 1½ pounds

Salt and freshly ground black pepper

1 Preheat the broiler or grill. Place a 10-inch skillet over medium-high heat for a minute or two. Add the tablespoon of olive oil, then the mushrooms and shallots, and turn the heat to high. Cook, stirring occasionally, until the mushrooms brown nicely on the edges, about 5 minutes.

2 Add the honey and stir until it evaporates, less than a minute. Add the vinegar and cook, stirring occasionally, until the mixture is dry, about 2 minutes. Add the sherry and cook, stirring once or twice, until the mixture is syrupy and nearly dry, about 5 minutes. Add the stock and cook, stirring once or twice, until the mixture thickens slightly, about 5 minutes. Reduce the heat to medium-low and keep warm.

3 Sprinkle the chicken breasts with salt and pepper and grill or broil them for about 6 minutes, or until cooked through.

4 When the chicken is done, season the sauce to taste with salt and pepper and strain it if you like; stir in the remaining olive oil. Serve the chicken with the sauce spooned over it.

With MINIMAL Effort

Mushrooms and Shallots with Sweet-and-Sour Sherry Sauce: Sauté about 1 pound fresh mushrooms, sliced (a combination of different mushrooms is best, but you can use all shiitakes or all button if you like) in 2 tablespoons olive oil over medium-high heat. The mushrooms will first give up their liquid, then begin to brown. When they start to crisp up, add ¼ cup minced shallots. Cook another 3 or 4 minutes, then serve with the sauce.

SAUTÉ the chicken breasts, using the recipe for Chicken Cutlets Meunière (page 136), and serve with the sauce.

SERVE the sauce with poached, grilled, or sautéed shrimp.

Chicken Cutlets Meunière
Crisp Chicken Breasts Made Easy

WORK TIME	15 minutes
PREP TIME	15 minutes
CAN BE	prepared in advance, easily multiplied
MAKES	4 servings

THE TERM *MEUNIÈRE* ONCE had a specific meaning, usually referring to fillets of sole that were floured and quickly sautéed in clarified butter, then finished with parsley, lemon juice, and a little melted butter. Over the years its definition has expanded, to the point where it describes a series of flexible techniques that can be applied to just about any thin cut of meat, poultry, or fish. All of which makes it more useful. While true sole—also called Dover sole—is ideal for this treatment, the softer-fleshed thin white fillets in our markets have a pronounced tendency to fall apart when sautéed. For this reason, the procedure is better suited to boneless, skinless chicken breasts.

Once you have this technique perfected (it won't take much practice, I promise), you'll be able to apply it to so many foods that months will pass before you repeat yourself. Vary the seasonings in some of the ways described below and the possibilities become even greater, and that's without finishing the dish with a pan-reduction sauce (see page 211).

There are several generally instructive points to learn here. For one thing, you must use a large, flat-bottomed skillet, preferably one with deep, sloping sides, which makes turning the cutlets easier and keeps the inevitable spattering to a minimum. Secondly, preheat the skillet before you add the oil, and make sure the fat is hot before you add the meat; a chopstick or a pinch of flour will sizzle when dipped or tossed into the oil. This is not just to prevent sticking—a nonstick skillet will achieve that without effort—but to brown the meat properly.

Always use enough oil (or clarified butter, if you're feeling extravagant) to cover the bottom of the skillet; meat that does not come in contact with the oil will essentially steam and turn soggy rather than sauté and become crisp. If your skillet is large, this will mean a half-cup or more of oil, although little of this will actually be absorbed. Next, do not crowd the food as it cooks; it's far preferable to work in batches (finished pieces keep well in a 200°F oven) than to cram pieces on top of one another. And keep the heat high (or medium-high, depending on your stove), at least when cooking the first side; lower it a bit when you turn the cutlets, as the second side will cook more quickly and have a tendency to scorch. Finally, keep the cooking time short. All of the foods mentioned above will cook through in the time it takes to develop a golden-brown crust. If you don't believe me, peek inside, using a thin-bladed knife, the first few times you try it; after that you won't bother.

The little bit of browned butter added at the end is obviously a luxury, but hearing and seeing the lemon juice and parsley sizzle when the butter hits them—preferably at the table, so everyone can enjoy it—is a thrill.

4 boneless, skinless chicken cutlets (2 breasts), 1 to 1½ pounds	Olive or other oil (or clarified butter) as needed
Salt and freshly ground black pepper	1 tablespoon fresh lemon juice
Flour or cornmeal for dredging	2 tablespoons minced parsley leaves
	1 to 2 tablespoons butter, optional

1 Heat a 12-inch skillet, preferably nonstick, over medium-high heat for about 2 minutes. While it is heating, sprinkle the chicken breasts with salt and pepper to taste and place the flour or cornmeal on a plate.

2 Place the oil or clarified butter in the skillet—it should coat the bottom well—and turn the heat to high. When the oil is hot, dredge a piece of the chicken in the coating, turning it over a few times and pressing it down so that it is well covered. Add the piece to the pan, then repeat with the rest of the chicken.

3 Cook until the chicken is nicely brown on the first side, 3 to 5 minutes, then turn. Cook on the second side 2 to 4 minutes—lower the heat a bit if the coating begins to scorch—until the chicken is firm to the touch. As the chicken is cooking, melt the optional butter over medium heat until it is nut-brown.

4 When the chicken is done, drain it briefly on a paper towel, then transfer to a warm platter. Drizzle with lemon juice and top with half the parsley. At the last minute, pour the browned butter over all, add the remaining parsley, and serve.

With MINIMAL Effort

FOR the chicken, you can substitute similarly shaped cutlets of pork, turkey, or veal, all of which will cook through in 6 to 8 minutes, just like the chicken. Shrimp, scallops, and calf's liver can also be cooked this way, all for somewhat less time—generally 4 to 6 minutes.

CHICKEN breasts made this way can be prepared in advance and served at room temperature; don't hold them for more than a couple of hours, however.

YOU can serve chicken cooked this way with almost any vegetable; sautéed mushrooms or cooked chopped greens such as spinach are my favorites.

To vary the flavor of the chicken itself:

SUBSTITUTE bread crumbs (season them with finely minced garlic and parsley if you like), ground nuts, or sesame seeds for the flour or cornmeal.

STIR a tablespoon or more of any spice mixture, such as chili powder or curry powder, into the coating.

ADD a clove of garlic and/or a small handful of chopped herbs to the browning butter.

ADD a teaspoon of balsamic vinegar and/or a tablespoon of capers to the browning butter (omit the lemon juice).

10-Minute Stir-Fried Chicken with Nuts
How Stir-frying Can Change Your Life

WORK TIME	10 minutes
PREP TIME	10 minutes
MAKES	4 servings

GENERALLY, STIR-FRYING IS THE fastest cooking method there is, especially if you have the same kind of high-powered wok burner as your neighborhood Chinese restaurant—which of course you don't. Nevertheless, if you keep ingredients—and, ironically, stirring—to a minimum, keep the heat high, and forget about a wok, you can keep the cooking time for a good stir-fry to just about five minutes.

You don't want to use a wok because, unlike the large pit burners seen in Chinese restaurants, home stoves are flat-topped. Thus, for best heat distribution a flat-bottomed skillet, the larger the better and preferably nonstick. The heat must be kept high to ensure nicely browned—even slightly charred—meat and vegetables; for the same reason, stirring should be minimized. The final key is to keep it simple; too many ingredients slow you down, and eventually overload the skillet so that browning becomes impossible.

For the sake of speed and simplicity, I often use hoisin sauce in stir-fries. Since it is made from fermented soybeans, chiles, sugar, ginger, and garlic, it contains pretty much the same ingredients you might spend an extra five or ten minutes measuring and preparing. And because it usually contains flour or cornstarch, it automatically glazes and thickens the dish. (Look for a brand of hoisin sauce whose first ingredient is fermented soybeans rather than sugar or water; the flavor will be more intense.)

For many stir-fries made at home, it's necessary to parboil—essentially precook—"hard" vegetables like broccoli or asparagus. So in this fastest-possible stir-fry, I use red bell peppers, onions, or both; they need no parboiling and become tender and sweet in three or four minutes. If you cut the meat in small cubes or thin slices, the cooking time is even less. I include nuts for three reasons: I love their flavor, their chunkiness adds great texture (I don't chop them at all), and the preparation time is zero.

This stir-fry is so fast that the first thing you need to do is start a batch of white rice. In the fifteen or twenty minutes it takes for that to cook, you can not only prepare the stir-fry but set the table and have a drink.

1 tablespoon peanut or vegetable oil	1 pound boneless skinless chicken breasts, cut into ½- to ¾-inch-thick chunks
2 cups red bell pepper strips, onion slices, or a combination of the two	1 cup halved walnuts, whole cashews, or other nuts
	3 tablespoons hoisin sauce

1 Place the oil in a large, nonstick skillet (12 inches is best) and turn the heat to high; a minute later, add the vegetable(s) in a single layer and cook, undisturbed, until they begin to char a little on the bottom, about 1 minute. Stir and cook 1 minute more.

2 Add the chicken and stir once or twice. Again, cook until the bottom begins to blacken a bit, about a minute. Stir and cook another minute; by this time the vegetables will have softened and the chicken will be done, or nearly so (cut into a piece to check). Lower the heat to medium.

3 Stir in the nuts and the hoisin sauce. Cook for about 15 seconds, then add 2 tablespoons water. Cook, stirring, until the sauce is bubbly and glazes all the chicken and vegetables. Serve immediately, with white rice.

With MINIMAL Effort

SUBSTITUTE any vegetable, or combination, for the onions and peppers. Try cut-up and parboiled (simmered in boiling water just until slightly tender) broccoli, asparagus, green beans, or dark leafy greens; shredded raw cabbage; raw snow peas; or chopped tomatoes.

USE any boneless meat in place of the chicken, or shrimp or scallops. Cooking time will remain the same.

SPRINKLE the meat with about 1 tablespoon curry powder as it cooks.

ALONG with the hoisin, add ground bean paste (about 1 tablespoon), plum sauce (about 1 tablespoon), or chili-garlic paste (about ½ teaspoon, or to taste) during the last minute of cooking.

REPLACE the hoisin with 3 or 4 dried hot red chiles (optional), 1 tablespoon minced garlic, 1 tablespoon soy sauce, and ½ cup chopped scallions, all added along with the nuts.

The Minimalist's Thanksgiving Turkey

WORK TIME	30 minutes
PREP TIME	2 hours 30 minutes
MAKES	at least 12 servings, with leftovers

ONE THANKSGIVING, I VOWED TO minimize everything: time, number of ingredients and, most of all, work. Heretical as it may seem, I thought it might be fun for this cook to have enough energy actually to enjoy the meal for a change. My goal was to buy all the food with one trip to the store and prepare the entire feast in the time it took to roast my twelve-pound turkey—less than three hours.

The results were as close to a traditional Thanksgiving dinner as I could get without spending an entire day—or more—in the kitchen. Without using convenience foods—I made both the stuffing and the cranberry sauce from scratch, each in less than ten minutes—I prepared a full-fledged feast for twelve with more food than anyone could possibly finish.

Here, the turkey gets a high-heat boost at the beginning so the bird gets a fast start. The high heat ensures browning and keeps roasting time well under three hours. The stuffing was inspired by a recipe from the late Pierre Franey, who often roasted a chicken with a "sandwich" of bread, chicken liver, and parsley. It took a little tinkering to adapt this to turkey, but the result is a light, almost pâtélike stuffing that even kids like. You can make it and stuff the bird in less time than it takes to preheat the oven.

The sauce relies on pan drippings, but is finished with nothing more than water, good sherry, and butter; it's made in ten minutes or so, while the turkey rests before carving.

You might serve this with oven-browned sweet potatoes, Green Beans with Lemon (page 190), some homemade cranberry-orange relish, and the Pear and Gorgonzola Green Salad (page 4). Start your guests off with cheese and crackers and pass mixed nuts and fresh fruit after the meal. You can do more work if you like . . . but I don't see the point.

| 12-pound turkey | Salt and freshly ground black |
| 1 recipe Bread Stuffing (below) | pepper |

1 Preheat the oven to 500° F. Rinse the turkey and remove the giblets; save the liver to make the stuffing. Loosely pack the turkey cavity with the stuffing, then tie the legs together to enclose the vent.

2 Place the turkey on a rack in a large roasting pan. Add ½ cup water to the bottom of the pan along with the turkey neck, gizzard, and any other trimmings. Place in the oven, legs first.

3 Roast 20 to 30 minutes, or until the top begins to brown, then turn the heat down to 350 degrees. Continue to roast, checking every 30 minutes or so; if the top threatens to brown too much, lay a piece of aluminum foil directly onto it. If the bottom dries out, add water, about ½ cup at a time. The turkey is done when an instant-read thermometer inserted into the thickest part of the thigh measures 165 degrees. If, when the turkey is nearly done, the top is not browned enough, turn the heat back up to 425 degrees for the last 20 to 30 minutes of cooking.

4 Remove the turkey from the oven. Take the bird off the rack and make Sherry Reduction Gravy, page 143, while the bird rests (let it sit for about 20 minutes before carving).

Fastest Bread Stuffing

WORK TIME	10 minutes
PREP TIME	2 hours 30 minutes
CAN BE	prepared in advance; easily multiplied
MAKES	about 12 servings

6 tablespoons butter	Salt and freshly ground black
3 chicken livers, about ¼ pound, or	pepper
an equivalent amount of turkey	8 slices good day- or two-day-old
liver	white bread, crusts trimmed
1 cup chopped parsley leaves	

1 Chop together (by hand or in a small food processor) the butter, livers, and parsley; season to taste.

2 Spread half of the mixture on 4 of the bread slices; use the remaining bread to make 4 sandwiches. Spread the remaining mixture on the outside of the sandwiches. Cut each of the sandwiches into 6 pieces.

3 Stuff the turkey as described above.

Sherry Reduction Gravy

WORK TIME	15 minutes
PREP TIME	15 minutes
CAN BE	easily multiplied
MAKES	4 servings

1½ cups Amontillado or Oloroso
  sherry
3 tablespoons butter, optional

Salt and freshly ground black
  pepper

1 Remove the giblets and pour off all but a tablespoon of the fat from the turkey's roasting pan; leave as many of the solids and as much of the dark liquid behind as possible. Place the roasting pan over two burners and turn the heat to high.

2 Add the sherry and cook, stirring and scraping all the brown bits off the bottom of the pan, until the liquid has reduced by about half, 5 minutes or so.

3 Add 3 cups water (or stock if you have it) and bring to a boil, stirring all the while. Turn the heat to medium and simmer for about 5 minutes.

4 Stir in the optional butter and, when it melts, salt and pepper to taste. Keep warm until ready to serve. Strain before serving if desired.

Roast Turkey Breast
Thanksgiving Made Easy

WORK TIME	15 minutes
PREP TIME	1 hour
CAN BE	prepared in advance
MAKES	4 to 10 servings

THERE ARE PLENTY OF REASONS to consider cooking a turkey breast for Thanksgiving rather than an entire bird. It minimizes fuss; cuts roasting time at least in half, and usually more; reduces the hassle of carving; and makes the overabundance of leftover turkey somewhat less absurd. It also deemphasizes the bird, which frees you to concentrate a little more on side dishes, always the most interesting part of the Thanksgiving table.

Smaller turkey breasts of about three pounds are perfectly adequate for a party of four or so, while the larger ones—they're available in sizes of six pounds and even more—can be counted on to serve about ten, especially because there is usually plenty of other food. Even though the breasts don't compare in size to gargantuan birds of 15 or 20 pounds, in my experience there are still usually enough leftovers to keep the sandwich crowd happy.

Perhaps the greatest advantage to roasting a turkey breast is that you can produce white meat that is truly moist—as opposed to the dried-out white meat that is the near-inevitable result of roasting a whole turkey until the legs are cooked through. Perfectly cooked white meat (all you need is an instant-read thermometer) does not require tons of gravy to become edible, although you may like to serve it with a light sauce.

If you prefer the kind of soggy dressing that results from stuffing it into the turkey, just pile it under the cavity formed by the breast bone. But dressing is best baked in a separate baking dish, or around the turkey, so that it crisps up. Cooking time for most dressing baked in this way is 30 to 45 minutes; if it appears in danger of becoming too dry and crisp on top, baste it with a little stock or simply stir it up so the less-crisp bottom portion comes to the top.

It's worth noting that although basting a turkey gives the skin added flavor, it does nothing to maintain interior moisture, let alone add to it; the only way to ensure moist meat is to avoid overcooking. So if one of your guests is on a serious low-fat diet—an increasingly common occurrence—baste with chicken stock or not at all.

Finally, for safety, the USDA recommends roasting white-meat poultry to 170 degrees, at which point it will be unpalatably dry (especially when you consider that the internal temperature typically rises at least five degrees during the resting period). Should you choose to do this, I strongly recommend that you serve the turkey with plenty of gravy. Personally, I take my chances with a slightly lower temperature and have never regretted it.

One 3- to 6-pound turkey breast	Salt and freshly ground black pepper
2 tablespoons olive oil, melted butter, or chicken stock, optional	

1 Preheat the oven to 450° F. Place the turkey in a roasting pan; you can place stuffing under its breastbone if you like; if you want crisp stuffing, however, add it to the pan (or bake it separately) when about 30 minutes of cooking time remain.

2 Brush the turkey with oil, butter, or stock if you like and season it with salt and pepper to taste. Place it in the oven. Roast for 40 to 60 minutes, depending on size, basting with the pan juices (or a little more chicken stock) every 15 minutes or so, then begin checking for doneness every few minutes with an instant-read thermometer. The turkey is ready when the thermometer reads 155 degrees. Let the turkey rest for 5 to 10 minutes (during which time its internal temperature will rise to about 160 degrees) before carving and serving.

With MINIMAL Effort

Herb Roasted Turkey Breast: Increase the melted butter, oil, or stock to ¼ cup, and combine with ¼ cup parsley, along with a mixture of other fresh herbs, such as tarragon (about a teaspoon), dill (about a tablespoon), celery or fennel leaves (a tablespoon or more), or other fresh herbs. Baste and roast as above.

Turkey Tonnato

An Elegant Classic Made from the Deli

WORK TIME	15 minutes
PREP TIME	at least 2 hours
CAN BE	prepared in advance; easily multiplied
MAKES	4 servings

I HAVE ALWAYS LOVED VITELLO TONNATO, a northern Italian specialty in which cold roast veal is marinated and then served in a creamy, mayonnaise-like sauce of canned tuna. (It didn't sound good the first time I heard of it either, but trust me, the combination is magical, and it's one of the great picnic dishes of all time.) But what a hassle: To make it, you begin by roasting a piece of leg of veal, or eye of veal round, or some other hard-to-find, fairly expensive cut. Then you chill it, slice it, layer it with the sauce, and chill it again.

After working on the preceding turkey breast recipe, I decided that turkey was enough like veal to give it a try, and marinated some slices of the leftover breast in a tonnato sauce. It worked well, but the next time I wanted to make turkey tonnato, once again I griped at having to roast a piece of meat first. Given that turkey was cheaper and easier to come by than veal, it wasn't quite so bad. But what seemed great as a dish that began with leftovers did not seem worth making from scratch.

Then I had a brainstorm: Why not buy the highest-quality deli turkey I could find, thick-sliced? The next time I was in the supermarket I bought some and gave it a try, and the results were great. I felt a slight tinge of guilt for not roasting the turkey breast from scratch, but I quickly got over it when I tasted the results.

1 cup fresh Mayonnaise (page 216) or bottled mayonnaise

2 tablespoons capers

6 anchovy fillets, minced

1 can (6 ounces) tuna packed in olive oil

¼ cup olive oil, more or less

Salt and freshly ground black pepper

Eight ¼- to ⅜-inch-thick slices white-meat turkey

Minced parsley for garnish

1 Combine the mayonnaise with the capers, anchovies, and tuna. Thin with olive oil (or hot water) to achieve a creamy consistency. Taste and add salt and pepper as necessary.

2 Make a thin layer of sauce on a platter; cover with turkey slices, then more sauce, then more turkey, and finally more sauce. Cover and refrigerate for at least 2 hours and up to 2 days; serve cold or at room temperature, garnished with parsley.

With MINIMAL Effort

Almost any spin you can put on mayonnaise will work here. Try folding in about ¼ cup of

> CHOPPED pitted olives (black, green, or a combination)
>
> MINCED shallots or scallions
>
> CHOPPED cornichons or other pickles
>
> MINCED red bell pepper
>
> OR GARNISH the dish with more capers or chopped olives.

Pan-fried Duck
No-Roast Duck

WORK TIME	15 minutes
PREP TIME	60 minutes
CAN BE	prepared in advance (and eaten at room temperature)
MAKES	4 servings

I'M SURE THAT WHAT KEEPS YOU from cooking duck more frequently—most people reserve it for special occasions—isn't that you don't like it, but that the roasting methods that efficiently rid duck of its thick layer of fat take a great deal of time and a fair amount of attention. (Not that roast duck is impossible; see page 150.)

Here's a method that takes less than an hour and results in a crisp bird from which nearly all of the fat has been rendered. It's accomplished by the simple procedure of cooking the duck, covered, on top of the stove. To do this, the bird is cut up before it is cooked.

By cutting the bird into serving pieces, you readily expose large chunks of surface fat, and can easily trim them. Cooking the duck with a cover renders the remaining fat while tenderizing the bird in a process that amounts to steaming (the cover also prevents spattering, a nice touch). When the bird is just about done, you uncover the skillet and crisp it up on both sides, using the duck's own fat as a cooking medium. Served hot or at room temperature, the bird is crisp, tender, and far more flavorful than any chicken.

Much as I'd love to take credit for this minimalist's dream of a technique, I cannot. I've been cooking duck this way for twenty-five years, after learning it from the brilliant *Peck's Art of Good Cooking,* which was first published in 1961. (The late Ms. Peck also wrote *Art of Fine Baking,* as succinct a general baking book as you'll ever see. Both books can occasionally be found on remainder tables at bookstores.)

I have made some changes in Ms. Peck's technique; her total cooking time is about one hour, but forty-five minutes is sufficient. She seasoned the duck with a mixture of soy sauce and sherry. Although I like this, and give a version of it as a variation below, I prefer to toss a few cloves of garlic and sprigs of thyme into the skillet, for a flavor more akin to that of duck confit.

If you have never cut up a raw duck, you will be relieved to know that it is nearly identical to cutting up a chicken (pages 118–119). Unlike chicken, you will also have a cup or more of duck fat. If you'd like to render it—it's great for cooking—cut it into pieces and cook it in a skillet, slowly, until all the fat has liquefied and the bits of skin have become crisp. Drain and eat the crispy bits, and refrigerate the fat; it will keep for weeks.

One 5- to 6-pound duck	**3 garlic cloves, optional**
Salt and freshly ground black pepper	**Several sprigs of fresh thyme, optional**

1 Cut the duck into 6 or 8 serving pieces, reserving the wing tips, back, and neck for the stockpot. (Cut the gizzard into slices and cook it along with the duck if you like; reserve the liver for another use.) Place the duck, skin side down, in a 12-inch skillet, and sprinkle it liberally with salt and pepper. Add the garlic and a few thyme sprigs if you like and turn the heat to medium-high. When the duck begins to sizzle, cover the skillet and turn the heat to medium.

2 After 15 minutes, turn the duck and season the skin side. After 15 more minutes, uncover the skillet and turn the heat back to medium-high. Cook the duck, turning as necessary, so that it browns nicely on both sides; this will take another 15 minutes.

3 Serve hot or at room temperature. Strip some of the leaves from the remaining thyme sprigs and use them as a garnish if you want.

With MINIMAL Effort

Soy Duck: Rub the duck with salt, pepper, 1 tablespoon soy sauce, and 1 tablespoon dry sherry before placing it in the pan. When it is done, garnish with minced fresh ginger or minced cilantro leaves.

Roast Duck in One Hour

WORK TIME	20 minutes
PREP TIME	60 to 70 minutes
MAKES	2 to 4 servings

WHAT SCARES MOST PEOPLE ABOUT roasting duck—its thick layer of subcutaneous fat—is actually its best feature, one that makes it a nearly foolproof dish, absolutely suitable for a weeknight meal. The fat keeps the meat juicy even when it's well done—a distinct advantage because the breast is best medium-rare, but the legs must be cooked through, or nearly so, to be palatable.

In fact, duck is so difficult to roast badly that all experienced cooks seem to claim their procedure is the best. Having tried many methods, I can say that the results are all about the same. So I usually rely upon the one presented here, which I believe is the easiest way to guarantee a succulent but beautifully browned bird. (The only method that works markedly better—steaming over hot water, followed by roasting—is much more of a production, but it's so good that I'll give a summary of it here: First, steam the duck on a rack over simmering water until it is nearly cooked, about forty-five minutes. Then chill it for up to a day; finally, roast it on a rack in a roasting pan at four hundred degrees for about thirty minutes until the skin is crisp.)

There are four discrete challenges in the simple method given here, all manageable. The first is spattering. All that fat can make a mess of your oven. The solution is simple: Keep a thin layer of water in the roasting pan. The fat drips into it and stays there. (You'll need a rack to elevate the duck, but you should be using one anyway.)

The second challenge is to achieve a uniformly brown color. I cheat a little bit here and brush the roasting duck with soy sauce, which works like a charm. The third challenge lies in carving; a duck is a little more complicated to carve than a chicken. The best thing to do is cut on either side of the rib cage to remove two boneless breast halves, then cut the legs from the carcass. The rest is for picking.

Finally, there's the basic challenge of having enough to go around; a roast duck can easily be finished by two people. If you want to serve four, roast two, or plan on a lot of side dishes.

One 4- to 5-pound duck   ¼ cup soy sauce, more or less
Freshly ground black pepper

1 Preheat the oven to 450° F. Discard the neck and giblets or keep them for another use; remove excess fat from the duck's cavity.

2 Place the duck, breast side down (wings up), on a rack in a roasting pan; add water to come to just below the rack (see headnote). Sprinkle with pepper and brush with a little soy sauce.

3 Roast for 30 minutes, undisturbed. Prick the back all over with the point of a sharp knife, then flip the bird onto its back. Sprinkle with pepper and brush with soy sauce again. Add a little more water to the bottom of the pan if the juices are spattering (carefully—you don't want to get water on the duck).

4 Roast 20 minutes, prick the breast all over with the point of a knife, and brush with soy sauce. Roast 10 minutes; brush with soy sauce. Roast another 5 or 10 minutes if necessary, or until the duck is a glorious brown all over and an instant-read thermometer inserted into the thigh measures at least 155 degrees. Let rest for 5 minutes before carving and serving.

With MINIMAL Effort

Follow the general rules for making a reduction sauce (page 211), and you can sauce this duck however you like (chicken stock and green peppercorns are always good; orange juice is classic). Just make sure to drain nearly all of the fat first. You can flavor the duck in a variety of ways while it's roasting:

LEMON: Put a whole lemon, cut in half, in the cavity while the bird roasts; squeeze the juice from that lemon over the bird after you carve it.

HERBS: Stuff the bird with a few sprigs of thyme or parsley.

VEGETABLES: Keep the pan juices moist with water or stock, and cook, along with the duck, a few chopped leeks, carrots, celery stalks, and/or onions.

Meat

Steak with Butter and Ginger Sauce

WORK TIME	15 minutes
PREP TIME	15 minutes
MAKES	4 servings

COOKING A STEAK SIMPLY, with good results, is easy as long as you have an outdoor grill—see the preceding recipe. But sometimes it's winter, or perhaps you don't own a grill, and cooking a steak in the broiler or oven usually means sacrificing a good crust; using the stovetop just sets off the smoke detector.

So the process is a tricky one. It's easy enough to get a crust on a steak before smoke fills the house, but unless you like raw steak this is not the perfect solution. It is, however, a good start. If you sear the steak quickly, then remove it from the pan before building a quick sauce, you can finish cooking the meat in that sauce. This reduces smoke while increasing flavor. It is such a good technique, with so many options, that you're sometimes likely to eschew the grill just to do it this way.

It isn't necessary to use butter in this preparation, but a small amount—there is little more than a teaspoon per person in the recipe—adds not only creaminess but also flavor. In this particular creation, that flavor combines with soy to produce an unusual, countertraditional marriage that is in its odd way uniquely American.

But the technique is not dependent on butter, ginger, or soy. As you can see from the variations, each of these three ingredients can be swapped, varied, even omitted, until the dish has nothing in common with the original recipe except the steak and the procedure used to cook it.

It is best to use fairly thin steaks here. Judging the doneness of thicker ones can be tricky, and inevitably the sauce evaporates before the meat is cooked through. The ideal setup for four people is four small, boneless steaks, cut from the top blade, sirloin, or rib. But two larger steaks will work nearly as well, as long as they're thin.

> 1 to 1½ pounds boneless top
> blade, skirt, sirloin or rib-eye,
> ¾ inch thick or less
>
> 1½ tablespoons butter
> 1 tablespoon minced fresh ginger
> 2 tablespoons soy sauce

1 Preheat a large, heavy skillet over medium-high heat until it begins to smoke. Add the steaks and cook until nicely browned, 1 to 2 minutes. Turn and brown the other side, another minute or two. Remove the skillet from the heat and the steaks to a plate.

2 When the skillet has cooled slightly, return it to the stove over medium heat. Add the butter and, when it melts, the ginger. About 30 seconds later, add the soy sauce and stir to blend. Return the steaks to the skillet, along with any of their accumulated juices. Turn the heat to medium and cook the steaks for a total of about 4 minutes, turning three or four times. (If at any time the pan threatens to dry out entirely, add a couple of tablespoons of water.) At this point, the steaks will be medium-rare; cook for a little longer if you like, and serve, with the pan juices spooned over.

With MINIMAL Effort

By varying the ingredients around the steak, you can give this recipe any number of different flavors. For example: substitute extra virgin olive oil for the butter, garlic for the ginger, and fresh lemon juice for the soy sauce; or stay with the butter, but use garlic or shallots and a few leaves of tarragon instead of the ginger, and vinegar in place of the soy sauce. Similarly,

FOR the ginger: Substitute minced garlic or any member of the onion family. Or use minced lemongrass or anchovies; whole capers or finely chopped mushrooms are also good.

FOR the butter: You can omit entirely or substitute any oil you like. Extra virgin olive oil and peanut oil are the most distinctive.

FOR the soy sauce: Use red wine, fresh lemon or lime juice, vinegar, or nam pla (fish sauce). Start with about a tablespoon (¼ cup in the case of wine) and add more to taste. Or thin with water.

FINALLY, add any minced herbs you like to the sauce, at about the same time you return the meat to the skillet.

Negima

Japanese Beef-Scallion Rolls

WORK TIME	20 minutes
PREP TIME	20 minutes
CAN BE	prepared in advance (up to cooking); easily multiplied
MAKES	4 servings

WRAPPING ONE FOOD WITH ANOTHER is a stimulating experience in both flavor and texture, as you bite through the outer layer and into the filling. It may be familiar, especially if meat, cheese, or vegetables comprise the filling—think of ravioli, stuffed cabbage, or egg rolls, for example. Making meat the wrapping is a nice role reversal, a neat twist that is extraordinary enough to allow a simple preparation to wow a crowd.

At Inagiku, the Japanese restaurant in New York's Waldorf Astoria, the perfect inside-out beef packages are served. The chef brushed wafer-thin slices of sirloin with teriyaki sauce before wrapping them around scallion greens and grilling them.

At first, it appeared that a couple of aspects of this seemingly simple dish were too far from the minimalist ideal for adaptation. But I've come up with a meat roll that closely mimics those negima, along with a number of variations.

The rolls comprise only three elements: meat, filling, and sauce. At home, chicken, veal, and pork are easier to work with than beef, because the cuts of beef that supermarkets most frequently slice thin are from the round, which is not only tough but relatively tasteless. I prodded a supermarket butcher to cut the thinnest possible slices of sirloin and they worked well enough. But chicken, veal, and pork are routinely sold as thin cutlets, which can be made even thinner with a little gentle pounding.

The flavor of store-bought teriyaki sauce can't compare with that made in a good Japanese restaurant, although it isn't bad. After a few tries I decided that I preferred the less complex but purer flavor of plain soy sauce. There are other options as well; see "With Minimal Effort."

8 thin slices of beef, chicken, veal, or pork, each about 3 inches wide and 5 to 6 inches long (about 1¼ pounds)	¼ cup soy sauce Green parts from about 2 dozen scallions

1 Preheat a grill or broiler; the fire should be quite hot.

2 Place the meat between two layers of wax paper or plastic wrap and pound it gently so that it is about ⅛ inch thick. Brush one side of each piece of meat with a little soy sauce.

3 Cut the scallions into lengths about the same width as the meat and place a small bundle of them at one of the narrow ends of each slice. Roll the long way, securing the roll with a toothpick or two. (You can prepare the rolls in advance up to this point; cover and refrigerate for up to 2 hours before proceeding.) Brush the exterior of the roll with a little more sauce.

4 Grill until brown on all sides, a total of about 6 minutes for chicken, 4 to 5 minutes for pork or veal, 4 minutes or less for beef.

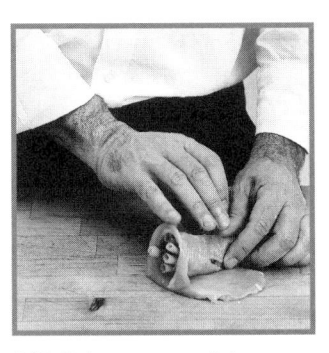

1 | Lightly pound the meat until it is flat and about ¼-inch thick. Stuff with scallions.

2 | Roll the meat around the scallions.

With MINIMAL Effort

Scallion greens are a wonderful filling, but chives work well, as do:

SMALL amounts of lightly cooked, chopped spinach or chard

COOKED, chopped shiitake (or other) mushrooms

JULIENNED and lightly cooked carrots

PARBOILED asparagus spears

As alternatives to soy sauce, you can use Asian fish sauce (nam pla or nuoc mam), Chinese hoisin sauce, or premade teriyaki sauce.

Perfect Grilled Steak

WORK TIME	15 minutes
PREP TIME	30 minutes
CAN BE	easily multiplied
MAKES	4 servings

YOU MIGHT THINK THAT YOU don't have the time to marinate meat or fish before grilling—I hear that complaint frequently—but the fact is that you don't need a marinade at all for grilled foods. No marinade in the world is going to "tenderize" a piece of meat that's too tough to grill in the first place. A long soak of twelve to twenty-four hours in a highly acidic marinade, one with lemon juice, vinegar, or the like, will begin to turn a tough piece of meat to mush—not exactly the texture you want. In less time, it will have little or even no impact on tenderness, which is fine, because grilling is a quick process, usually taking just a few minutes. It pays to stick to burgers, chicken, fish, vegetables, and those cuts of meat that need no coaxing to become tender when cooked.

What this means is that there are just two reasons for marinating before grilling: to add flavor and promote browning and crispness. Neither of these requires much time, although dunking the meat or fish for a few minutes in what is best labeled a grilling sauce may contribute to a slightly greater penetration of flavor. (On the other hand, if you really have no time at all, simply smear the food with the sauce as it's going on the grill.)

Which flavor to add is a matter of taste. My favorite is soy sauce; I love its taste, and it always seems to contribute exactly the right amount of saltiness. Its natural complements are garlic and ginger; for best flavor, each of these should be fresh rather than powdered.

Promoting browning is easy: Anything with sugar browns quickly—often too quickly, as you know if you've ever slathered a piece of chicken with barbecue sauce before grilling it. That's why ketchup, or a similar substance, forms the basis of so many commercial barbecue sauces; it contains so much sugar (or, more likely, corn syrup), that it browns in a flash. I prefer honey; it has a clean sweetness and allows the sauce to adhere better to the food. Molasses is also good, as is hoisin sauce, a kind of Chinese ketchup which contains a great deal of sugar but also soy.

The final ingredient is acid, not to tenderize the meat but to balance sweetness. Lime goes best with soy, but almost any acidic liquid will do, from lemon to white vinegar.

There is a safety issue here: Marinade that is applied to raw food should not be brushed on during the last few minutes of cooking, nor should it be used as a sauce unless it is boiled for a few minutes. And, as always, marinade brushes and other utensils that are used with raw food should not be used near the end of cooking.

¼ cup soy sauce	Freshly ground black pepper
1 teaspoon peeled and minced fresh ginger	Juice of ½ lime
½ teaspoon peeled and minced garlic	16 to 24 ounces boneless steak (such as rib eye, skirt, or strip), or 24 to 32 ounces bone-in steak (such as rib-eye or t-bone)
1 tablespoon honey, molasses, or hoisin sauce	

1 Start a charcoal or wood fire, or preheat a gas grill; the fire should be hot, and the rack no more than 4 inches from the heat source. Mix together the first 6 ingredients; taste and add more of anything you like. Turn the steak in the sauce once or twice, then let it sit in the sauce until the grill is hot.

2 Turn the steak one more time, then place on the grill; spoon any remaining sauce over it. For rare, grill about 3 minutes per side for steak under an inch thick. For larger or more well-done steak, increase the time slightly.

With MINIMAL Effort

This combination—soy and spices for flavor, honey for browning, body, and sweetness, lime for acidity—perfectly enhances not only steak but burgers, boneless chicken breasts or thighs, tuna, and swordfish. Longer-cooking meats, such as bone-in chicken, should be cooked to within 10 minutes of doneness before basting with the sauce.

There are many other ingredients that can contribute to this basic sauce to make it somewhat more complex in flavor. Add too many at once, however, and you run the risk of muddying the flavor.

MUSTARD, 1 teaspoon to 1 tablespoon

SESAME or other roasted-nut oil, about a teaspoon

PEANUT butter or tahini (sesame paste), about a tablespoon (some sesame seeds or finely chopped peanuts are good, too)

MINCED onion, scallion, or shallot

PREPARED horseradish (about a tablespoon) or wasabi powder (about a teaspoon)

MINCED zest of a lemon, lime, or orange

MINCED cilantro, about a tablespoon, plus more for garnish

GROUND cumin (up to a tablespoon) or coriander (up to a teaspoon), or a combination

MINCED jalapeño, crushed red chiles, or Tabasco or other hot sauce to taste

WORCESTERSHIRE or fish sauce (nuoc mam or nam pla, sold in most Asian markets), about a tablespoon

Osso Buco

WORK TIME	15 minutes
PREP TIME	at least 2 hours
CAN BE	prepared in advance; easily multiplied
MAKES	4 servings

THERE'S NO PROMISE OF SPEED here: Osso buco takes time. But this classic Italian dish of glorious, marrow-filled veal shanks (the name means "bone with hole"), braised until they are fork-tender, is dead easy to make and requires a total of no more than fifteen or twenty minutes of attention during its two hours or so of cooking. And it holds well enough overnight so that ninety percent of the process can be accomplished while you're watching television the night before you serve the dish.

As with many of the best simple meat dishes, the key to a delicious osso buco is not so much in the flavors you add but in the original purchase and careful handling. Buying any cut of veal, of course, requires a conscious choice. The standard, pale pink, "milk-fed" veal sold in supermarkets and most butcher shops remains a product of enforced confinement and formula feeding. It has mild flavor and good texture. The alternative, sold in natural foods stores and some supermarkets and butcher shops, is "natural" veal, in which the calf may be raised at its mother's side or at least allowed some room to roam and graze before slaughter. Its color is darker, its flavor a little more intense, its texture perhaps a bit tougher.

I prefer the stronger flavor of the latter, although I'm not altogether certain that my preference isn't influenced by guilt. When it comes to the shanks themselves, the decision is easier: You want slices taken from the center, about one and one half inches thick. The slices from the narrow end have very little meat on them; those from the thick end contain little or no marrow. Center cuts give you the best of both worlds.

Careful handling, when it comes to osso buco or almost any other braised meat, means slow cooking—almost the slower the better. After an initial browning and the addition of liquid, you cook the meat, covered, at a slow simmer. Turn the meat every thirty minutes or so, although the timing is unimportant; you just want to make sure that each side gets to spend some time bathed in the flavorful cooking liquid.

The liquid itself is worth a mention. As usual, the richest sauce results from using good-quality stock. But two hours of cooking veal shanks—

which are, after all, essentially veal bones—creates a very nice stock with no work, so I never hesitate to make osso buco with white wine or even water.

Most osso buco recipes call for flouring the meat before the initial browning, which helps create thicker pan juices. But cooking the pan juices over high heat for a few minutes after the meat is done results in a glossy, silken pan sauce that can barely be bettered. I say "barely" because the true hedonist will stir in a couple of teaspoons of butter to enhance the sauce even further. But since the dish is great as it stands, I usually manage to resist the impulse.

1 tablespoon olive oil

4 center-cut slices veal shank, 2 pounds or more

Salt and freshly ground black pepper

3 to 4 garlic cloves, lightly smashed and peeled

4 anchovy fillets

1 cup dry white wine, chicken or beef stock, or water

2 teaspoons butter, optional

1 Heat a large, deep skillet over medium-high heat for a couple of minutes. Add the oil, swirl it around, and pour out any excess. Add the veal and cook until nicely browned on the first side (for even browning, you can rotate the shanks, but try not to disturb them too much), about 5 minutes. Turn and brown the other side.

2 When the second side is just about completely browned, sprinkle the shanks with a little salt and pepper and add the garlic and anchovies to the pan. Cook, stirring a little, until the anchovies dissolve and the garlic browns, about 2 minutes. Add the liquid and let it bubble away for about a minute.

3 Turn the heat to low and cover the skillet. Five minutes later, check to see that the mixture is simmering—just a few bubbles appearing at once—and adjust the heat accordingly. Cook until the meat is very tender and pulling away from the bone, at least 90 minutes and probably somewhat more; turn the veal every half hour or so. (When the meat is tender you may turn off the heat and refrigerate the dish for up to 24 hours; reheat gently before proceeding.)

4 Remove the meat to a warm platter and turn the heat to high. Boil the sauce until it becomes thick and glossy, about 5 minutes. Stir in the butter if you like and serve the meat with the sauce spooned over it.

With MINIMAL Effort

Traditionally, osso buco is served with a condiment known as *gremolata*. To make gremolata, mix together 1 tablespoon minced lemon zest, 2 tablespoons minced fresh parsley leaves, and ¼ to 1 teaspoon minced garlic. Remember that this will not be cooked, so take it easy on the garlic.

Osso Buco with Vegetables: Omit the anchovy; the garlic is optional. Instead, cook 1 cup chopped onions; 1 chopped celery stalk; 2 medium carrots, peeled and chopped; a couple of sprigs of thyme (or about ½ teaspoon dried thyme) in the skillet over medium heat, after browning the meat. When the vegetables are tender, about 10 minutes, add the liquid and proceed as above.

Osso Buco with Tomatoes: Add about 2 cups chopped tomatoes (canned are fine; drain them first) to the skillet along with the liquid. Proceed as above. This version is excellent with about ½ cup roughly chopped basil added during the last few minutes of cooking, and some minced basil as a garnish.

Braised Veal Breast with Mushrooms

WORK TIME	15 minutes
PREP TIME	at least 90 minutes
CAN BE	prepared in advance; easily multiplied
MAKES	4 to 8 servings

FEW SLOW-COOKED FOODS ARE as rewarding as a well-cooked beef brisket, which at its best is tender, juicy, and flavorful. Doing it right takes so long—my favorite recipe is a twelve-hour job—that, at least in my house, a brisket is made only annually, or even less often than that. That's why I regret that I didn't make my "discovery" of veal brisket sooner. It had just never occurred to me until recently that you could get a delicious, tender, relatively quick-cooking form of brisket by removing the bones from a breast of veal.

The breast, a common cut that can be almost ludicrously cheap (as little as eighty-nine cents a pound), is also difficult to handle. To serve four requires buying a piece of meat that is too large to fit in most pots, and one that takes a long time to cook.

Unfortunately, boneless breast of veal—which can also be called veal brisket and, like brisket of beef, is the flap that covers the front part of a cow's chest—is rarely sold that way. But any butcher (and, yes, this includes virtually every supermarket butcher) can quickly remove the bones from a veal breast and present you with a flat, boneless, relatively compact cut that contains little fat and becomes tender in less than two hours of unattended cooking.

When the butcher makes you a veal brisket, first ask him to start with a piece of breast that weighs four to six pounds. The yield is about half that, a piece of boneless meat of two or three pounds that will easily fit in a large skillet. Consider asking the butcher for the bones, too—you're paying for them, and they are among the best for stock making.

Once the shopping is done, the battle is over, because this recipe requires time but almost no work or even attention. Slow cooking makes the veal breast wonderfully tender and moist, among the best briskets you've ever had. And since the dish is as good or better the day after cooking, it's a great candidate for those times when you're around the kitchen but not prepared to pay much attention—you might be working on a more labor-intensive recipe, or eating and cleaning up.

There are no tricks or subtleties here. I like to use dried mushrooms, largely because of their convenience and intensity of flavor, but you can substitute about a half-pound of fresh mushrooms if you prefer. And a not-too-dry white wine, such as a Riesling, adds a little complexity to the finished dish—although the difference is hardly pronounced.

> 1 ounce dried mushrooms, such as shiitakes, porcini, or a combination
>
> One 2- to 3-pound boneless veal breast
>
> ½ cup white wine
>
> Salt and freshly ground black pepper
>
> 1 tablespoon butter, optional

1 Reconstitute the mushrooms by covering them with very hot water. Turn the heat under a 12-inch skillet to medium-high and let the pan sit for a minute. Add the veal and brown it on both sides, turning once, for a total of about 6 minutes.

2 Remove the meat to a plate and turn the heat to medium. Add the mushrooms and about ½ cup of their liquid (strained, if necessary, to remove sediment) along with the wine. Bring to a boil and cook for about 30 seconds, then return the veal to the skillet. Season with salt and pepper, turn the heat to low, and cover.

3 Cook for 60 to 90 minutes, turning once or twice during that period and checking now and then to make sure the liquid is bubbling slowly; adjust the heat accordingly.

4 When the meat is tender, remove it to a cutting board. Turn the heat under the liquid in the skillet to high and reduce it to a thick, saucy consistency. Stir in the butter if you like and keep warm. Carve the meat against the grain into ¼-inch-thick slices and serve with the sauce.

With MINIMAL Effort

Veal Brisket with Fresh Mushrooms: Begin with at least ½ pound fresh mushrooms, button or other. Slice them, then cook them over medium-high heat in 2 tablespoons olive oil or butter, preferably with a couple of crushed, peeled garlic cloves and a few sprigs of thyme, until tender, about 15 minutes. Proceed as above, adding ½ cup water in place of the mushroom-cooking liquid.

Veal Brisket with Bacon and Onions: Render about ¼ pound cubed bacon, preferably cut from a slab, over medium heat, stirring, until nice and crisp. Then remove the bacon pieces with a slotted spoon. Brown the veal in the fat, as above. Remove the veal and cook 1½ cups chopped onions (or about 15 pearl onions) in the fat over medium heat until nicely browned. Proceed as above, beginning by adding the mushrooms and their liquid.

> **FOR** a richer sauce, substitute ½ cup good chicken or beef stock for the wine.

> **FOR** a *much* richer sauce, stir in up to 4 tablespoons of butter, a bit at a time, at the end of cooking.

> **YOU** can also cook the veal with fresh vegetables: After the meat has simmered for about 30 minutes, add 15 peeled pearl onions (or about 1½ cups chopped onions), 1 cup chopped carrots, ½ cup chopped celery, or any combination of vegetables that you like. You will probably have to add another ½ cup or so of liquid as well.

Crisp Roasted Rack of Lamb

WORK TIME	15 minutes
PREP TIME	30 minutes
CAN BE	easily multiplied
MAKES	4 servings

RACK OF LAMB—A ROW OF unseparated rib chops—has been a restaurant staple for so long that many people assume there is some trick to cooking it. But there is not. You trim the rack of excess (but not all) fat and roast it at high heat. Salt and pepper are good seasonings, there are a number of quick tricks for adding flavor to the exterior, and you can of course make a quick reduction sauce before serving. But these are options and by my standards unnecessary: The distinctive flavor of true lamb is an uncommonly fine treat.

Getting true lamb is part of the problem, because in shopping for racks of lamb I've been offered those ranging from just over a pound to well over two. More weight means a larger animal, and larger animals are not lamb but mutton. There is nothing intrinsically wrong with a rack of mutton, especially when it's relatively small (as the two-pounders are), but it isn't a rack of lamb: the meat and fat both taste stronger, and there's more of the latter.

Nor is this just a question for aficionados; the mild flavor of baby lamb has a more universal appeal than the gamier flavor of older meat. It's an easy enough decision to make; just tell the butcher you want a rack that weighs less than two pounds. Of course, if you enjoy the flavor of larger racks, this won't be an issue, and a larger rack certainly gives you more meat to tear into.

Because many restaurants offer a whole rack as a serving (six to eight ribs!), many people believe that to be a standard serving size. There are almost no circumstances where even a small rack will not serve two people; a larger rack can accommodate three and sometimes four. To serve more, just cook two racks at a time; they will fit comfortably side by side in most roasting pans. I like to cut each rack in half before roasting. This makes for slightly more uniform cooking, and also relieves you from separating each rack into individual ribs before serving.

The roasting itself is child's play. Your oven should be hot (it should also be well insulated, because high heat produces smoke). Cut the rack most of the way down between the ribs so that more meat is exposed to intense heat and therefore becomes crisp. ("Frenching" the ribs—scraping the meat off the bones to leave them naked and neater in appearance—is counterproductive; the crisp meat on the bones is one of the joys of rack of lamb.) Unless you're highly experienced, the most reliable method of judging doneness is with an instant-read thermometer; 125 degrees in the center will give you medium-rare meat.

2 racks of lamb, each about 1½ pounds	Salt and freshly ground black pepper

1 Preheat the oven to 500°F. Strip most of the surface fat from the lamb (your butcher may already have done this.) Cut between the ribs, almost down to the meaty eye. Divide each rack in half down the middle, sprinkle with salt and pepper to taste, and place in a roasting pan. (See photographs below.)

2 Roast for 15 minutes, then insert a meat thermometer straight in from one end into the meatiest part. If it reads 125 degrees or more, remove the lamb immediately. If it reads 120 degrees or less, put the lamb back for about 5 minutes. Remove and let sit for 5 minutes; this will give you medium- to medium-rare lamb on the outer ribs, medium-rare to rare in the center. Cook a little longer for more doneness. Serve, separating the ribs by cutting down straight through them.

  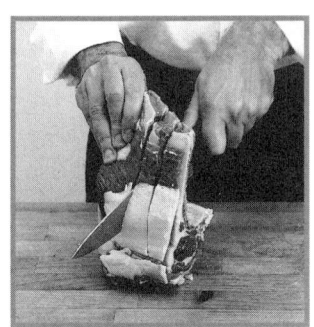

1 | Trim the lamb of excess surface fat.

2 | Cut the rack in half.

3 | Cut down about halfway between each of the ribs.

With MINIMAL Effort

Spice-Rubbed Rack of Lamb: Rub a teaspoon or more of your favorite spice rub—curry powder, chili powder, or anything else you find appealing—into the flat, fleshy side of the racks before roasting.

Rack of Lamb Persillade: Combine 2 tablespoons olive oil, 1 cup plain bread crumbs, 1 small peeled garlic clove, and about ½ cup fresh parsley leaves in a small food processor (or chop by hand). Process until minced, then rub into the flat, fleshy side of the racks before roasting.

Rack of Lamb with Red Wine or Port Sauce: When the lamb is done roasting, remove it to a warm platter. Pour off all but a tablespoon of its fat and place the roasting pan on a burner (or two burners, if it is big) over high heat. Add 1 cup good red wine or port and cook, stirring and scraping, until the liquid is reduced to about ⅓ cup. Add any of the liquid that has accumulated around the lamb and stir. Season to taste, then spoon a little of this over each serving of rib.

Braised, Then Grilled Lamb Shanks

WORK TIME	25 minutes
PREP TIME	at least 2½ hours
CAN BE	prepared in advance; easily multiplied
MAKES	4 servings

I'M OFTEN CONFUSED BY THE common "wisdom" of cooking. Why, for example, do so many recipes have you brown lamb shanks and other tough meats, when the subsequent two or more hours of braising needed to make them tender breaks down the lovely, crisp crust that the browning process created? The simple answer is that browning creates complex flavors—and it's true. (What is not true is that browning "seals in the juices," but that's another story entirely.)

Long, slow cooking also creates complex flavors. Furthermore, browning meat at the beginning of cooking creates a legion of hot, flying drops of fat, often accompanied by minor burns and a huge mess. Which explains why many people avoid it entirely.

Here's one solution: Cook lamb shanks (or short ribs, or any other really tough cut of meat on the bone) for a long time in liquid, without initial browning. The result is complexity of flavor, supreme tenderness, and little hassle. When the braising is done, grill or broil the shanks, which will give them the ultimate crust. The braising liquid serves as a succulent sauce.

All this takes, really, is time—the work is minimal. I find that a combination of port and garlic provides plenty of flavor, but if you want to add a few aromatic vegetables to the broth, like carrots, onions, and celery, they'll certainly make a contribution. Or you can change the character of the dish entirely; see the variations.

It pays to arrange your schedule to make this slow-cooked dish in leisurely fashion. I prefer to braise the shanks the night before serving them, while I'm cooking something else or even out of the kitchen entirely. They need occasional turning (I suggest every thirty minutes, but fifteen minutes more or less between turnings won't matter), but no more attention than that.

When they're done, refrigerate meat and sauce separately; well wrapped, they'll keep perfectly for two or three days. This allows you to skim the fat from the sauce before reheating; the shanks will reheat in the time it takes to brown them. The sauce needs nothing but salt, pepper, and a touch of vinegar or lemon juice to balance its sweetness.

4 lamb shanks, each about 1 pound	Salt and freshly ground black pepper
1 cup port or red wine	1 teaspoon red wine vinegar or fresh lemon juice, or to taste
8 garlic cloves (don't bother to peel them)	

1 Combine the lamb shanks, port or wine, and garlic in a skillet just large enough to hold the shanks. Turn the heat to high and bring to a boil; cover and turn down the heat so that the mixture simmers gently. Cook, turning about every 30 minutes, until the shanks are tender and a lovely mahogany color, at least 2 hours and more likely longer.

2 Remove the shanks and strain the sauce. If time allows, refrigerate both separately; skim the fat from the top of the sauce. Preheat a charcoal or gas grill, or the broiler; the rack should be 4 to 6 inches from the heat source, and the fire hot.

3 Grill or broil the shanks until nicely browned all over, sprinkling them with salt and pepper to taste and turning as necessary; total cooking time will be about 15 minutes. Meanwhile, reheat the sauce gently; season it with salt and pepper, then add the vinegar or lemon juice. Taste and add more seasoning if needed. Serve the shanks with the sauce.

With MINIMAL Effort

You can treat short ribs in exactly the same fashion; cooking time will be at least 30 minutes shorter. The ribs are done when the meat falls from the bone.

Anise-Flavored Lamb Shanks (or Short Ribs): Braise the meat in a mixture of ¼ cup soy sauce, 1 cup water, 5 thin slices fresh ginger, 5 whole star anise, 4 garlic cloves, and 1 tablespoon sugar. Proceed as above, finishing the sauce with rice or white wine vinegar.

Lamb Shanks with Carrots: Follow the original recipe, using red wine (the carrots are so sweet that port would be overkill). After 1 hour of cooking, add 2 cups peeled carrots, cut into chunks. Proceed as above; you may brown the carrots lightly or leave them in the sauce.

Braised Pork with Turnips

WORK TIME	15 minutes		
PREP TIME	60 minutes		
CAN BE	prepared in advance; frozen; easily multiplied		
MAKES	4 servings		

IN MUCH OF THE U.S., THERE'S A brief period in the spring during which fresh vegetables begin to flood the market while the weather remains cool enough to cook seriously even in non–air-conditioned kitchens. Like autumn—but on a smaller scale—it's a time when you can actually include local produce in the comforting, stewlike dishes of winter.

To me, a classic dish for this season is the simplest possible combination of pork in turnips, in which both are browned for perfect color and then simmered in a little liquid until tender. The pork should be boneless, and should contain at least a little fat to keep it moist; shoulder is the best cut, but loin is good, too. The turnips may be either white (the purple-topped variety is most common) or yellow rutabagas, usually considered coarser in flavor than true turnips but in truth equally good. White wine or chicken stock is the best liquid, because each contributes some flavor of its own to the dish, but the pork and turnips simmer long enough to produce good-tasting juice even if you use water.

That's nearly it for ingredients. Gardeners or those with ready access to greenmarkets can add a little lovage, whose intense, celerylike flavor shouts freshness, but celery leaves or parsley make a similar contribution.

The technique for this dish is also elementary, although it's always worth pointing out that meat does not brown automatically: It requires high heat and constant contact with the cooking surface. To get a nice brown surface on the meat properly, you must

PREHEAT the skillet for at least a minute;

ALLOW the cooking medium—butter, oil, or a combination—to become hot;

NOT CROWD the meat (one and one half pounds of cubed meat will just about fit in the bottom of a twelve-inch skillet);

ALLOW the meat to sear, undisturbed, for a few minutes before turning. (All stoves are different, but mine needs about five minutes to do the job here.)

These are cubes of meat, so theoretically you could brown six sides of each piece, but just make sure that the first side browns well and that the second is on its way to being browned before adding the turnips. The turnips themselves are so high in natural sugars that they brown almost instantly, and continue to gain color as they braise.

1 tablespoon neutral oil, such as canola

1 tablespoon butter (or use all oil)

1½ pounds boneless pork shoulder or loin, trimmed of excess fat and cut into 1- to 1½-inch chunks

1½ pounds purple-topped turnips or rutabaga, peeled and cut into 1-inch chunks

¾ cup white wine, chicken stock, or water

Salt and freshly ground black pepper

2 tablespoons minced fresh lovage, celery leaves, or parsley, optional

1 Place a 12-inch skillet, preferably nonstick, over medium-high heat and let sit for at least a minute. Add the oil and butter. When the butter foam subsides or the oil is hot, add the pork, a few chunks at a time. When it is all in the skillet, turn the heat to high. Cook for about 5 minutes, undisturbed, until the pork is nicely browned on one side. Turn each piece, return the heat to medium-high, and cook about 3 minutes more.

2 Add the turnip chunks and shake the skillet so that the pork and turnips are all sitting in one layer or nearly so. Cook for another 3 or 4 minutes, or until the turnips begin to brown. Add the liquid and stir once or twice. Add salt and pepper to taste and half the optional lovage, turn the heat to medium-low, and cover the skillet.

3 Cook, stirring every 10 minutes, until both pork and turnips are quite tender, about 30 minutes. Remove the cover and raise the heat to medium-high; boil the liquid until it is reduced to a syrupy glaze. Taste and add more salt and pepper if necessary, then garnish with the remaining herb if you like and serve.

With MINIMAL Effort

Creamy Pork with Turnips: In the final step, remove the pork and turnips to a warm platter. Do not quite reduce the liquid to a glaze; when there is about ½ cup left, reduce the heat to low, stir in 1 cup sour or sweet cream and slowly bring back to a boil over medium heat. Stir the pork and turnips back into the sauce; garnish and serve, preferably over rice.

Pork and Turnips with Mustard: You can do this in combination with the above variation if you like. Stir 1 tablespoon Dijon mustard, or more to taste, into the finished sauce. Heat through and serve.

Roast Pork with Fennel-Orange Compote

WORK TIME	40 minutes
PREP TIME	40 minutes
CAN BE	easily multiplied
MAKES	4 servings

IT ISN'T OFTEN YOU CAN COMBINE a few winter staples and create a novel, fresh-tasting dish that is easily varied, stands on its own, or forms the base for a variety of other foods. Yet a simple mélange of fennel and orange does all of these things, and without a lot of effort.

The basics couldn't be easier: You layer sliced fennel, sliced onion, and sliced orange, and poach them in orange juice and a bit of olive oil. The fennel and onion become tender, the orange juice and olive oil become saucy, and the orange flesh actually gains a bit of density, becoming deliciously jamlike. In its original version, the seasoning is rosemary (in addition, of course, to salt and pepper), but any herb, preferably fresh, will do nicely. And, by changing the seasoning, it's just as easy to steer this compote in an Asian direction.

When I first made the fennel-orange compote, I served it as a side dish. But it is so juicy, sweet, and gently acidic that its complexity made it perfect for serving under meat or fish, even those prepared in the most mundane ways imaginable. The synthesis is wonderful.

For example, when I marinated some slices of boneless pork in olive oil, lemon juice, garlic, salt, and pepper for just about 30 minutes, and pan-roasted them, then served them on a bed of the compote, the mingled juices were sheer delight. (I've offered the recipe that way here, but it is easy to cook the fennel-orange combination on its own.) Similarly, the compote worked nicely as a bed for simple roasted cod, sautéed duck breast, and grilled chicken. A week later, I was still working on the possibilities.

As for technique, there isn't much to speak of. You'll know the dish is done when the orange juice bubbles become scarce. Just make sure not to cook the compote entirely dry; the orange juice sauce is a nice touch.

4 boneless pork chops, 1 to 1½ pounds	1 fennel bulb, 1 pound or more
Salt and freshly ground black pepper	2 navel oranges, peeled
	1 medium onion, peeled
4 tablespoons extra virgin olive oil	1 tablespoon fresh rosemary or 1 teaspoon dried rosemary
Juice of 1 lemon	1½ cups orange juice

1 Sprinkle the pork chops with salt and pepper to taste and marinate them on a plate with 2 tablespoons of the olive oil and the lemon juice. Preheat the oven to 500 degrees.

2 Trim the fennel, reserving some of the dill-like fronds. Cut the fennel, oranges, and onion into ⅛- to ¼-inch-thick slices.

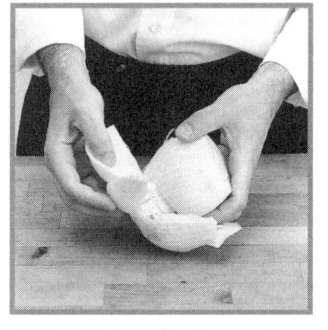

1 | Cut off the stalks, if any, and remove the tough outer layers from the fennel bulb.

2 | Cut slices through the bulb.

3 Place the remaining olive oil in an 8-inch skillet or a saucepan that is at least 4 inches deep. Place half the fennel in the skillet, then top with half the orange, the onion, and the rosemary. Sprinkle with salt and pepper, then top with the remaining fennel and orange. Pour in the juice, and add more salt and pepper.

4 Bring to a boil on top of the stove and cook over fairly lively heat, pressing the solids down into the liquid from time to time. When the mixture is no longer swimming in juice but not yet dry—about 20 minutes—it is done. Hold it at minimum heat while you finish the pork chops.

5 Just before you judge the compote to be done, heat an ovenproof skillet over high heat for 3 or 4 minutes. Add the pork chops with their marinade and immediately transfer the skillet to the oven (if you have a powerful vent, you can pan-grill the chops on top of the stove). Roast 2 minutes, then turn and roast another 2 to 3 minutes, or until the chops are done.

6 Serve the chops on a bed of the compote. Mince the reserved fennel fronds and use as a garnish.

With MINIMAL Effort

SUBSTITUTE grapefruit for the oranges, or add the juice of a lemon or a lime to the mix.

VARY the herb. Classic Western European herbs such as rosemary, thyme, tarragon, and parsley are all naturals, but cilantro or finely minced lemongrass also add nice touches.

ADD finely minced fresh ginger along with some garlic and soy sauce. A teaspoon or so of roasted sesame oil finishes the compote nicely. Substitute peanut oil for the olive oil if you have it, or use a neutral oil such as canola.

ANY meat, such as steak, can be cooked like the pork. Grilled chicken, on or off the bone, works well, as does sautéed duck breast.

YOU can also make the dish with fish: Try roasted delicate fillets, such as cod or red snapper; or grilled shrimp; or swordfish, tuna, or salmon steaks.

Roast Pork with Applesauce

WORK TIME	15 minutes
PREP TIME	about 60 minutes
CAN BE	easily multiplied
MAKES	4 servings

SPREADING A ROAST WITH A SUGARY coating—apricot jam comes to mind—serves a dual purpose. Its sweetness adds an element of flavor not often found in savory dishes, and the sugar encourages browning. But the results are often *too* sweet, at least for my tastes.

When I decided to experiment with alternative coatings for a small roast of pork—one that would cook quickly enough to be considered for weeknight dinners—I settled on applesauce, and quickly realized that it has an additional benefit. Because applesauce doesn't contain nearly the same percentage of sugar as jam, more of it can be used without overwhelming the meat with sweetness, and the thicker coating protects the meat and keeps it moist. This is important, because the superlean pork sold in supermarkets has an almost inexorable tendency to dry out as it cooks.

As is almost always the case in cooking, these benefits come with a trade-off: The lower-sugar applesauce (especially the unsweetened kind, which I prefer) did not brown as quickly or as well as jam. To counter this, I drained some of the liquid from the applesauce (this can be done while the oven is preheating), and roasted the pork at an extremely high oven temperature. The results were quite pleasing: A moist roast of pork, with a slightly sweet, nicely browned topping. Two ingredients and almost no work.

Although bone-in pork resists drying out better, the applesauce works so well that boneless pork becomes a good choice, which eliminates part of the hassle of carving. Steer clear, however, of tenderloin, which is so lean that it seems to dry out just by being in the vicinity of the oven. The lean end of the loin is nearly as bad, but a roast taken from the loin's center is acceptable. Best of all is a cut from the shoulder end of the loin, which contains a higher percentage of the darker, moister meat.

A word about cleanup, or minimizing cleanup: The small amounts of applesauce that drip off the pork onto the surface of the roasting pan will burn and stick; removing this mess is more work than the entire cooking process. You can avoid this by coating the bottom of the roasting pan with a double layer of aluminum foil, lightly brushed with a tiny bit of oil.

One 1½- to 2-pound pork loin

2 cups applesauce, preferably
  unsweetened

Salt and freshly ground black
  pepper

1 Preheat the oven to 500°F; set the oven rack as close to the top of the oven as is practical (take the thickness of the roast into account). Meanwhile, put the applesauce in a fine strainer over a bowl or in the sink to allow excess liquid to drain. Line a roasting pan with a double thickness of aluminum foil and brush the foil with a little oil.

2 When the oven is hot, sprinkle the roast with salt and pepper, then spread an even layer of the applesauce all over it, using up all the applesauce. Sprinkle with a little more salt and pepper and roast, checking every 15 minutes or so to make sure the applesauce doesn't burn. It's fine if it darkens and browns, or even turns dark brown, as long as the top doesn't blacken.

3 Begin checking the pork with an instant-read thermometer after 45 minutes. When the internal temperature reaches 155 degrees, remove the meat from the oven. Let it rest 5 minutes before carving. Serve the sliced meat with any accumulated juices.

With MINIMAL Effort

Roast Pork with Jam or Marmalade: This is the original version, which some will prefer: Substitute 1 cup apricot jam or orange marmalade for the applesauce; warm it over low heat, stirring in 1 tablespoon fresh lemon juice to thin it slightly. Proceed as above.

Sausage with Grapes

WORK TIME	30 minutes
PREP TIME	30 minutes
CAN BE	easily multiplied
MAKES	4 servings

A FEW YEARS AGO, I SAW *salsiccia all'uva*—with grapes—on a menu in a Tuscan trattoria, and ordered it strictly out of curiosity. My imagination could not prepare me for the utter simplicity of the dish: beautifully browned sausages nestled on a bed of grapes in varying stages of doneness—some lightly browned, some collapsed, some whole and nearly raw.

Although I was told the dish is Umbrian in origin, it seems as if many workers of the land who produced sausages and picked grapes would have created this, even if by accident, no matter where they lived. It is an often overlooked recipe in cookbooks, perhaps because there's almost nothing to it—there is neither the challenge nor the trendiness of sausages and polenta, for example. In any case, the wonderful marriage is incredibly easy to produce and easily worked into anyone's repertoire. With good bread and a salad, you've got a great weeknight meal in about half an hour.

Simple as the recipe is, there are some fine points to consider. You can brown sausages over raging high heat or more moderately. I recommend the latter method, which reduces spattering significantly. To minimize mess even further, don't prick the sausages to release their fat until they are almost cooked; they will brown perfectly even in a completely dry skillet.

Before cooking the grapes, you might drain off the excess fat. These days, however, many sausages are quite lean, and even a pound releases only a tablespoon of fat during cooking—the minimum you need for the grapes. As the grapes cook they release some of their liquid, which combines with the fat to form a lovely brown sauce. Because standard seedless grapes are somewhat one-dimensional in flavor and lacking in acidity, this sauce needs a minuscule amount of balsamic vinegar or lemon juice to balance it. That's it—even salt and pepper are unnecessary.

1 to 1½ pounds fresh Italian sausage	2 teaspoons balsamic vinegar or fresh lemon juice, or to taste
4 cups seedless grapes	

1 Place the sausages in a 10- or 12-inch skillet and turn the heat to medium. Cook the sausages, turning from time to time, until they are nicely browned, about 15 minutes. When they are brown all over, prick each sausage in a few places with a thin-bladed knife and cook for 5 minutes more.

2 Remove the sausages to a warm platter. If more than a tablespoon or two of fat remains in the pan, remove the excess. Add the grapes and turn the heat to medium-high. Cook, stirring occasionally, until some of the grapes collapse. Add the vinegar or lemon juice, stir, and turn off the heat. Serve the sausages nestled in the grapes and their juices.

With MINIMAL Effort

Sausage with Grapes and Pan Gravy: Before adding the grapes, add 1 cup white wine or chicken stock to the skillet. Raise the heat to high and cook, stirring, until the liquid is reduced by about half. Stir in the grapes and proceed as above. Serve with mashed potatoes (see below) or bread.

Bangers-and-Mash, Italian Style: Boil 1½ to 2 pounds peeled potatoes in water to cover until soft; drain, reserving some of the cooking liquid. While the potatoes are hot, mash them with ½ teaspoon minced garlic, 2 tablespoons extra virgin olive oil, and enough of the reserved cooking liquid to make them smooth. Season to taste with salt and pepper. Reheat if necessary and serve with the sausages and grapes. Especially good with the preceding variation.

The Minimalist's Choucroute

WORK TIME	15 minutes
PREP TIME	about 2 hours
CAN BE	prepared in advance; easily multiplied
MAKES	6 servings

IN ALSACE, ITS LAND OF ORIGIN, *choucroute garnie* is no more special than a frank and sauerkraut, with which it has much in common. But while the French treat this archetypically hearty combination of sauerkraut, spices, wine, and smoked meats as common fare, here it has become the province of restaurants. In any case, choucroute is a flexible combination of wintertime staples.

And no matter how—or where—it is made, choucroute is the perfect cold-weather dish, made with sauerkraut cooked in a little goose fat (or duck fat, or lard) and wine, then "garnished"—this is *some* garnish—with a variety of candidly heavy meats, some smoked, some fresh or salted. The seasonings are simple, usually little more than juniper and onion, but the meat and cabbage are assertive enough so that the dish screams for strong mustard.

Cooking a basic choucroute is an easy task, better handled at home than in restaurants. Nearly everything is up for grabs, especially if you imagine yourself in the positions of the people who first made this dish—in midwinter, with plenty of sauerkraut, some wine, and whatever meat or fish they could find to supplement the two. There is little right or wrong here and anyway, as Julia Child once said, "No one is watching."

3 pounds sauerkraut	1 pound kielbasa or similar dark sausage
1 large onion, peeled and chopped	
10 juniper berries	3 bratwursts or similar white sausage
2 cups dry white wine, preferably Alsatian Riesling	
	3 smoked loin pork chops
1 pound slab bacon, in one piece	Salt and freshly ground black pepper

1 Wash the sauerkraut and drain it well. Combine it with the onion, juniper berries, and wine in a large skillet or broad pot and add enough water to come about two-thirds of the way up the side of the sauerkraut (in some pots, the wine may provide enough liquid). Turn the heat to high and bring to a boil.

2 Turn down the heat and nestle the bacon in the sauerkraut. Cover and cook 60 minutes, then add the sausages and pork chops. Re-cover and cook another 30 minutes. The sauerkraut should be tender but retain some crunch; cook another 15 minutes if necessary, then taste and season with salt and pepper to taste.

3 To serve, cut the meat into pieces and serve it on a platter with the sauerkraut along with hot mustard.

With MINIMAL Effort

ADD several tablespoons of duck fat or lard to the simmering sauerkraut (a traditional addition).

USE any sausages you like, including those made from chicken, veal, turkey, or seafood.

ADD 12 small potatoes to the pot when about 45 minutes remain to cook.

ADD 2 to 3 peeled, cored, and grated apples to the sauerkraut when about 15 minutes of cooking remain.

STIR 2 tablespoons kirsch into the sauerkraut about 5 minutes before serving.

Grilled Lamb Ribs

WORK TIME	10 minutes
PREP TIME	30 minutes
CAN BE	easily multiplied
MAKES	4 servings

IF YOU DON'T SEE LAMB RIBS in your supermarket; the chances are that they're being tossed. Both demand and profit are evidently so slim that they are not worth processing and putting out in the case. Which is a shame, because next to pork (spare) ribs, lamb ribs are the best down-and-dirty grill item I know. They're also the cheapest. Where I live, it's hard to pay more than a dollar a pound for them.

Also, like pork ribs, lamb ribs require special treatment while grilling. They are loaded with fat, which, if not handled properly, will melt onto the coals (or open flame of a gas grill) and catch fire. To avoid this, parboil the ribs, just for ten minutes or so, to render enough of the fat so that it does-n't catch fire when you put the ribs on the grill.

Any brushing sauce or spice rub you like is suitable here. My choice is a sweet, but pungent amalgam of raw onion, strong mustard, and honey, marmalade, or maple syrup.

4 to 5 pounds lamb breast, cut
   into ribs
Salt and freshly ground black
   pepper

¼ cup honey, orange marmalade,
   or maple syrup
¼ cup Dijon mustard
1 small onion, peeled

1 Start a charcoal or wood fire or preheat a gas grill or broiler; the fire should only be moderately hot and the rack should be at least 4 inches from the heat source. Bring a large pot of water to the boil; salt it. Put in the lamb and simmer for ten minutes.

2 Drain the ribs. Grill or broil them for about 10 minutes, turning once or twice and sprinkling them with a little salt and pepper. Meanwhile, combine the honey, mustard, and onion in a blender and whiz until smooth.

3 When the ribs begin to brown, brush them with the sauce and continue to cook, watching carefully so they do not catch fire. When they are brown and crisp all over—a matter of no more than 10 or, at the most, 15 minutes—remove from the grill and serve.

Vegetables

Grilled Asparagus with
Lemon Dressing

WORK TIME	20 minutes
PREP TIME	20 minutes
CAN BE	prepared in advance; easily multiplied
MAKES	4 servings

MUCH AS I LIKE STEAMED ASPARAGUS, by mid-April I'm ready to move on to other ways of preparing this ancient symbol of spring. My first alternative is always the grill, another element of cooking that makes its appearance this time of year, and one which treats asparagus perfectly. I love the earthy, charred flavor added by the grill, a flavor that can also be achieved with stovetop pan-grilling, which combines high heat and a dry, heavy skillet.

Although it isn't always the case—see the following recipe, for example—here you want thick spears of asparagus, which remain tender and moist inside while their exteriors brown. Those that weigh an ounce or two each—that is, eight to sixteen per pound—are the best. Pencil-thin asparagus not only dry out during this treatment, they have a tendency to fall through the grill grates. (Outfitting a grill with a coarse-meshed screen is helpful in preventing this no matter what size asparagus you use.) The only disadvantage to thick asparagus is that they must be peeled before cooking in order to remove the relatively tough skin.

Asparagus works brilliantly with fish. And if you are grilling, the simplest thing to do is to pick a sturdy fish that can be grilled without falling apart, such as tuna, monkfish, or swordfish. Either of these can be lightly oiled, seasoned, and slapped on a grill, to be cooked in about the same time as the asparagus. (If you're pan-grilling, broil the fish at the same time.)

Both asparagus and fish go well with a strong, lemony dressing. The dressing here closely resembles one I've used regularly on grilled chicken: It's essentially lemon juice spiked with shallots, parsley, and black pepper tempered just slightly by olive oil. My guess is that if you sample it once it will become a staple.

1½ to 2 pounds large asparagus	Juice of 3 lemons
Olive oil as needed, about 2 tablespoons	2 tablespoons minced shallots or scallions
Salt and freshly ground black pepper	¼ cup minced fresh parsley leaves

1 Snap off the woody ends of the asparagus; most spears will break naturally an inch or two above the bottom. Peel the stalks up to the flower bud. Meanwhile, start a charcoal fire or preheat a gas grill; if you're cooking inside, preheat a cast-iron or other heavy skillet over medium-high heat until it smokes.

2 To grill the asparagus, toss them with about 1 tablespoon of the oil, mixing with your hands until they're coated. Season well with salt and pepper to taste. Grill until tender and browned in spots, turning once or twice, a total of 5 to 10 minutes.

3 To pan-grill the asparagus, do not oil or season them. Just toss them in the hot skillet and cook, turning the individual spears as they brown, until tender, 5 to 10 minutes. Remove as they finish, and season with salt and pepper.

4 Mix together the lemon juice and shallots, then stir in enough olive oil to add a little body and take the edge off the sharpness of the lemon; the mixture should still be quite strong. Season it with salt and plenty of black pepper and stir in the parsley. Serve the asparagus hot or at room temperature with grilled or broiled swordfish, monkfish, or other sturdy fish. Spoon the sauce over all.

With MINIMAL Effort

Asparagus with Soy-Ginger Dressing: Combine ¼ cup soy sauce with ½ teaspoon minced garlic, 1 teaspoon minced fresh ginger, ½ teaspoon sugar, 2 teaspoons rice or other mild vinegar, and a few drops of sesame oil. Serve over the asparagus.

SERVE the asparagus with any vinaigrette (pages 208–210) you like.

Roasted Asparagus
with Parmesan

The Skinny on Thin Asparagus

WORK TIME	10 minutes
PREP TIME	25 minutes
CAN BE	easily multiplied
MAKES	4 servings

THE ONGOING DEBATE ABOUT THE relative merits of asparagus spears usually centers on the sensual experience. Thick ones, adherents argue, have more flavor. I myself held that position until I began to think that perhaps it wasn't that their flavor was more intense but simply that the larger size meant that each bite delivered more asparagus into your mouth.

Whatever. There are two distinct advantages to pencil-thin asparagus that seem to get overlooked. One is that they require no peeling, because their outer sheaths are far more tender than those of their thick cousins. And the other is that they cook much faster. This is especially important when you turn to methods other than boiling or steaming—most notably roasting.

You can roast thin asparagus in 12 to 15 minutes. During that period, the spears shrivel, brown slightly, and gain complexity of flavor. It would take a least twice as long (not including the time it takes to peel) to achieve the same ends with thick spears. Even then the flavor gain will not be as great, because a pound of thick spears has less surface area than a pound of thin ones, and therefore less area to brown.

Enough of this discussion. What I like to do is roast thin spears until they're just about tender, then top them with a foolproof two-ingredient topping: coarse bread crumbs and Parmesan cheese. Run that under the broiler, and you get roasted asparagus with a crunchy, high-impact crust. The only trick is to keep your eye on the dish while it's under the broiler—the time needed there is only a minute or two.

There are a couple of minor considerations here. You can use any hard, grating cheese you like. Although I do think real Parmesan is best—especially if you combine it with butter—pecorino or other hard sheep's cheese does a nice job. Keep the crumbs coarse if you can; they might look slightly less attractive, but will give you more crunch.

1 thick slice good bread, about 1 ounce	3 tablespoons butter, extra virgin olive oil, or a combination
1 small chunk Parmesan cheese, about 1 ounce	Salt and freshly ground black pepper
1½ pounds thin asparagus, more or less	

1 Preheat the oven to 500°F; while it's preheating, put the bread in there, and check it frequently until it is lightly toasted and dry. Coarsely grind or grate the bread and Parmesan together (a small food processor is perfect for this)—if possible, keep the crumbs from becoming as small as commercial bread crumbs.

2 Rinse the asparagus and break off their woody bottoms. Lay them in a baking dish that will accommodate them in two or three layers. Toss with bits of the butter and/or oil, sprinkle lightly with salt and pepper, and place in the oven.

3 Roast for 5 minutes, then shake the pan to redistribute the butter or oil. Roast another 5 minutes, then test the asparagus for doneness by piercing a spear with the point of a sharp knife; it is done when the knife enters the asparagus but still meets a little resistance. You can prepare the recipe in advance up to this point up to a couple of hours before serving; allow the asparagus to sit at room temperature during that time.

4 Turn on the broiler and place the rack as close as possible to the heating element. Carefully brown the top—it will only take a minute or two—and serve the asparagus hot or at room temperature.

With MINIMAL Effort

Roast Asparagus with Garlic: Forget the topping; just toss the asparagus with 1 tablespoon minced garlic at the same time as you add the butter or olive oil.

Roast Asparagus with Soy and Sesame: Use 1 tablespoon peanut oil in place of the olive oil or butter. Halfway through the roasting, add 1 tablespoon soy sauce to the asparagus. Top with about 2 tablespoons sesame seeds; run under the broiler until they begin to pop, about 1 minute. Finish with a sprinkling of soy sauce, just a teaspoon or two.

Green Beans with Lemon

WORK TIME	15 minutes
PREP TIME	20 minutes
CAN BE	prepared in advance; easily multiplied
MAKES	4 servings

MANY PEOPLE FIND COOKING vegetables challenging, but there's one technique that is almost infallible, and works for almost every vegetable you can think of. You precook the vegetables—this is something you can do twenty minutes before you eat or twenty-four hours in advance—and then chill them. At the last minute, you reheat them in butter or oil (or, if you're especially fat-conscious, a dry nonstick skillet). That's it.

The advantages are numerous. You can precook a lot of vegetables at once, using the same water for each. You can store them, and cook as much as you need when you need it. You can finish the cooking in five minutes. And you can be pretty well assured that the cooking will be close to perfect, because this method is nearly foolproof.

I use green beans as an example, but this is as close to a generic recipe as there is; it will work with any vegetable that is suitable for cooking in water—beets, potatoes, turnips, broccoli, greens, cauliflower, fennel, snow peas, shell peas, carrots, or cabbage, to name just a few. The only precaution is to not overcook them. Since each vegetable cooks at different rates, the best guideline is to taste the vegetables as they cook; generally, you want the vegetables to be just short of perfectly cooked when you remove them from the boiling water and plunge them into the cold water (chefs call this "shocking" the vegetable). And then, when reheating, you can flavor the vegetables in countless ways. In fact, learn this technique and you will never again be at a loss when cooking vegetables.

| 1 pound green beans | 1 lemon |
| 1 to 2 tablespoons extra virgin olive oil or butter, or a combination | |

1 Bring a large pot of water to a boil and salt it; add the beans and cook until bright green and tender, about 5 minutes. Do not overcook.

2 Drain the beans, then plunge them into a large bowl filled with ice water to stop the cooking. When they're cool, drain again. Store, covered and refrigerated, for up to a couple of days, or proceed.

3 Zest the lemon and julienne or mince the zest. Juice the lemon. Place the oil and/or butter in a large skillet and turn the heat to medium-high. Add the beans and cook, tossing or stirring, until they are hot and glazed, 3 to 5 minutes. Toss in a serving bowl with the lemon juice, top with the zest, and serve.

With MINIMAL Effort

There's little you cannot do with precooked vegetables, but here are some good ideas:

SPRINKLE the cooked vegetable with toasted slivered nuts, bread crumbs, or sesame seeds.

ADD a teaspoon or so of garlic to the butter and/or oil as it is cooking; or use a tablespoon or two of minced shallot, onion, or scallion.

ADD a tablespoon or more of soy sauce to the finished vegetable, with or without the lemon.

SUBSTITUTE lime juice or vinegar for the lemon juice. Or use any vinaigrette (pages 208–210) as a dressing.

TOSS the vegetable with a couple of tablespoons of minced mild herbs—parsley, dill, basil, or chervil, for example—as it is heating.

Beet Roesti with Rosemary

A New Way with Beets

WORK TIME	30 minutes
PREP TIME	30 minutes
CAN BE	prepared in advance
MAKES	4 servings

ALTHOUGH SWEETNESS IS NOT AN unfamiliar sensation at the dinner table, no so-called savory food is quite like the beet, whose intensity is incomparable. This quality has typically led cooks to counter its sweetness with acidity or other sharp flavors, a natural inclination that has brought us beets with vinegar, beets with sour cream, beets with lemon, vinaigrette, ginger, and so on.

Showcasing the sweetness of beets is an attractive alternative, wonderfully exploited in this roesti, a dish, created about ten years ago by Michael Romano, the longstanding chef at Manhattan's Union Square Café. It's a thick beet pancake, cooked slowly on both sides until the beet sugars caramelize and a crunchy, sweet crust forms that, I swear, is reminiscent of crème brûlée. A touch of rosemary added to the mix does not diminish the sweetness at all, but simply adds another dimension.

Both concept and technique are unusual for beets, at least in my experience. Over the years, I've seen nothing like this in cookbooks, and everyone I've cooked the roesti for—or even mentioned it to—finds it surprising. The beets are peeled and grated raw; the grating disk of a food processor does this task quickly and easily, but a box grater works well also. They're then combined with flour, an essential ingredient; without it the pancake won't hold together.

There are some other fine points: In this dish, butter is really the fat of choice; it complements the beets perfectly. If you choose to substitute oil, use a neutral one, such as canola, rather than a strong-tasting olive oil. The roesti must be cooked in a nonstick skillet, preferably a large one measuring twelve inches across. (If you only have a ten-inch skillet, decrease the amount of beets in the recipe from two pounds to one and a half pounds; the quantity given for other ingredients can remain the same.) And keep the heat moderate. Too-quick cooking will burn the sugary outside of the pancake while leaving the inside raw.

Beets bleed, as you know. Peel them over the sink, and wash the grater or food processor as soon as you're done with it, and you won't have any serious consequences. Oh, and wear an apron.

2 pounds beets (about 3 very large or 4 to 6 medium)	½ cup flour
2 teaspoons coarsely chopped fresh rosemary	2 tablespoons butter or olive oil
Salt and freshly ground black pepper	Minced parsley or a few rosemary leaves for garnish

1 Trim the beets and peel them as you would potatoes; grate them in a food processor or by hand. Begin preheating a 12-inch nonstick skillet over medium heat.

2 Toss the grated beets in a bowl with the rosemary, salt, and pepper. Add about half the flour; toss well, add the rest of the flour, then toss again.

3 Place the butter in the skillet and heat until it begins to turn nut-brown. Scrape the beet mixture into the skillet, and press it down with a spatula to form a round. With the heat at medium to medium-high—the pancake should be gently sizzling—cook, shaking the pan occasionally, until the bottom of the beet cake is nicely crisp, 8 to 10 minutes. Slide the cake out onto a plate, top with another plate, invert the two plates, and return the cake to the pan. Continue to cook, adjusting the heat if necessary, until the second side is browned, another 10 minutes or so. Garnish, cut into wedges, and serve hot or at room temperature.

With MINIMAL Effort

Beet Salad with Vinaigrette: You don't need to cook the grated beets; simply toss them, raw, with any vinaigrette (pages 208–210). Given their sweetness, a strong, harsh vinaigrette, with a high percentage of vinegar, is best.

Fennel Gratin

WORK TIME	10 minutes
PREP TIME	20 minutes
CAN BE	prepared in advance; easily multiplied
MAKES	4 servings

A *GRATIN* HAS COME TO MEAN A kind of macaroni-and-cheese affair, a gooey dish in which the main ingredient—whether potatoes, noodles, or vegetables—is dominated by a mass of white sauce, cheese, and butter. The word *gratin* really refers to the crust that forms on the top and sides of a dish that has been browned under a flame.

Although gooey, cheesy dishes can be enjoyable, you can make honest, simple gratins with a topping of just a couple of ingredients, and it's a good, almost universal technique for vegetables.

The heat of a broiler can brown almost anything, but to create a good-looking, good-tasting crust, there are three more-or-less traditional ingredients used in simple gratins: butter, bread crumbs, and cheese. The butter, which adds an undeniably luxurious touch, can easily be dispensed with; there's plenty of flavor here without it. The bread crumbs are best when freshly made from good but slightly stale bread; coarse bread crumbs, such as those made in a food processor, are infinitely preferable to the finer store-bought variety.

The most important ingredient is cheese. In French-style dishes (on which most classic American dishes are based), the cheese is usually a mild, firm, but not hard cheese such as Emmenthal (Swiss) or Cantal, which is similar to cheddar. This type of cheese melts into a thick, sticky mass not unlike the topping on a pizza. Italian-style dishes often rely on freshly grated Parmesan, which combines perfectly with bread crumbs to form a crisp, salty topping as in the asparagus recipe on page 188.

Even more flavor can be added to a gratin dish of vegetables by mixing the bread crumbs with blue cheese. You can use Gorgonzola, the soft Italian cheese; bleu d'Auvergne, a mild cheese from France; Maytag blue, the premier domestic variety; Stilton, the classic English blue; and Roquefort, which is made from sheep's milk. All are good, but my preferences are for the stronger cheeses, such as Roquefort and Maytag. I don't use a lot of cheese on a gratin, just two ounces (about one quarter-cup) for a four-person serving, so I want as much impact as I can get on each bite.

| 1 fennel bulb, about 1 pound | ¼ cup crumbled blue cheese |
| ½ cup coarse bread crumbs | Freshly ground black pepper |

1 Preheat the oven to 400° F. Bring a pot of water to a boil.

2 Trim the fennel, then cut into about ¼-inch-thick slices and cook in the boiling water until just tender, less than 5 minutes. Drain and layer in a shallow baking dish. (You can also drain the vegetables, then stop their cooking by plunging them into ice water, then drain again. In this manner you can finish the cooking up to a day or two later; increase the baking time to 20 minutes.)

3 Top the fennel with the bread crumbs, then with the cheese; season all with pepper to taste (hold off on salt, because the cheese is salty). Place in the oven until the cheese melts, about 10 minutes.

4 Run the baking dish under the broiler until the top browns, checking every 30 seconds. Serve hot or at room temperature.

With MINIMAL Effort

Almost any vegetable will work here; some must be parboiled (see Green Beans with Lemon, page 190): green beans, broccoli, cauliflower, leeks, celery, etc. Some need not be (see Roast Asparagus with Parmesan, page 188): thin asparagus, zucchini, sliced tomatoes.

The flavoring can be changed by varying the cheese. Or toss a couple of tablespoons of minced parsley in with the bread crumbs, or a tiny bit (½ teaspoon or so) of minced garlic.

Tender Spinach, Crisp Shallots
How to Make Greens Appeal to Everyone

WORK TIME	30 minutes
PREP TIME	30 minutes
CAN BE	prepared in advance; easily multiplied
MAKES	4 servings

MY GUESS IS THAT MORE people eat greens because they think they should than because they actually like them, but there are a number of ways to make greens more appealing. First and foremost is to give them the treatment described in detail for green beans on page 191. You simmer the greens—spinach will take about a minute, collards a good ten—then drain them and toss them with oil, butter, and seasonings.

One of my favorite preparations involves a topping of crisp-fried shallots, which by themselves are irresistible and which, when combined with tender greens, create an alluring contrast in flavor and texture. Like the greens themselves, the shallots can be prepared well in advance. When you're ready to eat, you just reheat the greens and sprinkle them with the shallots.

The shallots must be thinly sliced, and this is the perfect occasion to use a mandoline if you have one. If you do not, just peel them, cut a thin slice off one of the long ends if necessary, then slice them as thinly as you can, using a small, sharp knife.

This preparation also serves as a good introduction to deep-frying, because the watchful eye can readily and infallibly detect when the shallots are ready—they turn brown. At that moment, they must be removed from the heat immediately or they will burn. The deliciously flavored oil should be strained and stored in the refrigerator; it can be used in vinaigrettes (pages 208–210), or in cooking.

1 cup or more neutral oil, such as grapeseed, canola, or corn	Salt and freshly ground black pepper
6 to 8 large shallots (about 6 ounces), peeled and thinly sliced	1 pound spinach, washed and trimmed
	2 tablespoons fresh lemon juice

1 Place the oil in a small-to-medium saucepan or narrow, deep skillet; the oil should be at least an inch deep. Turn the heat to high and wait a couple of minutes, then add the shallots and cook, adjusting the heat so that the bubbling is vigorous but not explosive. Cook, stirring, until the shallots begin to darken, 10 to 15 minutes. As soon as they turn golden brown, remove them immediately with a slotted spoon—be careful, because overcooking at this point will burn the shallots. Drain the shallots on paper towels and sprinkle with salt and pepper; they'll keep for a couple of hours this way.

2 Meanwhile, bring a large pot of water to a boil and salt it. When it is ready, add the spinach and cook until it wilts, about 1 minute. Remove the spinach with a strainer or slotted spoon and plunge it into a large bowl filled with ice water to stop the cooking. When it's cool, drain and chop. (You can store the spinach, covered and refrigerated, for up to a couple of days if you like.)

3 Take 1 tablespoon of the shallot oil and place it in a skillet; turn the heat to medium-high. Turn the spinach into this skillet and cook, stirring frequently and breaking up any clumps, until the spinach is hot, about 5 minutes. Season with salt and pepper, add the lemon juice, and serve, topped with the crisp shallots.

With MINIMAL Effort

You can use any leafy green you like here. Some, like collards and kale, will take up to 10 minutes to soften in the boiling water; just keep testing for doneness (sampling) until you're satisfied that they're tender. (Thick stems of 1/4 inch or more will take even longer; start them in the water a few minutes before adding the greens.)

And, of course, the crisp-fried shallots can be used as a garnish for almost any dish.

Piquillo Peppers
with Shiitakes and Spinach
A Canned Vegetable Worth Eating

WORK TIME	20 minutes
PREP TIME	20 to 40 minutes
CAN BE	prepared in advance; easily multiplied
MAKES	4 servings

TO THE LIST OF INGREDIENTS THAT have made the jump from regional specialty to international staple and from restaurant to home kitchen, you can add pimientos del piquillo, the brilliant crimson, cone-shaped peppers from Navarre, a region of western Spain. Piquillos have a lot going for them. Not only is their color stunning, their skin thin, and their flavor a near-perfect blend of sweet and hot, but one couldn't bioengineer a better shape for stuffing, and there's no preparation involved, because piquillo peppers are sold only in cans or bottles. All of this adds up to a terrific "new" ingredient for home cooks—at least those who don't mind the high price.

The best piquillos are from a town called Lodosa, and are so labeled; they are harvested by hand, then roasted over wood, hand-peeled—no water is allowed to touch them, for this would wash away some of the essential flavors—and canned or bottled with no other ingredients. Needless to say, this regal treatment makes top-quality peppers expensive, about fifteen dollars per pound. There are alternatives available: Some Lodosa peppers are roasted over gas, some have citric acid added as a mild preservative. There are also piquillo-style peppers from other parts of Spain. The differences are real but hardly worth fighting about.

Although they're great treated simply, piquillos have become popular largely because they are the perfect foil for full-flavored stuffings. Among the easiest to prepare is the one here, a combination of shiitake mushrooms and spinach. But you can use almost any stuffing you like.

Note: You can purchase piquillo peppers at many specialty food retailers, or by mail from Formaggio Kitchen in Cambridge, MA. (888-212-3224) or 86-17 Northern Boulevard Corp., Jackson Heights, NY (718-779-4971).

¼ cup extra virgin olive oil	1 cup cooked spinach, squeezed
2 garlic cloves, peeled and sliced	dry and chopped
1 dried hot red chile	Salt and freshly ground black
2 cups stemmed shiitake mush-	pepper
rooms, thinly sliced or chopped	12 piquillo peppers

1 Place the olive oil in a large skillet, turn the heat to medium, and add the garlic and chile. Cook, stirring occasionally, until the garlic browns lightly, about 5 minutes. Remove the chile and add the shiitakes. Cook, stirring occasionally, until the shiitakes release their liquid and become tender, about 10 minutes. Stir in the spinach and season to taste.

2 Stuff each of the peppers with a portion of this mixture. Serve at room temperature or warm gently in a 250°F oven for about 15 minutes.

With MINIMAL Effort

Sautéed Piquillos: Place 2 tablespoons extra virgin olive oil in a large skillet, turn the heat to medium-low, and add 2 teaspoons peeled and slivered garlic. Cook, shaking the pan occasionally, until the garlic turns light brown, about 5 minutes. Add 8 to 12 piquillo peppers, cut into strips, and cook just until the peppers begin to change color on the bottom; turn and repeat. Season and serve hot or at room temperature drizzled, if you like, with a little more olive oil and some sherry vinegar.

Piquillos with Anchovies: No cooking here, just place an anchovy fillet in each pepper and drizzle with olive oil, then serve.

Piquillo "Bruschetta": Toast a few rounds of good bread; rub each with a cut clove of garlic and top with a piquillo, or if the bread is small, half a piquillo. Drizzle with olive oil and serve.

Other stuffing suggestions for piquillo peppers:

SPINACH or other greens sautéed with raisins and pine nuts

COOKED and chopped tender fish fillets (such as cod or salmon), tossed with chopped tomatoes and a little oil and vinegar

STEWED and chopped or shredded meat

RICE bound with a little mayonnaise and chopped shrimp or chicken (good served cold)

Quick Scallion Pancakes

WORK TIME	20 minutes
PREP TIME	20 minutes
CAN BE	easily multiplied
MAKES	4 servings

THE SCALLION PANCAKE I'VE ALWAYS made, the one similar to that served in many Chinese restaurants, is essentially bread. And I like its tough, chewy, and slightly sharp nature. Still, I thought, as I made a batch recently, there are two problems with it: One is that the scallion flavor is never strong enough. And two, because the original scallion pancakes are made with what amounts to bread dough, actually requiring rising time, they take a couple of hours to make, making it hard to use them as a last-minute side dish.

I addressed both of these problems by making a simplified, scallion-laden pancake batter. In this batter, the liquid is scallion puree rather than milk, and the flour is just enough to hold the things together; the only thing you taste is scallion, a touch of soy, and the oil you use for cooking. The result is not the hand-held, pizza-dense scallion pancake we're accustomed to, but a fork-tender pancake reminiscent of a vegetable fritter. The flavor is great, and the preparation time is cut to about twenty minutes.

Because the batter is so delicate, it's better to make these as individual pancakes, which are easy to turn, than as one big cake. They're good not only as a side dish, but as a platform for stews and juicy roasts: Lay a couple on a plate and spoon the stew on top. And although I still associate them with Asian-flavored dishes, if you omit the optional soy sauce they're a perfect accompaniment to braised foods that use European seasonings.

Salt and freshly ground black
  pepper
4 bunches scallions or spring
  onions, about 1 pound
1 egg

1 teaspoon soy sauce
½ cup flour
Peanut, canola, or olive oil as
  needed

1 Bring a medium pot of salted water to a boil while you trim the scallions. Roughly chop about three-quarters of them, and mince the remainder.

2 Add the larger portion of scallions to the water and cook about 5 minutes, or until tender. Drain, reserving about ½ cup of the cooking liquid. Puree the cooked scallions in a blender, adding just enough of the cooking liquid to allow the machine to do its work.

3 Mix the puree with the egg and soy sauce, then gently stir in the flour until blended; add pepper and the reserved minced scallions. Film a nonstick or well-seasoned skillet with oil and turn the heat to medium-high. Drop the batter by the tablespoon or ¼ cup and cook the pancakes for about 2 minutes per side, or until lightly browned. If necessary, the pancakes can be kept warm in a 200°F oven for about 30 minutes.

With MINIMAL Effort

The same method can be used to make pancakes with many members of the onion family, especially shallots and spring onions (which look like scallions on steroids). I use peanut oil for this recipe, but that's only because I associate it with soy sauce. If you omit the soy you can use any vegetable oil you like, even good olive oil. There are also some quick additions to the batter to vary the pancakes:

TOASTED sesame seeds, about 1 tablespoon

ROUGHLY chopped peanuts, about 2 tablespoons

MINCED chives, added along with the uncooked scallions, about ¼ cup

¼ TEASPOON cayenne

1 TEASPOON minced fresh ginger

Spanish Tortilla

Turning Potatoes into a Meal

WORK TIME	40 minutes
PREP TIME	40 minutes
CAN BE	prepared in advance
MAKES	3 to 6 servings

THE SPANISH TORTILLA HAS NOTHING in common with the Mexican tortilla except its name, which comes from the Latin *torta*—a round cake. In its most basic form, the Spanish tortilla is a potato-and-egg frittata, or omelet, which derives most of its flavor from olive oil.

Although the ingredients are simple and minimal, when made correctly—and there is a straightforward but very definite series of techniques involved—this tortilla is wonderfully juicy. And because it is better at room temperature than hot, it can and in fact should be made in advance. (How much in advance is up to you. It can be fifteen minutes or a few hours.)

Most omelets rely on high heat, and most frittatas on low heat, but the tortilla is best cooked over moderate heat from start to finish. Potato and onion are cooked in lots of olive oil until soft but not at all crisp. Most of this olive oil is drained, and it should be reserved for other uses, especially sautéing and stir-frying. The potatoes are then combined with eggs and put in a not-too-broad pan to form a cake, which is firmed up slowly, again without browning.

Until recently, this procedure was quite challenging, especially to a novice. If the skillet was not at precisely the right temperature, or not enough oil was used, or the oil was not heated properly, the inevitable result was a stuck tortilla. The nonstick skillet has changed all that.

Now the procedure is pretty much foolproof. It's important to avoid browning the potatoes, which is easy enough, and to keep the omelet from overcooking—also not that difficult, as long as the heat is kept moderate and the cooking time relatively short. The only hard part is turning the partially formed cake, but I assure you that if you act swiftly and carefully you will succeed. The worst that will happen is that a couple of slices of potato and a dribble of egg will be left behind when you return the cake to the skillet, but this will not affect the final product. (If the process makes you nervous, you can finish the tortilla in the oven; see page 203.)

> 1¼ pounds potatoes, 3 to 4
>   medium
>
> 1 medium onion
>
> 1 cup olive oil
>
> Salt and freshly ground black
>   pepper
>
> 6 extra-large or jumbo eggs

1 Peel and thinly slice the potatoes and onion; it's easiest if you use a mandoline for slicing. Meanwhile, heat the oil in an 8- or 10-inch non-stick skillet over medium heat. After the oil has been heating for 3 or 4 minutes, drop in a slice of potato. When tiny bubbles appear around the edges of the potato, the oil is ready; add all of the potatoes and onion along with a good pinch of salt and a liberal sprinkling of pepper. Gently turn the potato mixture in the oil with a wooden spoon, and adjust the heat so that the oil bubbles lazily.

2 Cook, turning the potatoes gently every few minutes and adjusting the heat so they do not brown, until they are tender when pierced with the point of a small knife. If the potatoes begin to break, they are overdone—this is not a tragedy, but stop the cooking immediately. As the potatoes cook, beat the eggs with some salt and pepper in a large bowl.

3 Drain the potatoes in a colander, reserving the oil. Heat an 8- or 9-inch nonstick skillet (it can be the same one, but wipe it out first) over medium heat for a minute and add 2 tablespoons of the reserved oil. Gently mix the warm potatoes with the eggs and add them to the skillet. As soon as the edges firm up—this will only take a minute or so—reduce the heat to medium-low. Cook 5 minutes.

4 Insert a rubber spatula all around the edges of the cake to make sure it will slide from the pan. Carefully slide it out—the top will still be quite runny—onto a plate. Cover with another plate and, holding the plates tightly, invert them. Add another tablespoon of oil to the skillet and use a rubber spatula to coax the cake back in. Cook another 5 minutes, then slide the cake from the skillet to a plate. (Alternatively, finish the cooking by putting the tortilla in a 350°F oven for about 10 minutes.) Serve warm (not hot) or at room temperature. Do not refrigerate.

With MINIMAL Effort

Although potatoes are the most widely enjoyed filling, the tortilla is often filled with a variety of ingredients. Just make sure that any additions are either cooked in olive oil or thoroughly drained of other liquids.

REPLACE the potatoes with onions or scallions, in equal amounts.

REPLACE the potatoes with greens cooked like the spinach on page 196 (start with about a pound). Squeeze the greens dry and chop them, then sauté in just a couple of tablespoons of olive oil before adding the eggs.

ADD about a cup of red bell pepper strips to the potatoes as they cook.

ADD ¼ cup or more of diced chorizo, cooked bacon or shrimp, or dry cured ham like prosciutto to the eggs.

ADD ½ cup or more of canned or cooked fresh peas, lima beans, or chickpeas to the eggs.

Sauces and Condiments

Parsley-Vinegar Sauce

WORK TIME	10 minutes
PREP TIME	10 minutes
CAN BE	prepared in advance; easily multiplied
MAKES	4 servings, about 1 cup

PARSLEY IS, WITHOUT A DOUBT, THE most underrated herb in the United States. We fuss over basil, fall in and out of love with cilantro, experiment with lavender, and nearly ignore plentiful parsley. Still, the situation has improved somewhat; when I was growing up it wasn't even clear that parsley was edible—the few sprigs on the side of the plate merely served notice that the dish was somehow "fancy."

Yet when you get past using parsley as a garnish, and sprinkle a handful on top of a dish just before serving, you begin to appreciate the bright, clean flavor of this common herb. And when you realize that it remains in season far longer than basil, rosemary, or other popular herbs (many gardeners harvest parsley in the snow), you get a further sense of its value.

My passion for parsley increased even more when I learned how to feature it in sauces. You can, of course, make a parsley-based pesto, simply by substituting parsley for basil in any pesto recipe, and the results are quite good. Instead of combining the herb with olive oil, I blend it with vinegar to make a sharp, spiky sauce that complements simply prepared, full-flavored foods. I first had this sauce (or something very much like it) with *bollito misto,* the Italian dish of assorted boiled meats. It is an ideal accompaniment to the simplest grilled, broiled, or roasted meat—great on well-browned steaks, pork, or chicken.

There are a couple of simple technical aspects to this ten-minute preparation that are worth considering. First of all, although many sources insist that flat-leaf parsley is better than the curly-leaf variety, blind tastings have not borne out that myth. What matters more is freshness—limp parsley has no flavor. Secondly, parsley is sandy, so wash it well. In the quantity given here, it's worth using a salad spinner to dry it. Finally, the vinegar you use should be mild and not too intensely flavored; a good rice or sherry vinegar, with an acidity level of about six percent, works best. Stronger vinegar should be diluted even more than indicated in the recipe.

1 cup packed parsley leaves (about 1 ounce), washed and dried	Salt and freshly ground black pepper
1 tablespoon extra virgin olive oil	⅓ cup rice, sherry or other good, fairly mild vinegar
1 small garlic clove, peeled	

1 Place the parsley in a food processor along with the oil, garlic, a healthy pinch of salt, and about ¼ teaspoon pepper. With the machine on, drizzle the vinegar through the feed tube until the parsley is pureed.

2 Add 1 tablespoon water and pulse the machine on and off a couple of times; taste. The mixture should be sharp, but not overpoweringly so. If it seems too strong, add a little more water (the texture will be quite loose, something like thick orange juice). Taste and add more salt and pepper if necessary. Pass the sauce at the table, using a spoon to serve it.

With MINIMAL Effort

Most of the variations on this sauce make it richer, but they're worth considering:

INCREASE the amount of olive oil to as much as ½ cup; eliminate the water (you can also eliminate the vinegar if you like).

ADD toasted walnuts or pignolis, about 2 tablespoons, after the water. Pulse just until the nuts are chopped.

ADD the chopped white of a hard-cooked egg or two.

ADD grated Parmesan or other hard cheese to taste, at least 2 tablespoons.

SUBSTITUTE a shallot for the garlic.

Basic Vinaigrette
The Mother of All Dressings

WORK TIME	5 minutes
PREP TIME	5 minutes
CAN BE	prepared in advance; easily multiplied
MAKES	about ¾ cup

IT'S HARD TO IMAGINE FIVE MINUTES in the kitchen better spent than those making vinaigrette, the closest thing to an all-purpose sauce. At its most basic, vinaigrette is acid and oil, salt and pepper, plus additional flavors as desired. But behind this apparent simplicity lies a complex web of questions to be addressed: Which acid? Which oil? What else should be added? How should it all be combined?

Although the answers to all of these questions are subjective, there is a more-or-less standard vinaigrette that has evolved in the kitchens of many good cooks. It's simple, flavorful, flexible and, when made in a blender, so stable that it can be prepared hours before it is needed. Once made, it can be used on everything from a simple green salad to cold meat, vegetables, or fish dishes to anything that has been broiled or grilled, whether served hot or at room temperature.

My standard all-purpose vinaigrette begins, not surprisingly, with extra virgin olive oil. To vary the flavor, I sometimes use walnut or hazelnut oil or, if I want to downplay the flavor of oil altogether, a neutral oil such as grapeseed or canola. It continues with good wine vinegar, preferably but not necessarily Champagne vinegar, or with the extra-mild rice vinegar. (Balsamic and sherry vinegars, while delicious, are too dominant for some uses, fine for others.) Lemon juice is a fine substitute, but because it is less acidic than most vinegars—three or four percent compared to six or seven percent—you will need more of it.

The standard ratio for making vinaigrette is three parts oil to one part vinegar, but because the vinegars I use are mild and extra virgin olive oil is quite assertive, I usually wind up at about two parts oil to one part vinegar, or even a little stronger. Somewhere in that range you're going to find a home for your own taste; start by using a ratio of three to one and taste, adding more vinegar until you're happy. (You may even prefer more vinegar than olive oil; there's nothing wrong with that.)

There are two other ingredients I almost invariably add to vinaigrette: shallots and Dijon mustard. Shallots are to vinaigrette what garlic is to pesto—the miracle ingredient that ties everything together. There is almost no vinaigrette that is not improved by their addition. Dijon mustard, while not as essential, adds creaminess while fortifying and stabilizing the emulsion; it's a simple addition, and one that's worth it.

The ingredients may be combined with a spoon, a fork, a whisk, or a blender. Hand tools give you an unconvincing emulsion that must be used immediately. Blenders produce vinaigrettes that very much resemble thin mayonnaise in color and thickness—without using egg. They also dispose of the job of mincing the shallots; just peel, chop, and dump it into the container at the last minute (if you add it earlier it will be pureed, depriving you of the pleasure of its distinctive little crunch).

½ cup extra virgin olive oil

3 tablespoons or more good wine vinegar

Salt and freshly ground black pepper

1 heaping teaspoon Dijon mustard

1 large shallot (about 1 ounce), peeled and cut into chunks

1 Combine all ingredients except the shallot in a blender and turn the machine on; a creamy emulsion will form within 30 seconds. Taste and add more vinegar, a teaspoon or two at a time, until the balance tastes right to you.

2 Add the shallot and turn the machine on and off a few times until the shallot is minced within the dressing. Taste and adjust seasoning and serve. (This is best made fresh but will keep, refrigerated, for a few days; bring back to room temperature and whisk briefly before using.)

With MINIMAL Effort

You can integrate almost anything that appeals to you into your vinaigrette. Some quick ideas, many of which may be combined:

ANY fresh or dried herb, fresh by the teaspoon or tablespoon, dried by the pinch

MINCED fresh garlic and/or ginger to taste

SOY sauce, Worcestershire sauce, meat or vegetable stock, or other liquid seasonings, as much as 1 tablespoon

HONEY or other sweeteners to taste

WHOLE-grain mustards or dry mustard to taste

CAYENNE pepper or crushed red pepper flakes, minced fresh hot chiles, or grated or prepared horseradish to taste

FRESHLY grated Parmesan or other hard cheese, or crumbled Roquefort or other blue cheese, at least 1 tablespoon

CAPERS or minced pickles, preferably cornichons, at least 1 tablespoon

SOUR cream, yogurt, or pureed soft tofu, about 2 tablespoons

GROUND spices, such as curry powder, five-spice powder, or nutmeg, in very small quantities

Pan Gravy
How to Make a Reduction Sauce

WORK TIME	20 minutes
PREP TIME	20 minutes
MAKES	about 2 cups

PAN GRAVY—REAL GRAVY, WHETHER made from turkey or any other roasted meat or poultry—is just one of many possible variations on a basic reduction sauce. And reduction sauce is little more than a fancy term for degreasing (or, if you want to be nice, "deglazing") the pan.

When you roast or sauté meat or poultry at high heat, bits of skin, meat, and fat stick to the surface of the pan, becoming dark brown and concentrated; meat juices and rendered fat also gather at the bottom. If you remove the meat, add liquid to the pan, and place it over high heat while stirring, you incorporate these essences into that liquid. At the same time, some of the liquid you added evaporates—reduces—thereby intensifying its own flavor and thickening slightly.

While not essential, most reduction sauces are finished with a bit of butter or oil to add creaminess and even more flavor. Most traditional American gravies are thickened with flour, although cornstarch is a much simpler and more reliable thickening agent.

There are further options to make reduction sauces taste even better. Obviously, the more flavorful the liquid, the more intense the sauce. Thus stock is a common reduction liquid. In moderation, so are cream, milk, wine, fortified wine (like sherry or port), fruit or vegetable juice, or even the liquid used to soak dried mushrooms. Water, too, is perfectly acceptable, since the pan drippings contain plenty of flavor. This is especially true if you scatter aromatic vegetables, like carrots, onions, and celery, around the roasting meat.

In addition, there are many other flavors that can be incorporated into the sauce to boost its intensity. Cooking some chopped shallots or other aromatic vegetables in the pan drippings is a good option, as is adding mustard, herbs, bottled seasonings, or even strong-flavored ingredients like anchovies and capers. Finally, cooked bits of meat or vegetables can be incorporated into the finished sauce to add bulk and contrasting texture. (This is usual in making traditional turkey gravy, where the giblets that were simmered to produce stock are minced and added to the sauce.)

Having just made a simple process sound complicated, let me reiterate that reduction sauces are easy, and involve just a few basic steps. The basic recipe is followed by a variation for a thicker sauce, as well as some ideas for making it more complex. The basic recipe can be doubled or tripled in size, something you will want to consider when making gravy for a crowd.

2 tablespoons minced shallot, onion, or scallion	**2 tablespoons olive oil or softened butter, optional**
3 cups stock or water	**Salt and freshly ground black pepper**

1 Remove the meat from the roasting pan or skillet and pour off all but 1 or 2 tablespoons of the cooking fat (if there are nonfatty juices in the skillet or roasting pan, leave them in there). Place the pan over high heat (use two burners if the pan is large). Add the shallot and cook, stirring, until it softens, about 1 minute.

2 Add the liquid and cook, stirring and scraping to loosen the brown bits at the bottom of the pan. Allow the liquid to boil for about 5 minutes, or until about a third of it evaporates. (This is a good time to carve the meat, if necessary, as the boiling liquid need not be stirred except very occasionally.)

3 Turn the heat to medium-low and add the optional butter or oil, a little at a time, stirring well after each addition to incorporate it. Taste and season if necessary with salt and pepper to taste, then serve with the meat.

With MINIMAL Effort

Thickened Gravy: Combine 1 tablespoon cornstarch with ¼ cup cold water (it will dissolve easily). Stir this into the sauce after incorporating the optional butter or oil and heat, stirring, until thickened, just about a minute. If you want even thicker gravy, repeat with another tablespoon of cornstarch.

There are lots of ways to add weight to a reduction:

ADD 1 cup or more roughly chopped aromatic vegetables (carrots, onions, celery, etc.) to the roasting pan along with the meat, right from the beginning of cooking.

INCREASE the amount and kind of vegetables sautéed in the roasting fat. For example, add minced carrots and mushrooms along with the shallots. (You will probably want to strain the gravy if you do this; do so before adding butter or thickening, because it will pass through the strainer more easily; then reheat the sauce and enrich or thicken it as desired.)

REDUCE ½ to 1 cup of wine, fortified wine (like sherry or Port), or fruit or vegetable juice to just a couple of tablespoons before adding the stock or water.

MAKE the flavor even stronger by stirring in a teaspoon or more of prepared mustard, horseradish, soy sauce, or other condiment.

ADD minced fresh or dried herbs to the mixture along with the shallot: a few tablespoons of parsley or small amounts of sage, tarragon, or thyme are all good. You can also add capers, anchovies, chopped bell pepper, or minced garlic.

ADD bits of chopped meat to the sauce along with the shallot, or simply stir them into the finished sauce.

Sun-Dried Tomato Sauce

WORK TIME	10 minutes
PREP TIME	2 hours or so
CAN BE	prepared in advance; easily multiplied
MAKES	1 cup, about 4 servings

PESTO AND TAPENADE ARE well-known, all-purpose condiments that can be made in a few minutes and can transform any simply cooked meat, fish, or poultry—in fact, nearly any bland preparation from pasta to mashed potatoes. Yet another simple pounded sauce can be made from sun-dried tomatoes, those ultra-trendy eighties ingredients that faded from the scene largely because few Americans ever learned just what to do with them.

Fred Plotkin, who divides his time between New York and Italy and his career between opera and food, includes a sketchy but informative recipe for sun-dried tomato sauce in his inspiring *Recipes from Paradise*, a cookbook about Liguria, also known as the Italian Riviera. Mr. Plotkin is intentionally vague about the sauce's ingredients and their quantities, because he believes that everything beyond the distinct flavor of the dried tomato and the olive oil in which it soaks is nearly superfluous. With his guidance, and some experimentation, I've given the recipe a little more structure, but there remains plenty of latitude here in terms of quantities and additional ingredients.

You can buy sun-dried tomatoes already reconstituted and soaked in olive oil, and certainly that's the easiest way to begin preparing the sauce. On the other hand you may find, as I do, that the cost of those tomatoes is prohibitive. It's certainly easy enough—and only slightly less convenient if you think ahead—to begin with dried tomatoes, which are far less expensive. They're as tough as shoe leather when you buy them, but can be easily reconstituted.

Since they just about double in bulk once reconstituted, start with about one ounce (one-half cup) dried tomatoes to produce the amount you'll ultimately need for the recipe. Soak them in hot water to cover until they're soft, about an hour. (You might change the water once it cools to hasten the softening.) Drain the tomatoes and marinate them in a good, light, fruity olive oil to cover (one-half cup or more) for at least an hour.

After that, making the tomato paste takes just a moment. Traditionally, the tomatoes are pounded, usually with garlic, in a mortar and pestle. I use a small food processor and like the resulting texture very much. Mr. Plotkin adds a little lemon juice to the mixture as well as some pignoli nuts, and I think a touch of basil really brings the sauce to life.

1 cup sun-dried tomatoes, with their oil	**1 tablespoon fresh lemon juice, optional**
1 small or ½ large garlic clove, or to taste	**3 tablespoons pignoli nuts**
Salt	**Additional extra virgin olive oil if necessary**
4 chopped basil leaves, optional	

1 Place the tomatoes and a tablespoon or so of their oil in a small food processor along with the garlic and a good pinch of salt. Process until fairly smooth, stopping the machine and stirring down the mixture with a rubber spatula as necessary.

2 Add the basil and lemon juice if you like; pulse the machine a few times to blend. Remove the paste from the machine and stir in, by hand, the nuts and just enough additional oil to make the mixture silky rather than oily. Taste and adjust seasoning. The sauce will keep, covered with a thin layer of oil and refrigerated in a tightly covered container, for at least a week. But its flavor is best when served immediately.

With MINIMAL Effort

Some of the many uses for this sauce:

AS a pasta sauce, but sparingly, and thinned with a little of the hot pasta-cooking water

AS a spread on bread or sandwiches

AS a dip for raw vegetables or crackers

AS a condiment for chicken or fish

AS a sauce for cooked bland vegetables, such as boiled potatoes.

Mayonnaise
Why You Should Make It

WORK TIME	10 minutes
PREP TIME	10 minutes
CAN BE	prepared in advance; easily multiplied
MAKES	1 cup

WHETHER YOU DO IT BY HAND OR IN a blender or food processor, it takes just five minutes to make mayonnaise, and when you're done you have a flavorful, creamy dressing that is so far superior to the bottled stuff you may not recognize it as the same thing. Next to vinaigrette, it's the most useful of all dressings, and despite its luxurious nature it contains little saturated fat.

Mayonnaise, an emulsion of egg, oil, and acid (usually vinegar or fresh lemon juice), is best made with yolks for best color and flavor; you can use a whole egg if you prefer. Olive oil makes a great mayonnaise, but so do neutral oils like canola and grapeseed. (Make sure the oil is fresh, because this is an oil-dominated, uncooked sauce, and you'll notice any off flavors.) I generally use lemon juice because I love its flavor, but vinegar is just as good, and the quantity is so small it hardly makes a difference.

If you're worried about the health aspects of using a raw egg, start with bottled mayonnaise and beat in a little oil and/or any of the suggested additions.

1 egg or egg yolk

2 teaspoons Dijon mustard

Salt and freshly ground black
  pepper

1 cup olive or other oil

1 tablespoon freshly squeezed
  lemon juice or vinegar

1 To make the mayonnaise by hand: Combine the egg, mustard, and salt and pepper to taste in a medium bowl. Use a wire whisk to combine, then add the oil in a thin, steady stream, beating all the while. When the mixture becomes thick and creamy, you can add the oil a little faster. When it is all integrated, whisk in the lemon juice. Taste and adjust seasoning.

To make the mayonnaise in a blender or food processor: Combine the egg, mustard, and salt and pepper in the machine's container and pulse on and off a few times. With the machine running, add the oil, slowly, through the top or feed tube. When the mixture becomes thick and creamy, you can add the oil a little faster. When it is all integrated, pulse in the lemon juice. Taste and adjust seasoning.

2 If the mayonnaise is thicker than you like (a distinct possibility if you're using a machine), thin with warm water, sweet cream, or sour cream.

With MINIMAL Effort

Like vinaigrette, the flavor of mayonnaise can be almost infinitely varied. Many of the suggested ingredients can be combined; use your judgment.

ADD a clove of peeled garlic at the beginning. Try adding ½ cup roasted red peppers, (or canned pimiento) and a little cayenne pepper at the same time.

VARY the kind of acid you use: lime or orange juice, or any type of vinegar. If the acidity is too strong when you're done, beat in a little warm water.

ADD 2 or 3 anchovy fillets at the beginning.

ADD any fresh herbs you like. Start with a small amount and taste, adding more at the end if you like. If you're using a machine, they will turn the mayonnaise green. If you're working by hand, you will have herb-flecked mayonnaise.

ADD horseradish, Worcestershire sauce, or spices or spice mixes to the finished mayonnaise, tasting as you go.

Cumin-Tomato Relish and Pan-Grilled Tomato Salsa
What to Do with All Those Summer Tomatoes

IN JULY AND AUGUST, eventually, there are enough tomatoes. You've eaten them raw and cooked, and you're looking for something interesting to do with them. Here are two ideas—Cumin-Tomato Relish and Pan-Grilled Tomato Salsa—and both recipes are multipurpose.

The first is uncooked—chopped tomatoes combined with seasonings. I add onion, red bell pepper, and some cumin seeds for crunch, and serve it with grilled meats; it's also good on hamburgers and sandwiches. Pan-grilled tomato salsa is a charred tomato dish that's the type of thing you have in restaurants, but it is easy enough to make at home. The blackened tomatoes are combined with just enough oil and vinegar to make the whole thing juicy; it's great on top of grilled fish or chicken, or as a side dish.

Neither of these recipes requires peeling the tomatoes, but they should be cored: Use a paring knife to cut a cone-shaped wedge out of the stem end and remove it; see the photographs, page 37.

Cumin-Tomato Relish

WORK TIME	10 minutes
PREP TIME	10 minutes
CAN BE	prepared in advance; easily multiplied
MAKES	4 to 6 servings

2 teaspoons cumin seeds or ground cumin

1½ pounds plum or other tomatoes, cored and roughly chopped

½ red bell pepper, seeded, stemmed, and minced, optional

1 tablespoon minced onion

Salt and cayenne pepper

Juice of 1 lime

2 tablespoons chopped cilantro

1 If you're using cumin seeds, place them in a small skillet and toast over medium heat, shaking the pan occasionally, until they are fragrant, just a minute or two. Finely grind all but ½ teaspoon.

2 Combine the tomatoes, optional bell pepper, onion, salt, cayenne, ground cumin, and lime juice; taste and adjust seasoning if necessary. Just before serving, toss with the cilantro and reserved whole cumin seeds. (This can be refrigerated for up to a day or two; bring to room temperature before serving.)

Pan-Grilled Tomato Salsa

WORK TIME	20 minutes
PREP TIME	20 minutes
CAN BE	prepared in advance; easily multiplied
MAKES	4 servings

3 large, meaty tomatoes, cored and cut into thick slices

¼ cup extra virgin olive oil

2 tablespoons sherry or balsamic vinegar

Salt and freshly ground black pepper

1 Heat a large skillet, preferably cast-iron or nonstick, over medium-high heat for about 5 minutes. Add the tomatoes, raise the heat to high, and cook until lightly charred on one side, 3 to 5 minutes. Turn and cook the other side very lightly, about 1 minute. If necessary, work in batches to avoid crowding the tomatoes.

2 Combine the olive oil and vinegar in a large, shallow dish and, as the tomatoes are done, turn them in the mixture. Season and serve as a side dish, or as a sauce for grilled or roasted fish or chicken. (This can be refrigerated for up to a day or two; bring to room temperature before serving.)

Rosemary-Lemon White Bean Dip

WORK TIME	10 minutes (with precooked or canned beans)
PREP TIME	10 minutes (with precooked or canned beans)
CAN BE	prepared in advance; easily multiplied
MAKES	about 8 servings

LIDIA BASTIANICH, WHOSE FAMILY OWNS several great restaurants in New York City and elsewhere, including the well-known Felidia, makes a wonderful bean dip, with more life than most but without the harshness of raw garlic usually associated with Middle Eastern hummus or Southwestern purees. It turns out that the dip, which begins with white beans, is pretty simple, with the not-exactly-exotic "mystery" ingredient of grated lemon zest, which is quite substantial in both quantity and size of the pieces. The zest transforms the puree from something common into the bright substance I had admired at Lidia's restaurants.

Like most bean dishes, this puree is best if you use freshly cooked dried beans, but it is quite forgiving and can be made in about ten minutes with canned beans. One-half pound of dried beans will yield about two cups, the amount needed for this recipe, although you can double the quantities if you like. Cook the beans in unsalted water to cover (presoaking is unnecessary), with a couple of bay leaves, until very tender. Cooked beans can be frozen quite successfully in their cooking water. If you use canned beans, you'll need almost two full fifteen-ounce cans to get two cups (there's a lot of water in those cans).

The most obvious use for the puree is as a dip for breadsticks, pita or other bread, or raw vegetables, but there are many other uses; see "With Minimal Effort," for suggestions.

2 cups cooked cannellini or other white beans, drained but quite moist	¼ cup plus 1 tablespoon extra virgin olive oil
1 to 3 garlic cloves, peeled	2 teaspoons minced fresh rosemary
Salt and freshly ground black pepper	Grated zest of 2 lemons

1 Put the beans in the container of a food processor with 1 garlic clove and a healthy pinch of salt. Turn the machine on and add the ¼ cup olive oil in a steady stream through the feed tube; process until the mixture is smooth. Taste and add more garlic if you like, then puree again.

2 Place the mixture in a bowl and use a wooden spoon to beat in the rosemary, lemon zest, and remaining 1 tablespoon olive oil. Taste and add salt and pepper as needed. Use immediately or refrigerate up to 3 days.

With MINIMAL Effort

THE PUREE can form the basis of a wonderful sandwich. For example, combine a thick layer of puree with grilled vegetables and a little olive oil on rolls or between thick slices of crusty bread.

IT CAN be used to thicken and flavor cooked beans. Just stir a few spoonfuls of the puree into simmering white beans (if you have pesto, add some at the same time). Thinned with bean- or pasta-cooking water, this makes a good pasta sauce.

A SMALL mound of the puree served next to some braised escarole or other bitter greens, both drizzled with olive oil, makes a fine side dish.

SIMILARLY, serve it at the center of a plate of lightly and simply cooked vegetables—carrots, green beans, turnips, asparagus, potatoes, cauliflower, and so on.

LAYER it with grilled eggplant or zucchini and bake or broil to form a simple vegetable dish, which you can elaborate even more by incorporating thinly sliced toasted bread and grated Parmesan in the layers.

Fig Relish

WORK TIME	10 minutes
PREP TIME	10 minutes
CAN BE	prepared in advance; easily multiplied
MAKES	about 4 servings

I HAVE A LOUSY MEMORY, BUT I can vividly remember my first taste of a fresh fig. This is because I grew up at a time when this plump, succulent fruit was sold almost exclusively in its dried form. It took me twenty-plus years of life to encounter a fresh fig, and that was in Rome. In both appearance and taste, it was unexpected and spectacular.

Like chestnuts, fresh figs are so common in Mediterranean countries that they are taken for granted—there are places where you can hardly give them away—and yet I still encounter friends and family members who have never tried one. Now fresh figs are sold not only at pricey gourmet markets (where they cost as much as three dollars each!), but at Italian grocery stores everywhere (where the price is often a more acceptable two dollars per basket), and even at many supermarkets.

While the best way to eat figs is out of hand—few fruits are as luxurious tasting—there are rewarding ways to use them in recipes. Add them to sautéed and braised dishes, especially those made with dark, winey sauces, during the last few minutes of cooking, and the figs become even juicier and more tender than when they are raw.

In playing around with figs in cooking, it was impossible to ignore their tendency to add rather than absorb liquid. This reminded me of two other foods long associated with the Mediterranean, the olive and the eggplant. So I tried mashing the figs with a variety of herbs and spices and employing the results as a sauce or dip. Of course, I was inspired by eggplant caponata and olive tapenade, both of which are moist, highly seasoned, all-purpose relishes.

There are differences, of course: Unlike caponata and tapenade, fig relish does not make an especially good spread, or even a dip. And although the seasonings are similar, figs are sweet, a word that would hardly describe either olives or eggplant. This is not a problem, however; though balancing sweetness and acidity is one of the most important tasks in cooking, it is not a difficult one, just a matter of taste and judgment.

8 ounces fresh figs	Salt and freshly ground black pepper
1 tablespoon minced capers	
Zest of 1 lemon, minced	2 tablespoons chopped parsley
Juice of 1 lemon	2 tablespoons chopped basil, optional
2 tablespoons olive oil	

1 Gently rinse and stem the figs; chop them into about ¼-inch pieces, making sure to catch all of their juices. Toss in a bowl with the capers, lemon zest and juice, olive oil, salt, and pepper to taste. Just before serving (you can wait up to two hours), add the herbs, then taste and adjust the seasonings.

With MINIMAL Effort

The fig relish really shines as an impromptu sauce. It is especially brilliant on grilled swordfish or tuna, but nearly as good with grilled or broiled chicken (especially dark meat), pork, lamb, or beef. (Note that all of these foods contain some fat; because the relish is so lean, combining it with nonfatty meats or fish—such as boneless chicken or flounder—produces a dish that seems to lack substance.)

This recipe is hardly the last word on combining figs and seasonings. Possible additions and substitutions abound, and most of these can be used in combination. For example:

ADD a tiny amount (¼ teaspoon or so) of minced garlic. Alternatively, crush a garlic clove and let it sit in the mixture for a few minutes, then fish it out just before serving.

ADD a teaspoon or more of minced shallot.

ADD a couple of tablespoons of chopped olives or anchovies.

SUBSTITUTE lime zest and juice or mild vinegar for the lemon.

CHANGE the herbs; a teaspoon of minced thyme or rosemary in place of the basil makes the relish considerably more pungent.

Dried Mushroom Puree
The One-Ingredient Condiment

WORK TIME	10 minutes
PREP TIME	20 minutes
CAN BE	prepared in advance; easily multiplied
MAKES	4 servings

IT ISN'T OFTEN THAT YOU COME across a condiment that can be made with a single dried ingredient, but since dried mushrooms have become widely available, that is exactly what has happened. If you simmer dried mushrooms until tender, then toss them in a blender with their cooking liquid, you get a thick puree, potent and delicious.

The result is very much like the classic duxelles, in which fresh mushrooms and their scraps are cooked only until their essence remains. But this procedure requires almost no preparation: no cleaning, no chopping, and hardly any cooking, because the mushrooms have already been dried and there is no need to cook out their water.

You can use any dried mushrooms for this condiment, such as the extremely inexpensive shiitakes (also called black mushrooms) sold in Asian markets. Better, of course, is the prince of dried mushrooms, the porcini. Interestingly, however, the most expensive porcini—those from Italy—are not the best for this puree. That distinction belongs to dried porcini from Chile, which are dark, smoky, pulpy, and relatively inexpensive. Availability of these in retail stores is spotty, but you can buy them by mail from mushroom specialists.

Once made, the puree has many uses: Stir it into risotto or other grain preparations (be sure to use any of the leftover mushroom-cooking liquid in cooking the grain); include it in omelets or on pizzas; thin it with butter or olive oil to make a sauce for meat or fish; or simply use it as you would ketchup.

| 1 ounce dried porcini mushrooms | Salt and freshly ground black |
| (about ½ cup, loosely packed) | pepper |

1 Combine the mushrooms with 2½ cups water in a 4- or 6-cup saucepan and turn the heat to medium-high. Bring to a boil, then adjust the heat so the mixture simmers gently. Cook until the mushrooms are tender, about 15 minutes.

2 Remove the mushrooms with a slotted spoon and place in the container of a blender. Strain the liquid through a paper towel place in a sieve, or through a couple of layers of cheesecloth; there will be about 1 cup. Add most of the liquid to the mushrooms and puree, adding the remaining liquid if necessary to allow the machine to do its work.

3 Season to taste with salt and pepper and serve, or cover and refrigerate for up to a couple of days.

With MINIMAL Effort

The sauce can be made more complex by the addition of seasonings beyond salt and pepper, and the process is easy. When pureeing the mushrooms, add:

A PEELED shallot or small garlic clove

ONE teaspoon of thyme leaves (or ½ teaspoon dried thyme)

A TABLESPOON of Port, tomato paste, or soy sauce

Be sure to taste the puree before you remove it from the blender; the mushroom flavor is so strong that it may take a relatively large quantity of complementary seasoning to make its presence felt.

Red Pepper Puree
Better Than Ketchup

WORK TIME	20 minutes
PREP TIME	About 1 hour
CAN BE	prepared in advance; easily multiplied; frozen
MAKES	2 cups, at least 4 servings

WHY ISN'T ROASTED RED PEPPER puree a staple? It's more useful than ketchup, simpler in composition, and far more delicious—you can eat it with a spoon. It contains two basic ingredients, red bell peppers and olive oil, and both are always readily available. And since making a batch is about as difficult as scrambling an egg, and the puree stores fairly well, there's little reason not to have some on hand.

The only difficulty comes in roasting the peppers, which tenderizes them while concentrating and rendering their flavorful liquid, a task many recipes make needlessly complex. Some suggest broiling or grilling, but the first requires near-constant attention and the second is only worth it if the grill is already going. Others would have you char peppers over an open burner, which risks not only the stovetop but the hand. That's bad enough for one pepper; for two, the critical mass for making puree, or four (a nice amount to deal with), the process is absurd.

The best method, for puree or any other purpose, is to roast the peppers at high heat, turning occasionally. When the peppers collapse, they're done. You can skip this step entirely by beginning with canned or bottled pimientos, which are roasted peppers packed with natural or chemical preservatives. Their flavor, however, is relatively flat.

Once the peppers are roasted and peeled, pureeing them takes just a minute in a food processor. To aid the machine in its work and further enhance the flavor, use a little of the peppers' liquid along with salt and olive oil. You can even eliminate the oil if you like, but the flavor will suffer; the synthesis of pepper and oil is wondrous.

Of course, you can further flavor the puree with any number of herbs (thyme, basil, and parsley are fine) or spices—cumin, my mouth tells me, is a natural. Or add a little chile pepper, whose related flavor is perfect; try roasting one of the long, semihot finger peppers with the bell peppers. Some slow-cooked caramelized onions, or roasted or raw garlic, are also good additions.

| 4 large red bell peppers, about | Salt |
| 2 pounds | ½ cup extra virgin olive oil |

1 Preheat the oven to 500 degrees. Line a roasting pan with enough aluminum foil to fold over the top later. Place the bell peppers in the pan and the pan in the oven. Roast, turning the peppers about every 10 minutes, until they collapse, about 40 minutes.

2 Fold the foil over the peppers and allow them to cool. Working over a bowl, remove the core, skin, and seeds from each of the peppers, reserving some of the liquid.

3 Place the pepper pulp in the container of a food processor with about 2 tablespoons of the reserved liquid. Add a large pinch of salt and turn on the machine; drizzle the oil in through the feed tube. Stop the machine, then taste and add more salt and/or olive oil if necessary. Store, well covered, in the refrigerator (for several days) or the freezer (up to a month).

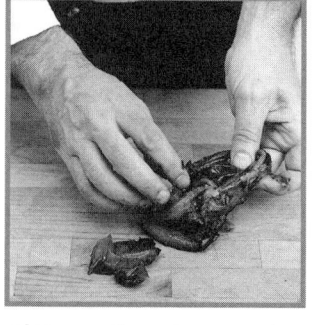 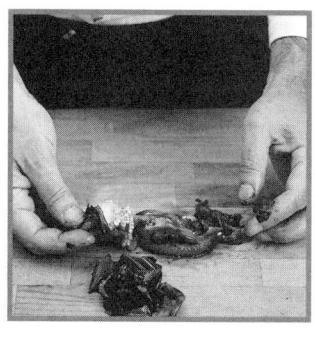 

1 | Use your fingers to remove the skin from the peppers.

2 | Gently pull out the core, bringing as many seeds as possible along with it.

3 | Remove all remaining seeds.

With MINIMAL Effort

ADD a couple of tablespoons of puree to the cooking liquid of any simmering grain—rice, couscous, or quinoa, for example. The color is glorious.

USE in place of or with tomatoes in pasta sauce. For example, sauté several vegetables and bind them with the puree during the last minute of cooking.

FOLD into omelets or scrambled eggs, with or without cooked vegetables.

COMBINE with chopped basil, grated Parmesan, and minced garlic for a pestolike pasta sauce.

EMULSIFY with fresh lemon juice, salt, and pepper to make a beautiful salad dressing.

SPREAD on crostini, bruschetta, or pizza before baking.

USE as a finishing sauce for roasted eggplant, zucchini, or other vegetables.

SERVE as a condiment with grilled or roasted fish, meat, or chicken.

STIR into soups or stews just before serving.

MASH a couple of tablespoons of puree, with a little olive oil, minced garlic, and cracked black pepper, into fresh, salty cheese—such as feta or goat—to make a dip for bread or vegetables.

Desserts

Strawberries with Balsamic Vinegar
A Sweet-and-Sour Dessert

WORK TIME	5 minutes
PREP TIME	15 minutes
CAN BE	easily multiplied
MAKES	4 to 6 servings

PRECIOUS AS THEY ARE, STRAWBERRIES are one fruit that is rarely eaten out of hand—they're delicate, their colors bleed, and in most instances they simply aren't sweet enough. These drawbacks, however minor, have combined to make strawberries the basis for some of the best fruit desserts, from strawberry shortcake to summer pudding. These, however, are the kind of rich and luxurious desserts you might regret eating after a heavy meal. This strawberry dessert is not only delicious and intriguing, but can compete with plain fruit in lightness. Strawberries are sugared to juice them up a bit, then drizzled with balsamic vinegar, and sprinkled with a pinch of black pepper. The result is so elegant that you'll find it in great restaurants from here to Emilia-Romagna, the home of balsamic vinegar.

All balsamic vinegar is slightly sweet. The authentic version, which is aged at least ten years, draws its velvety sweetness from the concentration of the unfermented wine that is its base. The subtle flavor of wood—the barrels are made from cherry, oak, apple, or other trees—lends an elusive vanilla quality that is also perceived as sweet. (Inexpensive balsamic vinegar, the kind that sells for two or three dollars a bottle, gains much of its flavor from sugar.)

Ideally, you'll make this dessert with ripe, local berries and authentic balsamic vinegar, which is expensive but used in tiny quantities—as it is here. Of course, it isn't always possible to get both, and we make the compromises we must. Even so, there is a combination of flavors here that is unlike any other, and is instantly likable, even to kids, as long as you take it easy on both vinegar and pepper and don't disclose the presence of either.

Strawberries with balsamic vinegar will not hold for any length of time. You can sugar the berries an hour or two before you want to serve them, but no longer.

1 quart strawberries, rinsed, hulled and sliced, or a mixture of strawberries, blueberries, and blackberries

1/4 cup sugar, or more to taste

1 teaspoon high-quality balsamic vinegar, or more to taste

About 1/8 teaspoon freshly ground black pepper

1 Toss the strawberries and optional blueberries or blackberries with 1/4 cup sugar and let sit for 10 minutes or longer. (Do not refrigerate.)

2 Sprinkle with the vinegar; toss gently, then taste and add more sugar or vinegar if necessary. Sprinkle with the pepper, toss again, and serve.

With MINIMAL Effort

GARNISH with chopped fresh mint leaves

SERVE with a few crisp cookies, or a slice of pound, sponge, or angel food cake.

SERVE with a glass of slightly sweet, lightly sparkling wine, such as Muscat.

Grilled Fruit Skewers with Ginger Syrup

WORK TIME	30 minutes
PREP TIME	30 minutes
CAN BE	easily multiplied
MAKES	4 servings

MY FRIEND JOHNNY EARLES IS A SELF-TRAINED chef who opened a restaurant eighteen years ago because he thought it would be "a hoot." His restaurant, Criolla's, is in Grayton Beach, Florida, and sits in the middle of the state's northwestern panhandle—an area locals self-mockingly call "The Redneck Riviera." When Criolla's first opened, it was funky indeed. The grill was outside, the primary means of cooking was an electric wok, and Johnny's tastes ran true to his roots—kind of Cajun-Caribbean.

Never mind. Johnny trusts his instincts for flavor combinations, and he's an expert in simplicity. One dish he created is a mélange of quickly grilled fruit brushed with a ginger sauce that itself takes about five minutes to put together. The sauce is a simple sugar syrup—equal parts sugar and water, boiled together until the sugar melts—and then infused with a lot of ginger. You could use other flavors instead—mint, lemon verbena, thyme, even chile—but ginger seems perfect to me.

The fruit can be varied, but Johnny and I have tried just about everything, and we agree that pineapple and bananas are the top choices. Carambola, also called starfruit, is another good selection, although not always easy to find. Many other fruits can be grilled, but pineapple browns beautifully and banana develops a luxurious creaminess. Johnny recommends using a gas grill—or a clean wood charcoal fire—for grilling fruit. "Real wood just overwhelms the fruit with flavor," he says, "and briquettes impart a weird taste." Whatever your fuel, make sure the fire is hot and keep the grilling time short.

½ cup sugar	4 bananas, not overly ripe
½ cup water	1 small pineapple
¼ cup thinly sliced fresh ginger (don't bother to peel it)	1 carambola, optional

1 Start a gas or charcoal fire; the fire should be quite hot, and the rack positioned 4 to 6 inches from the heat source. Combine the first three ingredients in a saucepan over medium heat. Bring to a boil and simmer for 3 minutes. Remove from the heat and let sit while you prepare the fruit. (Refrigerate the syrup if not using it right away; it'll keep for a week.)

2 Do not peel the bananas; cut them into 2-inch-long chunks and make a shallow vertical slit in the skin to facilitate peeling at the table. Peel and core the pineapple, then cut it into 2-inch chunks. Cut the carambola, if you're using it, into ½-inch-thick slices.

3 Skewer the fruit. Strain the syrup and brush the fruit lightly with it. Grill the fruit until the pineapple is nicely browned, 2 to 4 minutes per side. As it is grilling, brush occasionally with the syrup.

4 When the fruit is done, brush once more with syrup; serve hot or warm.

1 | Cut off the top and bottom of the pineapple, then cut it into quarters.

2 | Strip the woody core from all four quarters.

3 | Use a grapefruit or paring knife to separate the fruit from the peel.

4 | A quarter pineapple; cut into chunks for grilling.

Dried Fruit Poached in Port

WORK TIME	10 minutes
PREP TIME	45 minutes
CAN BE	prepared in advance; easily multiplied
MAKES	4 servings

I'M NOT SURE WHEN THE TRADITION OF poaching dried fruit dropped out of the average home cook's repertoire, but my guess is it was about the same time that fresh summer fruits started arriving from the Southern Hemisphere in midwinter. But nothing can match dried fruit for convenience and intensity of flavor. And when you poach an assortment with Port and a few spices, the results belie the ease of preparation. This is not a summer dessert—no one would mistake this for fresh fruit—but it is delicious, low-fat, and a welcome change from heavy winter desserts.

For breakfast I like fruit poached in water, with no spice at all, but adding Port and spices makes the dish special. This is especially true if you use some unexpected spices like black pepper, anise, and candied ginger, which becomes tender and delicious during poaching, more like a fruit than a spice. Consider the spices included in the recipe a guideline or series of suggestions rather than an absolute list (you might even try adding a dried chile if your tastes run in that direction), but be careful with especially strong spices like cloves, which can quickly overwhelm a dish.

Since the preparation of this dish is absolutely foolproof, the challenge lies entirely in the shopping. One of the great things about dried fruit is that organic specimens are readily available. Another is the incredible variety of fruits now being dried. In the course of fine-tuning this recipe, I tried not only the obvious prunes, figs, apricots, peaches, and pears, but cherries, blueberries, strawberries, pineapple, and even banana. I tend toward the traditional, but really enjoyed the tartness that dried pineapple added to the mixture.

I did not poach the fruit in mature vintage Port, because I'm not an eccentric millionaire. But I did try lighter, younger tawny Port—versus older, stronger (and more expensive) ruby and late-bottled-vintage Ports—and although I did like the intensity of flavor of the more powerful Ports, I don't think the difference is notable. Buy a Port you'll enjoy drinking, though, because you're going to use less than a third of the bottle in this recipe.

12 prunes	5 allspice berries
8 figs	5 peppercorns
4 apricot or peach halves	1 star anise
4 pear halves	1-inch cinnamon stick
3 pieces candied ginger	1 cup Port
1 clove	

1 Combine all ingredients in a medium saucepan and bring to a boil. Turn heat to very low and cover. Cook about 30 minutes, at which point most of the port will have been absorbed.

2 If the fruit is tender, it's done. If not, add ½ cup water, bring to a boil again, cover, and cook another 15 minutes. Repeat once more if necessary.

3 Remove the fruit with a slotted spoon, then strain the liquid to remove the spices. Serve a portion of the fruit warm, cold, or at room temperature with a spoonful or two of its juice.

With MINIMAL Effort

SUBSTITUTE almost any sweet or neutral liquid for the Port: water, Oloroso sherry, red wine (add a tablespoon of sugar), sweet white wine, orange juice, and so on.

IF YOU prefer less-than-sweet results, add a squeeze of fresh lemon juice at the end of cooking.

VARY the spices. Try a tiny grating of nutmeg in place of the allspice, peppercorns, and anise, for example. Some coriander seeds are also nice.

SERVE with a bit of sweet or sour cream, yogurt, or crème fraîche.

15-Minute Fruit Gratin
An Elegant Summer Dessert

WORK TIME	15 minutes
PREP TIME	15 minutes
CAN BE	easily multiplied
MAKES	4 servings

TAKE SOFT, RIPE FRUIT; top it with crème Anglaise (essentially a thin custard), sabayon (a frothy egg-and-wine mixture), or another sweet sauce. Run the whole thing under the broiler, and you have a four-star dessert. The only problem is that luxurious sauces like these take a fair amount of time and attention to prepare.

Suppose you topped the fruit with something fast and easy? Like sweetened heavy cream, whipped just enough so that it holds some body when broiled? Even simpler is sweetened sour cream, which barely needs to be whisked.

The toppings produce strikingly different results. Sour cream is thick, rich, flavorful, and (obviously) sour; sweet cream becomes thinner and saucier in texture. It also browns beautifully, and—especially if you begin with really good cream, that which hasn't been ultra-pasteurized—has a fresh subtlety that cannot be matched. I like both alternatives, and between the two of them I may never prepare another sabayon, at least for this purpose.

To make this dessert, I've used figs, pitted prune plums, strawberries, raspberries, blueberries, peaches, and these same fruits in various combinations. They were all great, but if I had to pick a favorite I suppose it would be peaches spiked with a few raspberries and blueberries. In any case, be sure that the fruit you use is perfectly ripe. You're going to serve this dish with spoons, and the last thing you want is to have to reach for a knife and fork.

Although this preparation is lightning-quick, it has to be constantly watched while cooking. Get the broiler hot, place the dish right under the heating element, and keep your eyes open. You want the topping to burn a little bit—it will smell like toasting marshmallows—but obviously not too much. When the topping is nearly uniformly brown, with a few black spots, it's done. The fruit will not have cooked at all.

> 1 to 1½ pounds perfectly ripe soft fruit, such as peaches, plums, berries, figs, or a combination
>
> 1 cup heavy cream
>
> 3 tablespoons sugar
>
> 1 teaspoon vanilla extract

1 Preheat the broiler; set the rack as close to the heat source as possible (even 2 inches is not too close).

2 Wash, pit, stem, and peel the fruit as necessary. Cut stone fruit in halves or slices as you prefer. Cut strawberries in thick slices; leave smaller berries whole. Place the fruit—there should be at least 2 cups—in a baking or gratin dish just large enough to hold it.

3 Whip the cream with 2 tablespoons of the sugar until it is thick and just barely holding soft peaks. Pour it over and around the fruit. Sprinkle with the remaining 1 tablespoon sugar.

4 Broil carefully, allowing the cream to brown all over and even burn in a couple of spots; rotate the baking dish during broiling if necessary. Remove and serve.

With MINIMAL Effort

Gratin with Sour Cream: Combine 1 cup sour cream with just enough milk—about ¼ cup—that you can whisk it smooth. Add 2 tablespoons sugar and proceed as above, using 1 tablespoon brown sugar for the topping.

One Batter, Many Cookies

WORK TIME	30 minutes
PREP TIME	30 minutes (assuming you can bake 24 cookies at once)
CAN BE	prepared in advance; frozen
MAKES	about 4 dozen cookies

COOKIES ARE ALWAYS EASY, BUT EVEN they can use streamlining. One solution is to whip up a single batter—in the food processor—and finish it in different ways. (You might call this "the mother of all butter cookies.") With this one dough you can flavor some, roll some, bake them at different temperatures, and fill a cookie plate with variety in no time.

In fact, with one batch of batter you can make four different types of cookies—add lemon juice and zest to one-fourth of it, for example, chopped walnuts to the second, raisins to the third, and coconut to the fourth. The basic batter can also be varied with ginger or a mix of spices, chocolate chips, or orange. It's also great plain, made with white sugar or brown, or even molasses. Finally, this batter can make rolled-out, cut, and decorated cookies; just chill it first to make it easier to handle.

The standard—and perfectly wonderful—butter cookie recipe contains equal weights of flour and butter, sugar to taste (usually about half as much as the flour), an egg for every two cups of flour, enough milk to produce a batter, and any flavorings. The proportions of the basic ingredients—the flour, butter, sugar, egg, and milk—determine the underlying taste and texture of the cookies. Make them with more flour and they're cakey; use more butter and they're delicate, with better flavor; here, I go for the second option.

I've refined the classic recipe to do all the mixing in the food processor, which is fast and easy. (You can, of course, make this batter in a standing mixer, or by hand. In either case, cream together the butter and sugar first, then add the mixed dry ingredients.) Because the processor is such a powerful machine, it's easy to overdevelop the gluten in the flour, which leads to tough cookies. (This is also a problem with electric mixers, but rarely with cookies that are made entirely by hand.)

My solution is to replace a quarter of the flour with cornstarch, which develops no gluten and, as a bonus, adds a silken quality to the cookies (and baked goods in general). Even so, it's still important to process the ingredients gently, letting the machine run no longer than necessary at each stage.

The baking procedure is determined by the results you prefer. At

375° F, the edges brown nicely and the center of each cookie remains pale and tender after about eleven minutes of baking; at 350° F, there will be no browning and the cookies will take a minute or two longer. In either case, slightly longer baking times will produce crisp cookies. These times assume, of course, that your oven is reasonably accurate; since most ovens are not, check the cookies every minute or so after eight minutes have passed. Note the timing of the first batch and subsequent batches will require less attention.

1½ cups all-purpose flour	2 sticks chilled butter, cut into bits
½ cup cornstarch	1 teaspoon vanilla extract
¾ cup sugar	1 egg
Pinch salt	½ cup milk, more or less

1 Preheat the oven to 375° F.

2 Combine the flour, cornstarch, sugar, and salt in a food processor and pulse once or twice. Add the butter and pulse 10 or 20 times until the butter and flour are well combined. Add the vanilla and the egg and pulse 3 or 4 times. Add about half the milk and pulse 2 or 3 times. Add the remaining milk a little at a time, pulsing once or twice after each addition, until the dough holds together in a sticky mass.

3 Remove the dough from the machine to one or more bowls. Make cookies as described in Step 4, or make any of the cookies listed in "With Minimal Effort."

4 Drop rounded teaspoons of dough (you can make the cookies larger or smaller if you like) onto a nonstick baking sheet, a sheet lined with parchment paper, or a lightly buttered baking sheet. If you want flat cookies, press the balls down a bit with your fingers or the back of a spatula or wooden spoon. Bake 11 minutes, or until the cookies are done as you like them. Cool on a rack, then store, if necessary, in a covered container.

With MINIMAL Effort

Butterscotch Cookies: Substitute half or more brown sugar for the white sugar, or simply add 1 tablespoon molasses along with the egg.

Citrus Cookies: Do not use the vanilla; add 1 tablespoon lemon juice and 2 teaspoons grated lemon zest along with the egg. The same can be done with orange juice and zest. A couple of tablespoons of poppy seeds go well here also.

Chocolate Chip Cookies: Stir about 1 cup of chocolate chips into the finished batter. (The butterscotch batter variation, is good here.)

Chunky Cookies: To the finished batter, add about a cup of M&Ms (or other similar candy), or roughly chopped walnuts, pecans, or cashews; slivered almonds; raisins; coconut; dried cherries; and so on. Or combine any chunky ingredients you like.

Ginger Cookies: Add 1 tablespoon ground ginger to the dry ingredients. For even better flavor, add $1/4$ cup minced crystallized ginger to the batter by hand (this works well in addition to or in place of the ground ginger).

Spice Cookies: Add 1 teaspoon ground cinnamon, $1/4$ teaspoon each ground allspice and ground ginger, and 1 pinch ground cloves and mace or nutmeg to the dry ingredients.

Rolled Cookies: Freeze the dough batter for 15 minutes or refrigerate it for about 1 hour (or longer). Work half the batter at a time, and roll it on a lightly floured surface; it will absorb some flour at first but will soon become less sticky. Do not add more flour than necessary. Roll about $1/4$ inch thick and cut with any cookie cutters; decorate as you like. Bake as above, reducing the cooking time to 8 to 10 minutes.

Puffy Cookies: The basic cookies are flat. For airier cookies, add $1/2$ teaspoon baking powder to the dry ingredients.

Index

Man and the Horse

Man and the Horse

An Illustrated History of Equestrian Apparel

Alexander Mackay-Smith

Jean R. Druesedow

Thomas Ryder

The Metropolitan Museum of Art
Simon and Schuster
New York

This book was published in connection with an exhibition at The Costume Institute of The Metropolitan Museum of Art, New York, from December 3, 1984, through September 1, 1985.

The exhibition is presented by Polo/Ralph Lauren.

Published by The Metropolitan Museum of Art, New York,
and
Simon and Schuster
A Division of Simon & Schuster, Inc.
Simon & Schuster Building
Rockefeller Center
1230 Avenue of the Americas
New York, New York 10020

Bradford D. Kelleher, Publisher
John P. O'Neill, Editor in Chief
Barbara Burn, Project Supervisor
Michael Shroyer, Designer

Type set by National Photocomposition Services
Printed by Princeton Polychrome Press
Bound by A. Horowitz & Sons

Library of Congress Cataloging in Publication Data
Mackay-Smith, Alexander.
  Man and the horse.

  1. Horsemen and horsewomen—Costume.   2. Horseman-
ship—Equipment and supplies.   3. Riding habit.
I. Druesedow, Jean R.   II. Ryder, Thomas.
III. Metropolitan Museum of Art (New York, N.Y.)
IV. Title.
GT5885.M33   1984   391'.0088798   84-22734

ISBN 0-87099-411-5 (MMA)
ISBN 0-671-55520-0 (S&S)

On the jacket: *Mme et M. Mosselman et leurs filles*
by Alfred de Dreux (detail). Petit Palais, Paris.

Contents

Foreword

Man has always assigned a special place to the horse in the hierarchy of the animal kingdom. Esteemed for elegance of line and proportion, for speed, intelligence, and strength, this majestic creature has been, at least until this century, central to virtually all human occupations—agriculture, commerce, travel, and warfare—and even today is associated with many of our most beautiful sporting events and noblest ceremonial occasions. The physical alliance between man and the horse extends to a special symbolic relationship for, in mastering the art of equitation, man invests himself with precisely those attributes of grace and power for which horses are known.

Throughout history the splendor of equestrian attire has reflected man's desire to emulate the nobility of the horse. Unlike other costumes designed and worn to achieve a merely fashionable effect, riding clothes have always shared a unique quality, regardless of their place or period of origin. Because of the specific functions they serve, riding costumes require above all superior design, materials, and workmanship—a harmonious blend of efficient cut, durability, and meaningful decoration—the essence of true style. As they indicate social status and incorporate contemporary fashion, the clothing and accessories of the horseman make an important statement about the era in which they evolved.

In many ways the world of the horse constitutes the epitome of social decorum, not only in the age of chivalry, to which the horse gave its name, or in the eighteenth century, when Beau Brummel turned the riding habit into high fashion for all gentlemen, but in our own time as well, when forms of dress traditionally associated with equestrian activity—the cutaway and top hat, the hacking jacket and high boots, the three-piece suit and blue jeans—are considered appropriately stylish even for those who have never sat upon a horse.

For each of the past ten years, as Special Consultant to The Costume Institute, Diana Vreeland has selected key periods in the history of costume and fashion for the Museum's annual exhibition. That she should choose the theme of "man and the horse" is a natural extension of her lifelong commitment to the definition of style of the highest order. At every stage in the selection and preparation of costumes, accessories, and equipment, Mrs. Vreeland has had the support of lenders, many of them fine horsemen and horsewomen whose enthusiasm for the realization of this rich display has made the exhibition possible.

This publication has also benefited from the extensive knowledge of numerous individuals, foremost among them its three authors, Alexander Mackay-Smith, author and editor of many publications about horses; Jean

Druesedow, Associate Curator in Charge of The Costume Institute; and Thomas Ryder, editor of *The Carriage Journal* and an important contributor to the revival of the sport of coaching. Their essays, together with the abundant illustrations, provide the historical and social context for many of the costumes to be seen in the exhibition. Helmut Nickel, Curator in the Department of Arms and Armor, Walter Liedtke of our Department of European Paintings, who is the author of a forthcoming book on equestrian portraiture, and Mrs. Vladimir Littauer, with her profound knowledge of the historical aspects of horsemanship, have generously given their time to review the text. Merri Farrell, Curator of the Carriage Museum at Stony Brook, was extremely helpful in providing information and assistance, and Katell le Bourhis, Associate Researcher in The Costume Institute, played a key role in coordinating the illustrations in this book with the objects in the exhibition. I also wish to thank the editor of the publication, Barbara Burn, who brought to bear her own considerable knowledge in this field as well as her editorial skills.

The exhibition could not have been realized without the generous support of Ralph Lauren, whose appreciation for the world of the horse and of art will be shared by countless visitors.

Philippe de Montebello
Director
The Metropolitan Musem of Art

Introduction

Round-hoof'd, short-jointed, fetlocks shag and long,
Broad breast, full eye, small head and nostril wide,
High crest, short ears, straight legs and passing strong,
Thin mane, thick tail, broad buttock, tender hide:
Look, what a horse should have he did not lack,
Save a proud rider on so proud a back.

Shakespeare, Venus and Adonis

Nothing is more marvelous than sitting at a little table in the gathering dusk in the Piazza di San Marco, the guest of the six golden-bronze horses prancing away—to paradise. Then you know you are in the presence of the most immaculately beautiful creature on earth.

Through the periods of history the horse has heralded the arrival of the great event. He has carried the hero of the hour—Alexander, Caesar, Washington, Bolívar—along the paths of discovery and conflict and together they have returned triumphant—and history continues. A man mounted on his horse is twice the man he is on the ground. Indeed, the Arabs tell us that one aspect of earthly paradise is to be astride a horse. Such a man holds the reins of power and progress in his hands, for the horse has been the basis of the mobility of culture.

The horse possesses the fluid power of the perfect athlete, gleaming in regal movements. The horse is the most sensitive piece of living beauty. The projection of the muscular jaw, the tension and arc of the neck, the sinuous line of the back, and splendid power of the leg—nothing is more enthralling than a well-loved horse. Man has long recognized the breeding of this animal. When a horse in ancient Arabia was seized in battle, the owner would present the conqueror with a pedigree so that, though himself vanquished, his horse might still receive the proper honors. Strength, stamina, size, spirit, power: it is the horse's splendid perfection that inspires man.

The history of horse and rider is the history of the intense regard each has for the other. Churchill said, "When you are on a great horse, you have the best seat you will ever have." It is said that Bucephalus, the favorite steed of Alexander the Great, was unmanageable and disagreeable to any save his master; Bucephalus would calmly kneel so that Alexander might more easily climb upon his sturdy back. We know that the saddest sight in all the world is the solitary, riderless horse in a state procession.

The horse has created for man a particular and glorious world; in turn men and women have created a world appropriate to the intelli-gence and *esprit* of this remarkable animal. Nothing is too good for a horse. In the tackrooms of the great stables, everything is attuned to his needs. Sensing the completeness of the horse, man has sought to equal, in raiment and accouterment, that simple splendor, that physical ideal. The highly refined domain of the horse is a polished, highly stylized realm reflecting the glory and exhilaration he inspires.

That domain calls forth the inherent glory of man. Tailors, bootmakers, and hatmakers alike know that men and women will never look as good as they do in their riding gear. The fit of the boots, the white suede breeches and racing silks, the saddle blankets thick with embroidery, the silver, gold, and bronze spurs and bits oiled and polished—there is nothing haphazard about the equestrian world. It is not a theatrical world; one dresses down to perfection. One dresses not for display but to meet the inspiration of the ideal. The splendid attire of the world of the horse is the fulfillment of man's half of a covenant.

Diana Vreeland
Special Consultant
The Costume Institute

Man and the Horse

The Evolution of Riding and Its Influence on Equestrian Costume

*H*istorians have called the horse the noblest conquest of man, yet horsemen know that man is not the horse's conqueror but a partner in a relationship that has had a profound and far-reaching effect on the history of civilization. It was cavalry that made possible the extraordinary achievements of Alexander the Great in the fourth century B.C. and of the Mongol Genghis Khan in the thirteenth century A.D. When the Plains Indians of North America began acquiring horses during the seventeenth century, they gradually became a nomadic rather than an agricultural people, and it was a fine horseman, General George Washington, who led his colonial army to victory over the British in the American Revolution.

Although the image of horse and rider is one of the most powerful in the human mind, man did not learn to ride this magnificent animal until relatively late in his history. It is believed, according to evidence found in the Ukraine, that horses were domesticated by the middle of the fourth millennium B.C., but the earliest representations of ridden horses cannot be dated earlier than about 1900 B.C. Eventually, the horse would become man's most important means of transportation and source of power, remaining so until the advent of the steam engine in the early nineteenth century; even today, engine capacity is measured in terms of horsepower. And, although the horse has been largely replaced by motor-driven vehicles, we still revere this splendid creature, not simply for his beauty and spirit but also for his continuing role as our partner in some of our most pleasurable activities.

The techniques of riding, which until the Renaissance in western Europe was considered primarily a utilitarian skill for use in travel, warfare, and hunting, have evolved in accordance with the various tasks that horses have been asked to perform. As the training of horses became more sophisticated and riders were able to achieve harmony between themselves and their mounts—using their hands, legs, seat, and balance to promote rhythm of movement, mental understanding, and sympathy—equitation became more than a mere necessity but developed as a sport and, in courtly circles, as an art form. The clothes worn by the rider and the equipment (or tack) worn by the horse played a significant role in this evolution of riding, enabling riders to attain a high degree of horsemanship as well as serving the functional purposes of protection, security, and comfort.

This bas-relief from the palace at Nineveh of Ashurbanipal, king of Assyria (668–627 B.C.), shows a mounted archer drawing his bow. He is dressed for battle with a conical helmet and body armor (a cuirass) from which hang lappets that protect his legs. The horse is wearing a snaffle bridle and a pad held by two surcingles and resting on leather armor that covers most of the horse's body. Stirrups had not yet been invented, but the fact that this rider is using both hands to manage his weapon rather than his horse speaks well for Assyrian horsemanship. Although this horse is standing still, other reliefs show archers at a full gallop, but it is difficult to imagine that their shots were always on the mark. *Musée du Louvre, Paris*

Saint George (icon), possibly seventeenth century, painted by an unknown Russian artist. *The Metropolitan Museum of Art*

Many types of material, from textiles to buckskin, have been used for riding apparel, and most articles of tack have been fashioned from leather, although wood has also been used in making saddle trees (frames) and certain kinds of stirrups. Because of the perishable nature of such organic materials, only a few examples of riding clothes and tack dating from before the seventeenth century have survived, although metal and bone (or antler) components of harnesses have been found dating back to the fifteenth century B.C. or earlier. Fortunately, however, the history of equestrian costume, tack, and riding styles is splendidly illustrated in works of art. This brief essay will reproduce a large number of such works—ranging in date from the seventh century B.C. in Assyria to the twentieth century in America—to help describe this colorful and dramatic history. In the essay various aspects of the development of equitation will be discussed, and the selection of plates that follows will be accompanied by specific comments on costumes and equipment.

Because different styles of riding depicted in equestrian works of art have been adapted to the natural gaits of the horse, the viewer must be familiar with equine gaits, as determined by the sequence of footfalls, in order to understand these images. The two gaits common to all horses are the four-beat walk (right hind, right front, left hind, left front) and the three-beat canter or gallop (right hind, left front, and—simulta-neously—left hind and right front, or vice versa). There are also three types of natural gait faster than the walk but slower than the canter: the diagonal two-beat trot (right hind and left front hitting the ground simultaneously, followed by left hind and right front, also hitting simultaneously); and the two lateral gaits, known as the pace (or amble) and the rack (or singlefoot). The pace is a two-beat gait in which the right hind and right front move together to hit the ground simulta-neously, followed by the left legs; in the four-beat rack, the sequence is much the same as in the slower four-beat walk.

These intermediate gaits affect the rider in very different ways. In the diagonal trot, the horse's back rises and falls, whereas in the lateral gaits the back remains level, swaying slightly from side to side. Before

The most famous equestrian portrait of the classical era, this large bronze depicts the Roman emperor Marcus Aurelius (A.D. 121–180) sitting his horse with ease, his legs firmly held against the horse's flanks. He wears a ceremonial imperial costume—a short tunic girded with a military belt—and on his feet are short, laced sandals. In accordance with classical tradition, the horse's neck is raised toward the vertical and the head is overbent slightly because of the bit's pressure; he is trotting, the appropriate gait for the charger of a military leader. *Piazza del Campidoglio, Rome*

the introduction of "posting" (rising in the stirrups) in the middle of the eighteenth century, the trot was a decidedly uncomfortable gait, yet it provided a good deal of stability since at any given time the horse was balanced with one foot on each side placed on the ground. The lateral gaits, while less stable, were far more comfortable for the rider. Horses are naturally either diagonally or laterally gaited—few strains can perform both gaits—so the rider's selection of a horse was determined by the function he wished his mount to perform. For military service, where stability was more important than comfort, the rider would select a trotter; for travel or hunting, where comfort was desirable, he would select a laterally gaited pacer or racker. Although these differences may seem unimportant to us, patrons commissioning portraits were fully aware of them, and it is often possible to identify the role of a rider by observing the gait that the artist has been instructed to depict. A man seated on a trotting horse was most likely displaying his military prowess, as well as considerable horsemanship in remaining balanced and in harmony with the horse. A man on a pacer was likely to be playing a civilian role where less skill was required to achieve a comfortable seat.

*I*n the history of riding, the first significant development was undoubtedly the invention of the stirrup, for it enabled riders to remain securely on their horses while carrying or using weapons, even at high speed. While its origin is unknown, the first evidence of rigid stirrups like those in use today are metal-sheathed wooden devices found in Chinese tombs of the fourth century A.D. It is likely, however, that soft, straplike stirrups existed before that time, probably among the nomadic horsemen of Asia and perhaps elsewhere, but no examples have survived. The first appearance of the stirrup in western Europe is a type similar to the Chinese and was uncovered in seventh-century Avar tombs in Hungary, leading scholars to suspect that the Avars, and possibly other nomadic tribes, brought the stirrup with them from the Far East across the grassy steppes of northern Asia. The stability provided by stirrups virtually revolutionized the history of warfare. Thanks to a cavalry equipped with stirrups, Charles Martel, ruler of the Franks, was able to consolidate his kindgom and, at a battle near Poitiers in 732, to defeat Abd-el-Rahman, ruler of Cordova, the last of the Muslims to lead an army to France.

Another important piece of horse equipment that appeared first in China was a saddle built on a wooden tree, with a pommel in front and a cantle in back to help keep the rider secure in his seat. For centuries the horse had been ridden with a saddle cloth attached by a surcingle (girth) passing under the belly; the addition of cushions and rolls or leather-covered metal arches in front and back, such as those used in ancient Rome, tended to increase comfort but did not give as much stability as the treed saddle, which made its appearance in Europe during medieval times. The heavily armored knight required a well-built saddle tree to support a high pommel and cantle to keep him in place as he charged with couched lance at a knight similarly armed.

Bits and bridles, used to control and guide the horse, have probably been in use since the first time man decided to use such a lively animal. The bridle is a set of straps, usually made of leather, which holds a bit in the horse's mouth on the flat gums between front and back teeth; in its earliest form, the bit was a straight metal bar or bone with a ring at each end to hold the reins. By 1400 B.C. this bar was constructed in two pieces, with a joint in the middle, virtually the same as the modern jointed-snaffle bit, which enables the rider (or driver) to apply pressure to various points in the horse's mouth. Many different types of bits have been used over the years, some of them exceptionally severe, since early riders, especially those carrying weapons and concentrating on their foes, had little time and no inclination to struggle with running horses in the middle of battle.

Stopping a horse was one problem; getting him to move quickly was another. Whips and spurs, developed as aids to the horseman's legs, seat, hands, and voice, are also of ancient origin. Iron prick-type spurs, which were attached to the heels of the rider's boots and applied to the flanks of the horse, appear in Celtic graves dating from about 400 B.C. These were gradually replaced by rowel spurs, which were equipped with wheels of radiating points, first found in Spain in the ninth century A.D. and still in use today throughout the world.

The history of ancient riding clothes is difficult to trace except through the evidence of works of art. As the Greeks and Romans had no stirrups or treed saddles and often rode bareback or on a simple saddle

The saddle in this painted pottery figurine of the T'ang dynasty is clearly furnished with stirrups. It was found in the tomb of Princess Yung T'ai, who died in A.D. 706, although figurines of horses wearing saddles with stirrups occur as early as the fourth century. The bearded rider, whose coat with broad lapels and baggy trousers are typical of western Asian fashion, undoubtedly represents one of the many central Asian horsemen who served as retainers in the great Chinese households.
Shaanxi Provincial Museum, China

pad (the latter to prevent the horse's sweat from soaking the rider's legs), we find riders wearing everyday robes and sandals (or nothing at all). The earliest trousers seem to have been used by the Achaemenids, who ruled Persia from 550 to 330 B.C., but their use, and the wearing of boots, was most likely spread by the nomadic Asian tribes, who had to protect their legs and feet from severe weather, and it is from these steppe riders—the Huns, Alans, and Sarmations of the Migration Period—that our modern riding costume of trousers and jacket derives. Certainly, ancient warriors had to protect themselves with armor, and this too had to be adapted for use on horseback, but it is unlikely that special riding clothes, as we know them today, were in common use until well into the Renaissance in Europe, when riding became an activity performed for its own sake as well as for the requirements of travel, hunting, and warfare.

With its high pommel in front and cantle behind, this elegant saddle of Hungarian origin dating from the first half of the fifteenth century is shaped like a practical war saddle, but its veneer of staghorn plaques, delicately carved with chivalrous scenes, suggests that it was most likely a decorative piece of fine equipment befitting a horseman of status.
The Metropolitan Museum of Art

This is one of seventy-two scenes on the Bayeux tapestry, woven about 1092, which tells the story of the Norman conquest of England. Here, William, duke of Normandy, leads his troops to victory over the Saxons. He is clad in a type of armor called a hauberk, with sleeves, hood, and leggings that reach below the knee. The armor is made of mail, which was developed by the Parthians and continued to be the primary means of protecting the body and limbs

through the thirteenth century A.D. Although the king is in battle, he is mounted on a pacing horse, the gait clearly indicated by the embroiderers' use of one color for the left legs and another for the right. Military horsemen often preferred trotters for stability, but pacers were far more comfortable to ride and more valuable because of the great demand for them. Kings would therefore be more likely to ride pacing horses even into battle. *Bayeux Cathedral*

From China the stirrup moved westward with nomadic horsemen across Asia. This late seventh-century Near Eastern silver plate shows a mounted archer at the gallop discharging an arrow at a lion. Thanks to his stirrups, the rider is in perfect balance with his horse and capable of aiming his weapon accurately. *Hermitage, Leningrad*

This plate, from Antoine de Pluvinel's book, *L'Instruction du Roy...* (1625), shows the horse being trained between two pillars, a technique that Pluvinel popularized.

During the fourteenth century in Europe, chain mail was gradually replaced by plate armor, and by about 1450 armorers were fashioning complete steel-plate armor for horses as well as riders. The horse armor prompted a special vocabulary: chamfron for the head, crinet for the neck, peytrel for chest and body, and crupper for the hindquarters. The example illustrated here was made in about 1575 in the armory of the counts of Collalto, an ancient dynastic family of northern Italy. This type of armor was very expensive, but well-trained horses were valuable to the knights who rode them and worthy of protection. The armor worn by the rider is also Italian, dating from about 1575, but it shows the influence of Spanish fashion in the use of decorative etched stripes that imitate the seams of a Spanish doublet. The helmet was designed for use in the battlefield, although this set also has another helmet (not shown) suitable for use in tournaments.
The Metropolitan Museum of Art

The only riding manual to have survived from classical antiquity was written by the Greek historian Xenophon in the fourth century B.C. While containing much valuable information regarding the training and care of horses, it was addressed to military horsemen, who considered riding a necessary skill rather than an art form. Not until the sixteenth century did riding become the art known today as "dressage." (From the French word for training). In 1550 a riding master named Federigo Grisone published a book entitled *Gli Ordini di Cavalcare (The Principles of Riding)* under the aegis of the king of Naples and Pope Julius III. Within seventy years, the book had appeared in sixteen Italian editions and fourteen editions in French, Spanish, German, Portuguese, and English. Thus Grisone first put the art of dressage into print and inspired subsequent riding masters and manuals. One influential follower was Antoine de Pluvinel, who founded an academy in Paris in 1594 and became director of Henri IV's Grandes Écuries and later riding instructor to the dauphin, who would become Louis XIII. Pluvinel's treatise, *L'Instruction du Roy en l'exercise de monter à cheval,* was published in 1625, five years after the author's death, with engravings by the Dutch artist Crispin de Pas, and it became the most significant work of its kind to date from the seventeenth century. The ultimate text, *L'École de Cavalerie,* by François Robichon de La Guérinière, was published in Paris in 1733, with engravings by Charles Parrocel. The methods outlined by La Guérinière are still practiced today in their original form at the Spanish Riding School in Vienna and by the Cadre Noir at the French national riding school at Saumur.

The riding academies established by Grisone and his followers were much more than riding schools in the modern sense. They were courtly institutions in which formal refinement became the mark of a gentleman (indeed, commoners were excluded). Proficiency in *haute-école* riding became an essential element in the education of young noblemen and

The Lipizzan stallion ridden by this Spanish Riding School master is performing the *levade,* one of the "airs above the ground" in advanced dressage.

François Robichon de La Guérinière, the eighteenth-century riding master, was the first to describe and teach the lateral dressage movement known as the shoulder-in (*épaule en dedans*), which is illustrated in this plate (far left) from his book *L'École de Cavalerie*; the rider is said to be the author himself. The clothing seen here and in the Pluvinel plate was designed specifically for riding, adapted from the style of military uniforms.

When Louis XV became king of France in 1715, at the age of five, La Guérinière was given a royal appointment as riding master. This portrait of the king by J. B. van Loo and Charles Parrocel (the latter illustrated La Guérinière's book) shows Louis XV at the age of thirteen, mounted on a well-trained horse performing a stately trot or perhaps a *piaffe* (trotting in place). His riding costume includes armor, as would befit a king, but the jackboots are the same as those worn by La Guérinière and other horsemen of the time. *Musée de Versailles*

*H*unting from horseback, which dates back to at least 1300 B.C., quickly became as much sport as necessity, and hunting scenes have long been a favorite subject for artists and patrons. The speed of the horse, combined with man's ability to use spears, bows, swords, and later firearms, made for an exciting chase, whether the quarry was lion, wolf, wild boar, stag, roebuck, or the smaller species—fox, hare, and otter. Even a wide variety of birds have been hunted from horseback, often with the help of a falcon. Other partners in the hunt have been the various types of hounds, some bred to hunt by scent (foxhounds and harriers) and those known as coursing or sight hounds (greyhounds, whippets, salukis, wolfhounds, and so on). Feudal lords in Europe especially enjoyed hunting the larger animals and reserved the privilege of doing so for themselves and their households, and some species, such as the stag and roebuck, were often kept in parks or reserves to assure

European stag hunts were often held in special reserves where hounds and riders pursued their quarry through thickly wooded forests, as in this painting, *The Hunt* (ca. 1460), by Paolo Uccello (Italian, 1396/97–1475). Uccello was one of the first Renaissance painters to depict horses, a subject that would later fascinate Leonardo and many other artists. *Ashmolean Museum, Oxford*

gentlemen, on a par with dancing, fencing, court tennis, and singing or playing a musical instrument. The equestrian art was designed to display rider and horse at their harmonious best, performing not only collected and extended forms of the ordinary gaits (walk, trot, and canter) and lateral movements such as the shoulder-in, but also the spectacular "airs above the ground," exercises in which the horse lifts the forehand alone, as in the *levade*, or leaps entirely off the ground, as in the *courbette* and *capriole*. Of all forms of riding, dressage is the most demanding; to reach the upper levels requires talent and temperament, on the part of both horse and rider, and years of patient and skillful training. Today it is one of the three equestrian disciplines of the Olympic Games.

From the middle of the sixteenth century, monarchs, noblemen, and other subjects of equestrian portraits could be expected to request one of three poses for the horse: standing still, trotting sedately, or performing a more difficult air above the ground, usually the *levade*, in which the horse rises on its hindlegs and remains motionless for a few moments. Because this pose requires considerable skill and control of the horse, the image of a ruler on horseback performing the *levade* not only conveyed to the viewer his mastery of the courtly art of riding but also served to symbolize his command over his subjects.

The French national riding school at Saumur in the Loire Valley is one of the few places where *haute-école* dressage is still performed as it was centuries earlier. This nineteenth-century illustration shows a horse performing a *capriole* between pillars, as described by Pluvinel; the costumes seen here are the same as those worn by members of the Cadre Noir today.

their availability for the hunt. Eventually, the privilege of stag hunting (*la grande vénerie* in France) became the king's alone, and only members of the court or his guests could be granted permission to join him. In France, Louis XIV decreed that anyone permitted to participate in the royal hunt should wear a special hunting uniform, and during the reign of Louis XVI noble families were allowed to devise their own uniforms, known as *boutons*, because an important part of the costume was an elaborate set of engraved buttons. These *boutons* have been traditionally passed from one generation to the next. In England and America today, fox-hunting associations also use distinctive "colors," a reference to the colored collar worn on the coat with the permission of the Master of Hounds.

During the eighteenth century in England, the British Parliament passed the so-called Enclosure Acts, which transferred to private ownership the common lands that had been used by medieval villagers for farming and grazing their livestock. Property owners consequently built hedges, banks, and stout fences to enclose their lands, a development that brought about a dramatic change in the sport of hunting on horseback. Within a short time, fox hunting became extremely popular among young men of fashion, who took great pleasure in jumping their

horses over the newly constructed obstacles in pursuit of foxes, which were considered verminous pests by farmers but a lively and challenging quarry by sportsmen. Riding styles and hence riding clothes and equipment were altered to accommodate the new demands of riding over obstacles across country. Saddles lost their high pommels and cantles, and riders dispensed with dressage movements to take up what they called a "safety seat." Early in the twentieth century, an Italian cavalry officer, Federigo Caprilli, developed what is now called the "forward seat," a position in the saddle that enables the rider to remain over the horse's center of balance during the gallop and the jump and to interfere less with the animal's forward momentum. This style of riding is now common practice among all those who jump, not only during the hunt but also in the show ring. Two of the three Olympic equestrian disciplines—show jumping and three-day eventing—include the sport of jumping.

The introduction of hedges and fences into the eighteenth-century English landscape revolutionized the sport of hunting on horseback, which quickly became a spirited cross-country chase over obstacles. This print was made by Henry Alken (British, 1774/85 – 1850/51), one of the best-known producers of sporting prints in the nineteenth century.

The romantic image of Arabs riding their splendid horses appealed to many European artists of the nineteenth century, including Adolf Schreyer (German, 1828 – 1899), whose painting of a battle scene shows horsemen wearing their traditional robes. *The Metropolitan Museum of Art*

*A*side from the four principal tasks that horses and men have performed in partnership through the centuries—traveling, fighting, dressage, and hunting—there is another, the herding of livestock, that has an important place in the history of equitation. Herding was first—and is still—practiced in Mongolia but is perhaps most familiar to us today in its American context, as a significant part of the development of the West. The style of so-called western riding, however, is a continuation of a tradition that began with the Bedouins of Arabia, who used their magnificent Arabian horses for warfare. The Muslim armies brought the horses to North Africa where, mixed with native stock, they became known as Barbs. When the Moors overran the Iberian peninsula, where cattle-herding was an important way of life, the horses, as well as the riding style, were used for herding and eventually bullfighting, which later became the national sport of Spain. The interbreeding of the Barbs with local Andalusian horses resulted in an exceptionally fine strain of riding horses that became prized all over Europe. (The Spanish Riding School in Vienna was named for these animals.) In 1493, on his second voyage to the New World, Christopher Columbus brought Spanish horses to the West Indies, and in 1519, Cortés took sixteen of them with him to Mexico. Over the next three centuries, the horse became an integral part of life on the North American continent, not only in furthering the

Horsemen in Peru, Columbia, Brazil, and Puerto Rico have assiduously cultivated the lateral gaits in their pleasure horses, which they use for working cattle and sheep and exhibit with great pride in horse shows. This photograph shows a Peruvian paso fino horse pacing with his left foreleg thrown outward, a much-esteemed element of the gait known as the *termino*. The costume is a characteristic feature of paso fino show classes.

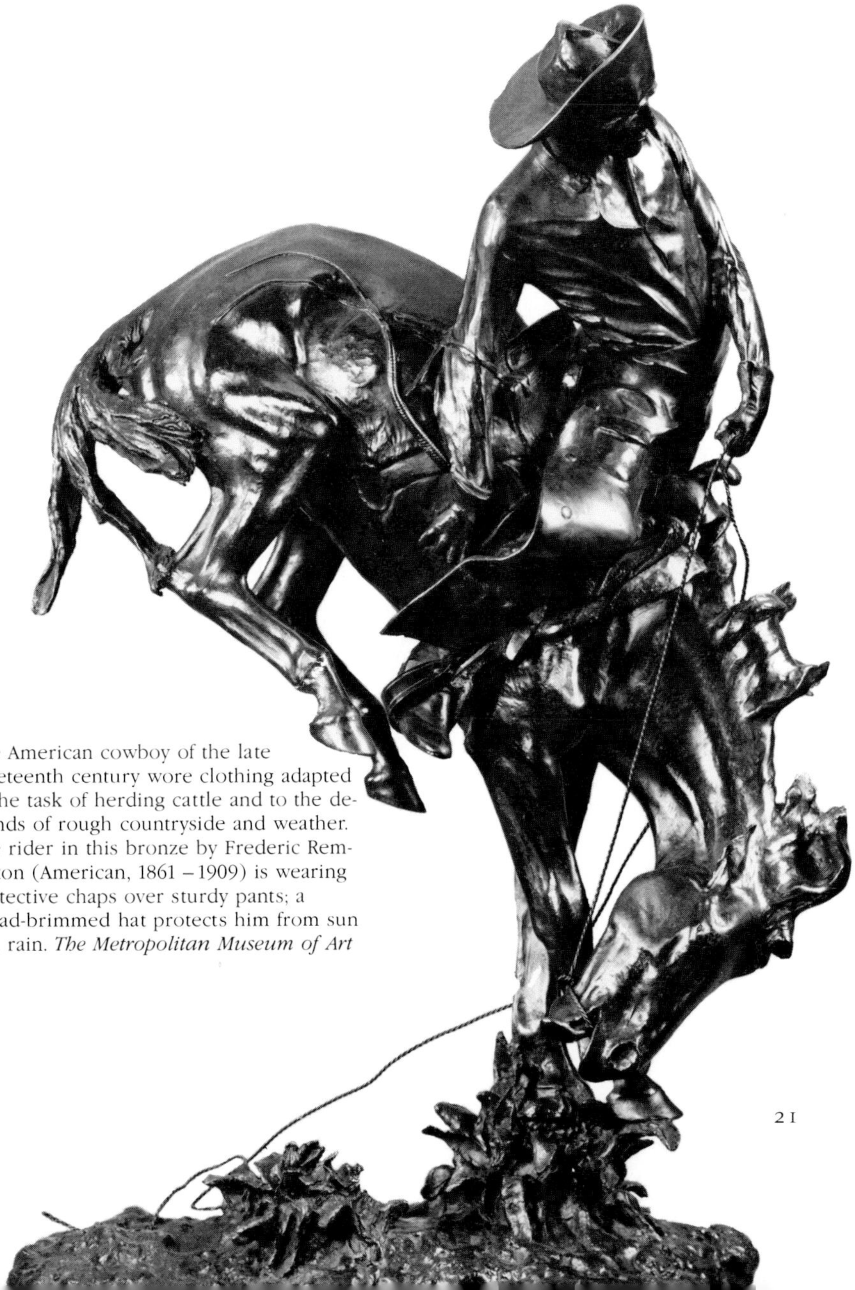

The American cowboy of the late nineteenth century wore clothing adapted to the task of herding cattle and to the demands of rough countryside and weather. The rider in this bronze by Frederic Remington (American, 1861–1909) is wearing protective chaps over sturdy pants; a broad-brimmed hat protects him from sun and rain. *The Metropolitan Museum of Art*

Spanish conquests but also in herding cattle and sheep. Although the training and riding techniques, as well as the clothing and equipment, used by cowboys underwent considerable adaptation from the Spanish tradition, the original source is still apparent in the long, straight legs and erect posture of the rider, the wide brim and tall crown of the hat, the high-heeled boots with roweled spurs, and the curb bit and loose rein of the bridle. And, in some areas, such as Mexico, California, and even parts of South and Central America, the Spanish styles of clothing and riding remained much the same and can still be seen at horse shows and parades, where horses and riders are dressed to resemble their equine and equestrian ancestors.

Alexander MacKay-Smith

Equestrian Portraits

The over-life-size equestrian bronze portrait below by Donatello (Italian, ca. 1386–1466), commissioned in 1447 and installed six years later in front of the Church of San Antonio in Padua, was the first colossal equestrian statue produced after classical times. Representing Erasmo da Narni, popularly known as Gattamelata, it became a prototype for hosts of equestrian monuments erected from the fifteenth through twentieth centuries. Donatello has created a perceptive portrait of this condottiere—the leader of a band of mercenary soldiers; the manner in which he sits his pacing horse reveals that he is a confident rider. He holds a baton of authority in his right hand and carries a broadsword on his left thigh; he wears pseudo-classical armor, and on his feet, which are thrust forward in the stirrups, are long spurs with sharp rowels. The horse wears a bridle with a browband and throat latch but no noseband; in his mouth is a severe curb bit. The high pommel and cantle of the saddle, which rests on a thick pad, provide the rider with maximum support. Although Donatello has clearly imbued his portrait with the spirit of classical antiquity, perhaps inspired by the Roman statue of Marcus Aurelius, the spurs, bit, and saddle of the rider did not exist in western Europe until years after the fall of the Roman Empire.

The principal figure in this fresco entitled *The Procession of the Magi* is actually Lorenzo de' Medici. The fresco, which covers the walls of the chapel in the Medici-Riccardi palace in Florence, was commissioned in 1459 and painted by Benozzo Gozzoli (Italian, 1420–1497). Lorenzo shows his superior horsemanship by sitting securely on his trotting white horse. He wears Florentine red, like the others in his retinue, and the horses are brilliantly turned out in caparisons (decorative trappings) of red and gold, blue and yellow.

22

Henri II of France, who reigned from 1547 to 1559, was also an accomplished horseman, and he is seen at left on a trotting horse in a painting from the workshop of François Clouet (French, 1515/20 – 1572), who made a number of similar portraits. The king is dressed in black velvet and white satin decorated with gold, the mourning colors he wore in sympathy with his mistress, Diane de Poitiers, whose husband has died. He wears military-style jackboots and carries a riding stick similar to those described and illustrated in contemporary riding manuals. His black horse, whose bridle has a massive curb bit, is equally splendid: the tail is tied up in an

ornamental fashion, and the saddle and caparison are embroidered in gold with silk tassels that show the king's monogram *H* combined with a *D* for Diane de Poitiers and a *C,* the monogram of his queen, Catherine de' Medici. The queen was herself a fine rider and is credited with having been the first woman to wrap her right leg around the pommel of the saddle, thereby inventing the first true side saddle. This would have allowed her not only to maintain a more secure seat at faster gaits than the walk while riding sideways but also to face the horse's head and effectively control the reins herself. *The Metropolitan Museum of Art*

Prince Maurice of Orange, here depicted by Pauwels van Hillegaert the Elder (Dutch, ca. 1595 – 1640) before a field of battle, is clearly more concerned with making a handsome appearance than with displaying his military prowess. His stocky horse has been bred not only for the ability to carry a rider wearing heavy armor but also for his long, silky mane and tail, a concession to fashion rather than practicality.
Rijksmuseum, Amsterdam

This sketch for a portrait (now apparently lost) of the first duke of Buckingham was painted in Paris in 1625 by Peter Paul Rubens (Flemish, 1577 – 1640), an artist clearly aware of the fine points of *haute-école* riding. Buckingham was an excellent rider who was appointed Master of the Horse by James I in 1616; he was also a patron of racing, and many pedigrees of today's thoroughbreds can be traced to the Bucking-ham stud at Helmsley. In this portrait Buckingham holds a staff in his upraised right hand in classical fashion; he wears a doublet and hose with a cloak, but the over-the-knee jackboots of Pluvinel are absent. His horse is executing a *levade*, indicating that both horse and rider were accomplished in the art of dressage. *Kimbell Art Museum, Fort Worth*

Count Duke Olivares, like the duke of Buckingham, was a chief minister to his sovereign; Philip IV of Spain appointed him Master of the Horse *(General de la Caballeria de España)* in 1625, and he became known as the best horseman in the country. In this portrait (ca. 1634) by Diego Velázquez (Spanish, 1599 – 1660), Olivares is riding a favorite white horse, the subject of other studies by Spain's court painter, who has chosen to depict the duke's skill and authority and the high degree of training of the horse. Olivares is wearing the high boots of the horseman; his armor is today in the collection of the duke of Alba.
The Metropolitan Museum of Art

While court painters chose kings and noblemen as their subjects for equestrian portraits, Rembrandt van Rijn (Dutch, 1606–1669), the son of a miller and a baker's daughter, selected a humbler sitter. In this, his only equestrian portrait, he has depicted a young cavalryman, whose dress and style of riding differ sharply from those of the upper classes. The fur hat, long coat, and short boots seem to be of central European origin, and art historians have speculated that he represents one of the Polish soldiers who fought gallantly in the Holy Wars to repel the Turks during their repeated invasions of central Europe. It is possible, however, that Rembrandt simply chose as his model one of the mercenary soldiers who were being imported at the time by the rulers of western Europe from Hungary and other eastern European countries. Unlike the riders painted by Rubens and Velázquez, who are shown sitting squarely in the center of the saddle to distribute their weight evenly and enable their horses to perform dressage movements, Rembrandt's so-called *Polish Rider* (1655) sits well forward, balancing his horse on the forehand, essential for speed at the gallop. The horse is eastern European in type, suitable for warfare in rugged climates but far removed from the finely bred stallions of the Turkish and Polish cavalry. In fact, the horse is probably a gelding, for it was the Hungarians who first used them regularly in battle. (The French word for gelding is *hongre,* meaning Hungarian.) *The Frick Collection, New York*

The spirit of the eighteenth century survives today at the famous Spanish Riding School in Vienna, where horsemen regularly perform their ballet-like quadrille in its magnificent hall, a triumph of rococo architecture built in 1735. The riders wear a nineteenth-century costume, which includes a brown cutaway coat ornamented with a double row of gilt buttons, full skirts, white buckskin breeches, black boots covering the knees, and bicorne hats.

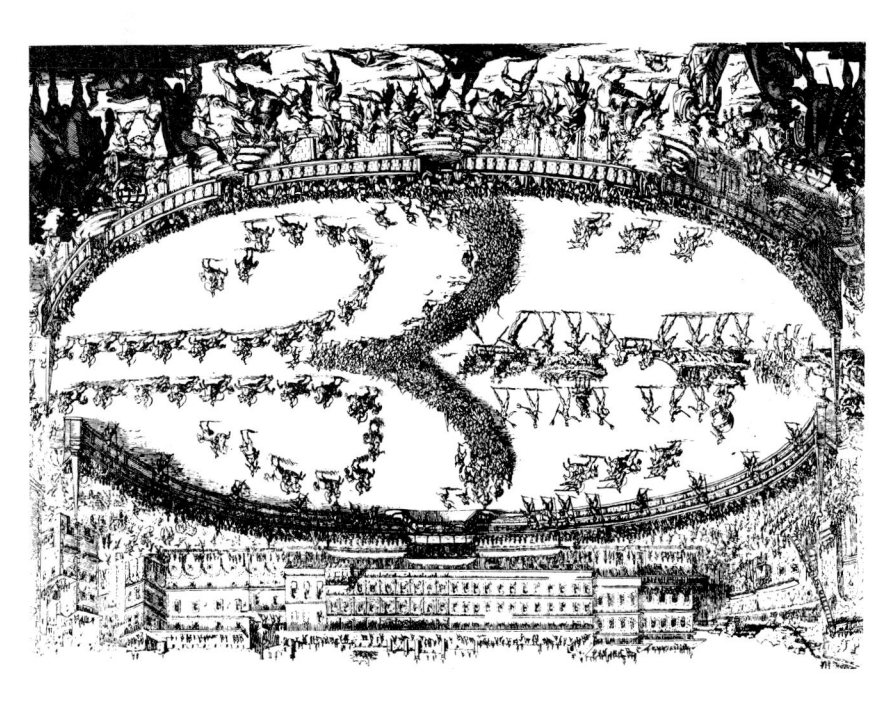

The seventeenth century was the era of the equestrian ballet, in which a large group of costumed horses and riders would perform a series of intricate figures to music, similar to the quadrilles performed today by the riders of the Spanish Riding School and by the Royal Canadian Mounted Police. The early ballets are known to us through paintings and engravings as well as descriptions by contemporary writers. This print by Jacques Callot (French, 1592 – 1635) after a design of Giulio Parigi (Italian, 1571 – 1635) shows a ballet entitled "La Guerra di Bellezza," held in 1616 in the Piazza Santa Croce in Florence to celebrate the arrival of the prince of Urbino. The ballet was choreographed by Angelo Ricci, dancing master to the grand duke, Cosimo de' Medici, who led the ballet on horseback, supported by four quadrilles of forty-two riders each.

As part of the celebration of the birth of the dauphin, Louis XIV organized an equestrian ballet which took place on June 5 and 6, 1662, in Paris in front of the Palace of the Tuileries. The ballet or carrousel included 655 horses and riders, drummers, trumpeters, footmen, squires, pages, and grooms. There were five quadrilles, each with fanciful, exotic costumes: the "Romans" were led by the king, the "Persians" by his brother, Philippe d'Orléans, the "Turks" by the prince de Condé, the "Indians" by the duke d'Enghien, and the "American Indians" by the duke de Guise. A folio volume of plates illustrating the carrousel was published in 1670, with text by Charles Perrault and engravings by Israel Silvestre and François Chauveau and illuminated by Jacques Bailly in the king's personal copy. This colorful portrait by Chauveau shows the king flanked by his attendants. Perrault described his costume: "The King was dressed like a Roman, in a corset of silver brocade embroidered with gold.... He wore a silver helmet with gold leaf, enhanced by two large diamonds ... [and] a crest of feathers the color of fire, from which emerged four herons." The horse, as if it were a physical extension of the king, wore "a saddle of brocade .. the whole caparison of the neck, chest, flanks, and croup was nothing but bands of gold brocade embroidered with silver, trimmed with diamonds...."

The exotic nature of this equestrian portrait is completely authentic, a product of the Mughal court, which supported one of the most famous schools of Indian painting. This splendid miniature shows Shah Jahan, who reigned from 1627 to 1658 and was known in Europe as the Grand Mogul. (It was Shah Jahan who commissioned the building of the Taj Mahal, in memory of his wife, Mumtaz Mahal.) He is seen here riding a piebald horse at the collected trot, a picture of pure magnificence, not only in the richness and color of the costume and equipment but also in the way in which the Shah sits his mount and in the conformation and controlled cadence of the horse in motion. *The Metropolitan Museum of Art*

The Tournament

One of the most splendid and romantic activities of the Age of Chivalry (derived from the French word *chevalier,* meaning horseman) was the tournament, in which armored knights engaged in contests on horseback to display their skill and courage. Originally organized as war games in which the knights could train for battle, tournaments are known to have taken place as early as the ninth century in France and Germany, but they became formal events in eleventh-century France, and continued well into the sixteenth century, with increasingly complicated rules and specialized armor. Jousting was the principal equestrian exercise of the tournament. Two knights carrying lances and shields and riding heavy horses dressed in full armor would charge one another, the object being to unhorse the opponent or, failing this, to score the best hit on the other's shield while remaining in perfect balance on one's horse. The joust, which was limited to contestants of noble birth, became gradually less dangerous, but it was no mere game; Henri II, king of France, was wounded in a tournament in 1559, not long after the portrait on page 24 was painted, and he died of the injury a few days later.

To sharpen their accuracy with the lance, jousting participants used two practice devices. The first was the quintain, a wooden figure armed with shield and sword and modeled after a Saracen, the name given by the Crusaders to their Muslim opponents in the Holy Land. If the "Saracen" was hit with the tip of the lance exactly between the eyes, it would be knocked over, but if the rider missed, the figure would revolve on a swivel and strike the luckless horseman on the head with its sword. The second device, above right, was a suspended ring through which the rider would attempt to pass the point of his lance as he galloped past. These illustrations showing the quintain and ring come from Pluvinel's *L'Instruction du Roy . . . ,* indicating that success in tournament games was as important an equestrian accomplishment as the art of dressage.

Tournaments were popular throughout Europe and were often occasions for grand social events, such as parades, pageants, and feasting. This colorful page from a tournament book, made to commemorate a procession that took place in Nuremberg in 1561, shows two knights riding elegantly caparisoned pacing horses, followed by attendants dressed in the same colors as the animals. Because knights in helmets were not recognizable to either friend or foe, they would wear distinctive colors and patterns (or coats-of-arms) to facilitate identification, and their horses and servants would do likewise, in what would eventually come to be known as livery.
The Metropolitan Museum of Art

Ao. 1561. Andres Schmid

The Hunt

Another popular equestrian activity, but one in which women could participate as well, was hunting on horseback. In the sport of falconry, which has a long tradition going back to the steppe riders of the Dark Ages, different species of birds of prey are used to capture the quarry. In this scene, a lady with a hawk on her wrist rides astride, while two others ride sideways (pillion) behind gentlemen. At least two of the horses are pacers of the type known as palfreys, which were used for pleasure riding as well as for hunting. The elaborate, colorful costumes are not specially designed for riding but could be worn on many different social occasions. This meticulously painted illustration represents the month of August in the manuscript known as the *Très Riches Heures*, commissioned by the duke of Berry about 1415 and executed by the Limbourg brothers of Burgundy and Jean Colombe. *Musée Condé, Chantilly*

By the eighteenth century, clothes worn for riding had become specialized in terms of design and fabric, as seen in equestrian portraits and riding-manual illustrations, and the same was true for clothes worn while hunting on horseback. In France *la grande vénerie* was the stag, roebuck, or boar, which were then (as now) hunted in great forests through which were cut wide paths (*allées*) that converged like the spokes of a wheel on a central axis. This tapestry, made after a design by Jean-Baptiste Oudry (French, 1686–1755), official painter of the royal hunts, clearly shows the costume of participants in *la chasse à courre* (the hunt with running hounds): a long-skirted coat made of sturdy fabrics afforded protection from branches and mud, as did the knee-covering boots, while the tricorne (cocked hat) and colors,

buttons, and trim on the coat identified each rider according to rank and hunting society. The circular horn is one of the most striking components of French hunting costume, carried over the shoulder not only by the Master of Hounds and hunt servants but also by members of the hunt. In the thick forest those who follow catch only occasional glimpses of the stag and hounds, but the musical range of the horn enables everyone who carries one to blow the particular series of notes that describes exactly what they have seen. French hunting is thus largely a matter of the ear rather than the eye. Hunting in France is still pursued in the traditional manner, although the tricornes and hunting horns have become smaller, following court fashion of the late eighteenth century. *Musée de Versailles*

British riding clothes of the eighteenth century derived from French hunting dress. In this 1740 portrait by James Seymour (British, 1702–1752), Sir Roger Burgoyne of Sutton Park, Bedfordshire, aboard his favorite horse, Badger, wears a cocked hat over a wig, a coat of blue camlet lined with red and richly ornamented with gold braid, a white lace cravat, and black boots with spurs. As the sport came to demand more athletic ability, the clothing became more practical, with long-skirted coats cut away at the waist (cutaways), sturdier hats, and plainer cuffs and cravats. The military jackboot, which extended over the knee for protection, was also adapted to the need for greater flexibility: the tops were rolled down to reveal a colored leather lining, though eventually the tops disappeared and only a band of colored leather (usually brown) below the knee and the term *top boot* remained as reminders of the earlier style. *Yale Center for British Art, New Haven*

During the first half of the nineteenth century, an era often called the golden age of fox hunting, it took a bold and determined rider on a fast horse to keep up with the crack packs of hounds that raced across the British countryside. Most of the young bloods hunted six days a week, requiring several sets of hunting clothes and boots and a full-time, experienced valet to turn out his master impeccably clean and well pressed. In this portrait, painted in 1806 by Benjamin Marshall (British, 1768–1836), George Gordon, marquess of Huntly, sits astride his bay hunter, Tiny. Two hunt servants, the huntsman (on the bay horse) and the whipper-in (on the gray), wear black hunt caps but are otherwise dressed like their master, with white stock ties and waistcoats, long scarlet coats with square skirts, white breeches, and black boots with colored tops and spurs. The pattern, cut, and material of Huntly's clothes and boots differ little from those worn at fashionable hunts today. *Yale Center for British Art, New Haven*

This hunting scene, entitled *Two Busvines and a Cutaway,* was painted by Sir Alfred Munnings (British, 1879 – 1959), president of the Royal Academy and unquestionably the most successful horse painter of the twentieth century. He made many portraits and was especially fond of racing and hunting subjects. Busvine was a British tailor who, for many years, was the most fashionable maker of sidesaddle habits. The gentleman wears a hunting cutaway, which is somewhat impractical for bad weather, having no protective skirts on the jacket; however, it was considered the epitome of elegance in the hunting field. *Private collection*

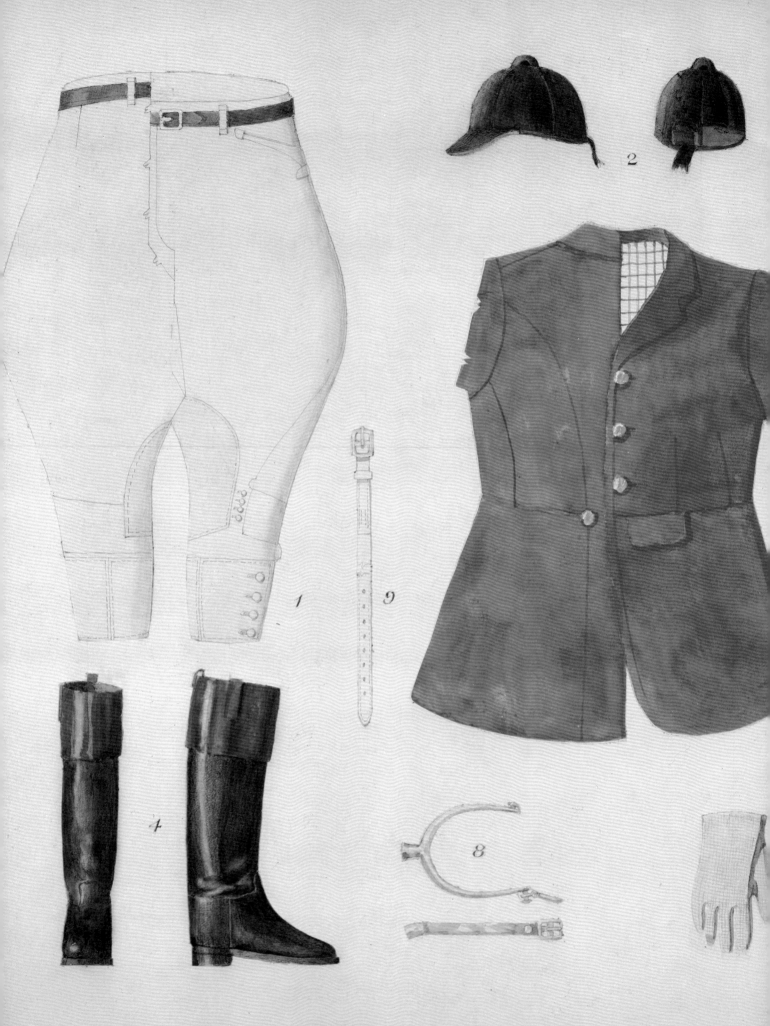

2

1   9

4   8

Ferner del et pinx.

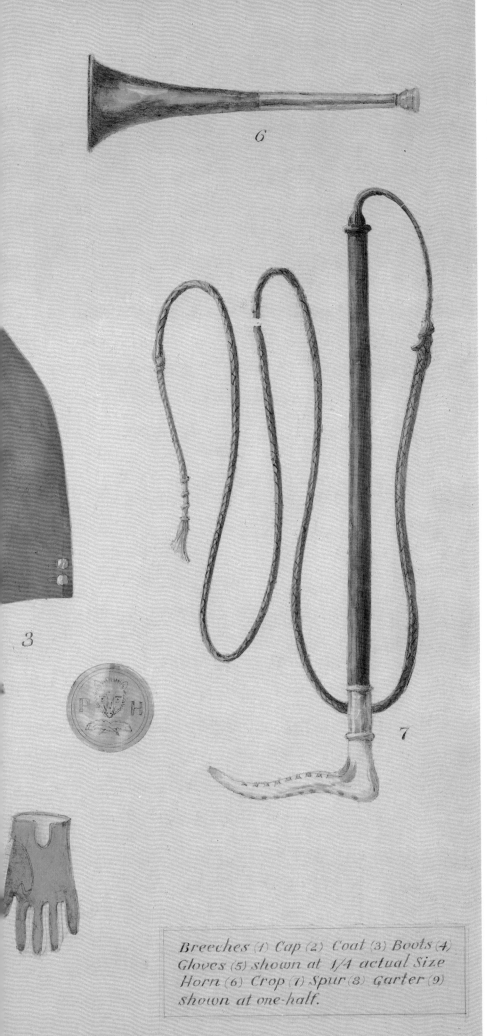

Breeches (1) Cap (2) Coat (3) Boots (4)
Gloves (5) shown at 1/4 actual Size
Horn (6) Crop (7) Spur (8) Garter (9)
shown at one-half.

Fox hunting was no less popular among gentlemen in the British colonies in America than in England, and George Washington was one of its most enthusiastic participants. His hunting clothes, custom-made by a London tailor, were described by his step-grandson, George Washington Parke Custis: "Washington [was] always superbly mounted, in true sporting costume of blue coat, scarlet waistcoat, buckskin breeches, top boots, velvet cap, and whip with long thong." In 1766, a group of Philadelphia gentlemen founded the Gloucester Fox Hunting Club, and in 1774 they adopted a hunt uniform which, perhaps because of Quaker influence, called for a "dark brown cloth coatee, with lapelled dragoon pockets, white buttons and frock sleeves, buff waistcoat, white or tan colored breeches, and a black velvet hunting cap." Eventually, however, American hunting clothes became virtually identical to the accepted British style, as illustrated in this watercolor by Harold Sterner (1895–1976) made for Paul Mellon, Master of Foxhounds of the Piedmont Hunt in Upperville, Virginia. His rank is indicated by the four brass buttons on his scarlet coat and his velvet cap (a member of the hunt would have five buttons and wear a top hat or a bowler whereas a guest would wear a black coat with a plain black collar and a bowler or top hat rather than a cap). *Paul Mellon Collection, Upperville, Virginia*

Racing

Horseracing has probably existed as a sport since men first mounted horses. It was a popular activity in ancient Greece and draws the largest crowds of any sport in America today, where it is big business. But from the Renaissance to the early twentieth century, horseracing deserved to be called the sport of kings or at least of the nobility. Light horses called "hobbies" were bred in England and Ireland from the fourteenth through the sixteenth centuries, and Italian noblemen imported them in considerable numbers to compete in *palio* races in the principal cities of Italy. Before a race, the horses would walk in a procession through town, wearing elaborate trappings in colors that represented different districts or *contrada* of the city. Then they would be disrobed and run through the streets or around the central square, with or without riders, cheered on by citizens of their respective districts. This panel painting, from a *cassone* ("chest") painted by Giovanni di Francesco Toscani (Italian, ca. 1370 – 1470), shows such a race in the city of Florence. The forward-seat position of the riders resembles that of today's jockeys, except for the absence of stirrups, which forces these riders to keep their lower legs back in an effort to maintain balance. *Palio* races are still run twice a year in Siena, staged with all the pageantry of old. *The Cleveland Museum of Art*

A traditional feature of the annual Carnival season in Rome was the race of riderless horses, here portrayed by Horace Vernet (French, 1789 – 1863) in a sketch for a painting (now lost) completed in 1820. The race, which also inspired Goethe and Géricault, took place along a mile and a half of the via Flamina, now known as the Corso, and the horses—small Barbs imported from North Africa—were driven not by jockeys but by noisemakers and the shouts of the crowd. *The Metropolitan Museum of Art*

Under the Tudor kings, races in England were held between the native-bred English and Irish hobbies, whose natural intermediate gait was the pace. Henry VIII maintained a stable of racing hobbies at Greenwich, but it was the house of Stuart that laid the foundations of the thoroughbred. Charles II established Newmarket as the racing center shortly after he regained the throne in 1660, and he instituted the King's Plate as a prize. Private breeders imported stallions from the Barbary coast of North Africa by way of Spain, as well as a few Arabian stallions from the Near East. One of the most influential of these was the Darley Arabian, who was brought in 1704 from Aleppo and is an ancestor of most modern thoroughbreds, the hackney pony, and even the standardbred, America's trotting racehorses. This portrait by James Seymour (British, 1702 – 1752) is of England's first great racehorse, Devonshire or Flying Childers. He was foaled in 1715, sired by the Darley Arabian out of a mare whose ancestry can be traced back to the duke of Buckingham's stud. The cap and clothes of the jockey are typical of the period, lightweight and bare of decoration but brightly colored to match the colors of the horse's owner, the duke of Devonshire. *Private collection*

Overleaf:

In 1766 George Stubbs (British, 1724 – 1806) published his *Anatomy of the Horse,* with plates that he himself drew and engraved. The first book to deal adequately with the subject, it ushered in a new era in equestrian painting. Stubbs, an artist of the first rank, is considered by most critics the greatest painter of horses in history. In this painting of 1760 – 61, Stubbs shows the racehorses of the third duke of Richmond exercising in Goodwood Park, observed from horseback by the duke and duchess and Lady Louisa Lennox attired in clothing suitable for pleasure riding. The racehorses wear heavy yellow blankets and hoods trimmed with red (the duke's colors) in order to induce a good sweat that will help them lose surplus weight. Stubbs, despite his grasp of equine anatomy, has depicted the racehorses in a "flying gallop," a stylistic device typical of sporting artists until a photographer, Eadweard Muybridge, demonstrated in the late nineteenth century that galloping horses do not run with all four legs off the ground in this manner. Goodwood House has been an important site for equestrian activities for nearly three hundred years. There, the first duke of Richmond (a natural son of Charles II) established the Charlton hunt, the first formal British fox hunt, and the third duke initiated the Goodwood races in 1801, described by a journalist in the 1830s as "the most glorious meeting that ever man attended." Today Goodwood is one of the most popular centers for racing and dressage competitions. *Private collection*

43

John Hay Whitney, a great American art collector and former ambassador to the Court of St. James, was also a fine horseman; he owned and bred many of the finest racehorses of our time, including Triple-Crown winner Twenty Grand, and was himself a superb polo player. He bought this racing scene painted by Sir Alfred Munnings in part because it shows the Whitney racing silks, although the racetrack and the horses and riders are not identified. Munnings painted many racehorses on commission but this painting was apparently executed for his own pleasure; a skilled colorist, he was perhaps attracted to the distinctive Whitney colors because of their aesthetic value. The Whitney family maintains a racing stable in England as well as America. The British racing silks are shown here; the American silks are slightly different, with pink and black on the sleeves and a black cap. *Mrs. John Hay Whitney Collection, New York*

Steeplechasing as a sport grew out of fox hunting in Ireland and England during the first half of the nineteenth century and is now popular throughout the world, both as a professional sport at major racetracks and as an amateur activity at hunt meetings. The professional steeplechase jockeys above are wearing the silks of their horses' owners, adding color to the excitement of the final jump at Saratoga. The photograph at left of an amateur point-to-point race at Pytchley, England, in 1911, shows gentlemen dressed in their formal hunting clothes.

Hunting and other equestrian sports require certain types of apparel for the sake of tradition as well as practicality, but riding for pleasure has offered the wealthy an opportunity to dress in the most fashionable garb of the day. In this 1777 painting, George Stubbs has portrayed John Musters, High Sheriff of Nottingham, and his wife, Sophia, in front of their home, Colwick Hall, in Nottinghamshire. Musters wears a round black hat with a medium brim, a brown frock coat with a white stock, white breeches, and black boots with wide tops. Mrs. Musters wears a black fur hat and a red habit with a fitted coat and voluminous skirts, not unlike the riding habit of Lady Worsley, painted by Sir Joshua Reynolds only a few years later (see page 65). John Musters altered this painting by eliminating the figures of himself and his wife, presumably because of her infidelity, and replacing them with grooms leading the horses, but the painting was restored to its original form in 1938. *Major Musters Collection, Nottingham*

Riding for Pleasure

Along with Eugène Delacroix (see page 54), Théodore Géricault (French, 1791 – 1824) was a leading Romantic painter who was attracted to horses as a subject. Famed for his military and racing scenes, Géricault also made many sketches of horses and riders, including a number of *chevaliers* riding for pleasure, often accompanied by *amazones* (ladies on horseback). This horseman is wearing a typical French suit of the period, complete with top hat, and his horse's tail is fashionably docked, as was the custom in the nineteenth century. *The Metropolitan Museum of Art*

Unlike Géricault, who knew how to depict horses accurately, Edouard Manet (French, 1832 – 1883) adapted his horses from British sporting prints. As he explained to his friend Berthe Morisot, "Not being in the habit of painting horses, I copied mine from those who knew best how to do them." This may explain why Manet has omitted much of the horse in this 1870 portrait of an artist friend, Emile Guillaudin, who wears a fashionable white linen suit of the sort worn by Frenchmen who rode for pleasure rather than for the hunt. *Private collection*

The origin of polo, one of the oldest of stick-and-ball games, is unknown; the first representation we know of dates from the T'ang dynasty (A.D. 618–906) in China, but it was probably played before that in other parts of Asia. (The name of the game comes from *pulu,* the Tibetan word for ball.) It was during the period of polo's greatest popularity in Persia, the Safavid dynasty (A.D. 1501–1726), that this beautiful manuscript illumination was painted. Iran's national epic is the *Shah-nameh (Book of Kings),* written by the poet Firdowsi in the tenth century, and perhaps the greatest copy of the poem was the one commissioned by Shah Isma'il for his son in 1522 with 258 illustrations painted by artists of the court. This page, *Siyavush Plays Polo Before Afrasiyab,* shows the players with their weight in the stirrups leaning well forward, the most efficient position for a man on horseback who must swing his mallet at a ball resting on the playing field below. *The Metropolitan Museum of Art*

Polo

British officers in India took up the game of polo in the mid-nineteenth century and brought it to England in 1869. Called "hockey on horseback," it became very popular among those who could afford the necessary strings of ponies. In 1876, the first polo game in America was played at Jerome Park, outside New York (see page 104). The heyday of polo in America took place between the two world wars when tremendous crowds were drawn to Meadow Brook, Long Island, to watch dashing young gentlemen compete with tremendous enthusiasm and skill. The danger and excitement of the game are boldly expressed in this powerful drawing by George Bellows (1882–1925), an American artist renowned for his dramatic paintings of boxing matches. *The Metropolitan Museum of Art*

This photograph dating from the 1920s shows, left to right, some of the finest American polo players of the time, Pete Bostwick, Gerald Balding, Tommy Hitchcock, and John Hay Whitney of the Greentree team, resting between chukkers. Polo is still played internationally today, the best teams being those from Argentina, the United States, and Great Britain, where the game has been a favorite among members of the royal family. Clothing for polo, designed for maximum flexibility and protection, includes helmets and knee pads, as well as the classic polo shirt, which has become a favorite article of sportswear even for those who have never mounted a horse.

The golden age of polo has passed, but the game is still a popular spectacle at clubs and playing fields around the world. The gentleman pictured above is the most honorable marquess of Cholmondeley, who played polo in England during the 1920s. The aggressive action of the game is scarcely apparent in the appearance of this elegant pair—the rider dressed in pristine white breeches and shirt with polished boots and the beautifully groomed horse with neatly wrapped protective leg bandages and impeccable bridle and saddle.

"Western" Riding

When the Muslims invaded Andalusia in the eighth century, they introduced their techniques for bullfighting on horseback, and great tournaments were held in which Moorish chieftains competed against Iberian knights. After the Muslims were driven out in the fifteenth century, the sport continued to be a favorite among Spanish aristocrats and formed an integral part of court life. By 1700, the bull was no longer lanced from the back of a highly trained horse but was fought on foot; horsemen were thereafter relegated to a subordinate position as picadors, while the star of the show was the matador. Francisco Goya (Spanish, 1747 – 1828), who was official court painter, actually designed a professional uniform for use in bullfighting, and he made a series of etchings called *Tauromachia* in which he celebrated the history of the sport. This plate shows El Cid Campeador, a great hero of the eleventh century, who was supposedly the first Castilian to lance a bull from the back of a horse.

Arabian horses, originally bred by the Bedouins, are highly prized for their great speed over long distances, quality, and endurance, and many fine breeds used for riding today can trace their ancestry to them. This painting by Eugène Delacroix (French, 1798 – 1863) shows an Arab rider, probably a cavalryman, signaling from the back of his fiery steed. In 1832 Delacroix was sent by King Louis Philippe of France as part of a diplomatic mission to the sultan of Morocco, and thereafter North African horses and riders became one of his favorite subjects. *The Chrysler Museum, Norfolk, Virginia*

The conquistadors introduced horses to the New World and, along with the animals, brought their distinctive style of riding. Their clothing and equipment were adapted not only for battle but also for herding cattle and sheep. By the 1860s, when Maximilian of Austria became emperor of Mexico, Mexican riding clothes had become all the rage in Europe. In these paintings by the British-American painter James Walker (1819–1889), a typical California ranch owner (*patron*) and cowboy (*vaquero*) are depicted in their characteristic costumes. The saddles are high in front and behind, like those used by European knights in armor, and the men sit their horses with straight legs, feet thrust forward. *The Bancroft Library, Berkeley, California*

Aside and Astride

A History of Ladies' Riding Apparel

From the earliest records of women on horseback, one learns that the rationale for women riding has been the same as that for men: war, transportation, sport, and pleasure. From the legendary Amazons onward, women rode astride as well as sideways—depending on the nature of the activity and the daring of the woman. Chaucer's description of the Wife of Bath on her way to Canterbury implies a pair of spurs, and an illustration from the Ellesmere manuscript of 1407 shows her with skirts hiked up riding astride:

> *Easily on an ambling horse she sat*
> *Well wimpled up, and on her head a hat*
> *As broad as is a buckler or a shield,*
> *She had a flowing mantle that concealed*
> *Large hips, her heels sharply spurred under that.*

One could hardly have expected Joan of Arc to have accomplished her mission in 1429 had she been seated sideways, encumbered by skirts, on a docile palfrey. Equally daring, the mistress of Henri II of France, Diane de Poitiers (1499–1566), was an avid rider and hunter and is thought to have ridden astride. However, since classical times, as evidenced by Greek vase paintings depicting Amazons riding astride and goddesses riding sideways, there has been a strong implication that only a woman as masculine as an Amazon, as earthy as the Wife of Bath, as heretical as Joan of Arc, or as notorious as Diane de Poitiers would have dared to ride astride. This left the vast majority of ladies sitting sideways on horseback with their skirts spread modestly about them.

The first true sidesaddle, thought to have been inspired by Henri II's wife, Catherine de' Medici, in the early sixteenth century, was a decided improvement over the various pads and platforms upon which ladies had sat for untold centuries. Not only was it considerably safer than sitting sideways on a man's saddle, but it responded to aesthetic considerations as well, for a woman's wide hips were considered unseemly and unattractive when she was riding astride. This first type of sidesaddle, with the single pommel or crutch moved a little to the saddle's left side and curved to hold the rider's right leg, continued in use until the invention of the "leaping-head" at the end of the eighteenth century. Legend has it that Thomas Oldaker, huntsman to an English earl, broke

This illustration of the Wife of Bath, from the 1407 Ellesmere manuscript of Chaucer's *Canterbury Tales*, clearly shows her broad-brimmed hat, spurs, and whip, some of the accessories essential for a woman riding alone and astride on a pilgrimage during the early fifteenth century. Many women at this time would have ridden pillion (behind a man on a special cushion designed for the purpose, as in the falconry scene from the *Très Riches Heures*, page 34), or been led while seated sideways on a pad or platform. *Huntington Library, San Marino, California*

Marie Antoinette by Louis-Auguste Brun
(Swiss, 1758–1815). *Musée de Versailles*

his leg and devised this contraption to enable him to jump his horse while hunting. He placed a second crutch below the first so that it would curve over his left thigh. This saddle, which firmly controlled the position of the legs, became popular with women and led to the development of a special sidesaddle skirt cut, which allowed the rider's hemline to be perfectly horizontal when mounted but contained minimal yardage for a neat appearance. By the twentieth century, this had become an "apron-skirt," which was open in the back and had a weighted hem that hung parallel to the ground when mounted but when dismounted fell back over the breeches, making a partial skirt.

The first concessions by fashion to the development of specialized riding apparel came from a need to protect the rider from the hazards of traveling: wind, weather, and dirt. By the second half of the sixteenth century, such protective clothing included an overskirt or "safeguard," cloaks, capes, boots, masks to protect the complexion, and hats. In addition to protection from the elements, the rider also needed to guard his or her legs from the sweat of the horse and from chafing caused by the saddle. Riding pants, apparently first worn in ancient Persia, were widely used by the nomadic horsemen of Asia, and breeches gradually became standard dress for horsemen throughout Europe. Women choosing to ride, whether astride or aside, needed some form of this "masculine" garment. An eighteenth-century inventory of Mme de Pompadour's possessions lists several pairs of silk knitted *pantalons*, which might well have been used for warmth and comfort under her riding skirt.

Women, attracted to the style of men's clothing for psychological as well as practical reasons, found early in the seventeenth century that riding provided the opportunity to adapt masculine attire for their own

This seventeenth-century French saddle was intended for a woman riding aside. While it resembles a chair, with a back and a platform to support the feet, it also has the high pommel and cantle of the man's saddle. This saddle was designed to be used on either side of the horse, not just on the left side, as is the case with the true sidesaddle, which enables the rider to face the horse's head and manage the reins herself. *Hermès Collection, Paris*

This delightful painting by Claude Deruet (French, 1588–1662) vividly shows the perils involved in riding sideways. The elegant ladies, probably of the court of the duke de Lorraine, are disporting themselves on a falconry hunt (though one woman uses an owl), wearing their finest dresses, which are not at all adapted to riding on horseback. (It was not until the end of the seventeenth century that special clothes were developed for the purpose.) The artist has provided us with a rare opportunity to view what was worn beneath the skirt—a refined pair of shoes, stockings, and beribboned garters—hardly a practical outfit for the chase. The fanciful nature of seventeenth-century taste can also be seen in the long, silky manes and tails of the horses, which were specially bred at this time to present an elegant appearance, matching that of their riders. *Musée de Chartres*

purposes. Samuel Pepys in a diary entry dated June 12, 1666, wrote, "I find the Ladies of Honour dressed in their riding garb, with coats and doublets with deep skirts, just, for all the world, like mine . . . so that, only for a long petticoat dragging under their men's coats, nobody could take them for women. . . ."

An early illustration of a woman in specialized dress for the hunt, *Dame en habit de chasse* (1676), shows, in terms of line, the traditional accommodation of a man's style to feminine attire. The shape of the upper body—coat, hat, and accessories—is adapted from the lines and ornamentation of the stylish men's fashions of the time; the lower body—the skirt—establishes the femininity of the wearer. The eighteenth century in particular saw the development of a specialized costume for *l'amazone*—the woman on horseback. In France as well as England, this consisted of coat, waistcoat, tie, shirt, hat, gloves, and skirt with or without train, corresponding in line to men's fashions. The 1704 portrait of the duchesse de Bourgogne and the painting *Départ pour la Chasse à Courre* illustrate this relationship clearly. The style of ornamentation is also related to the development of men's riding clothes, for equitation was recognized as an art at this time and specialized riding apparel had become associated with dressage as a courtly pastime. Englishwomen were no less aware of what their gentlemen on horseback (or their French *amazone* counterparts) were wearing at this time. One young equestrienne moved *The Spectator* in 1716 to describe "a coat and a waistcoat of blue camlet trimmed and embroidered with silver, with a petticoat of the same stuff, by which alone her sex was recognized, as she wore a smartly cocked beaver hat, edged with silver and rendered more sprightly with a feather, while her hair, curled and powdered, hung to a considerable length down her shoulders, tied like that of a rakish young gentleman, with a long streaming scarlet riband."

Alan Mansfield, in a history of English sporting costume, speculates that there may even have been a reciprocal relationship between such a costume and eighteenth-century military dress: "Some ladies in the 1780s and 1790s modeled their habits on military uniforms; perhaps in revenge for the adoption by the Royal Navy of dark blue and white for its officers' coats, said to have been inspired by the riding habit of the duchess of Bedford some forty years earlier." (Phillis Cunnington and Alan Mansfield, *English Costume for Sports and Outdoor Recreation from the 16th to the 19th Centuries* [London: Black, 1969], p. 105.) Royal ladies, including Marie Antoinette, found occasion to have their portraits painted wearing fully masculine attire and riding astride, perhaps to emphasize their status as well as to astonish their more conservative contemporaries.

However, not all who rode or hunted in the eighteenth century followed these specialized styles. Carle van Loo's painting in 1737, *Halte de Chasse,* shows a royal hunting party in which the ladies have made only minor concessions to the nature of the activity. The setting for this festive picnic is the forest of Compiègne, where Louis XV enjoyed exercising his royal prerogative of stag hunting—*la grande vénerie.* After a morning devoted to the chase, the king's party would stop during the afternoon at a pleasant spot, often by a stream, for relaxation and luncheon. The king, who can be seen standing in the center, is wearing a richly embroidered red coat. Mme de Pompadour sits in the foreground, elegantly costumed in a flowing skirt, with only slight masculine touches—the short jacket, open blouse, and small bow at her neck—to

Dame en habit de chasse, a fashion plate of 1676. *Musée de la Vénerie, Senlis*

indicate that she too has participated in the hunt. She is surrounded by noblemen dressed in royal blue, trimmed with red and silver, which was the livery worn by all members of the king's hunting party by his express permission. Louis XIV was the first to regulate the use of such uniforms to control participation in the royal hunt.

As the eighteenth century progressed, the major inspiration for men's fashionable apparel and therefore for women's riding habits switched from the French court to the English countryside. The English country gentleman rode and hunted over a course filled with obstacles in a climate that demanded rugged, weatherproof clothing. He was so enamored of this sporting life that even at court he did not give up his country clothes. It was this plain fabric and severity of cut that was to

Départ pour la Chasse à Courre, painter unknown, ca. 1700. *Location unknown*

Halte de Chasse by Carle van Loo (French, 1705 – 1765), 1737. *Musée du Louvre, Paris*

influence men's and women's fashions of subsequent centuries. Alan Mansfield traces another source of this fashion creation: "A quite new development occurred in about 1785 when the Great Coat or Riding Coat dress was introduced. It has a close-fitting bodice with lapels and a deep double or triple cape-collar, after the style of a coachman's coat; and a long straight, full skirt, buttoned through: the bottom button often left undone to show the underpetticoat. The fashion apparently crossed the Channel and returned from France as the 'Redingote' at the end of the century."

Lady Worsley, who sat for Sir Joshua
Reynolds (British, 1723 – 1792) in June 1779,
chose to have herself portrayed in a riding
habit based on the uniform of her husband's regiment, the Hants Militia, a practice followed by a number of other Englishwomen of her day. *Earl of Harewood
Collection, Harewood House, Leeds*

La Duchesse de Bourgogne by Pierre
Gobert (French, 1662 – 1744), 1704. *Musée
de Versailles*

Galeries des Modes, 1779.   *Galeries des Modes*, 1787.

The 1787 plate from *Galerie des Modes* shows a French version of this costume, adapted for women's riding apparel, but labeled "in a German style." In the 1779 plate the man is wearing a French interpretation of the influential English country gentleman's costume. Never lagging in fashion sense, equestriennes conformed to current feminine fashions in their riding apparel through the placement of the waistline, the configuration of the bodice, the shape of the sleeve, and the style of the skirt. After the eighteenth century, the cut of women's riding clothes did follow male fashions by becoming less voluminous, with jackets shorter, narrower, and more cutaway. Even so, sensitivity to feminine fashions persisted throughout the nineteenth century. The rise of the English tailor and availability of high-quality English woolen cloth meant that women's riding habits exuded the same kind of sartorial elegance epitomized by George Bryan ("Beau") Brummell (1778–1840). By refining the cut of the country gentleman's costume, insisting on impeccable cleanliness of linen, and demanding only dark colors contrasted with neutral shades and brilliant white, Brummell created an enduring standard of appearance in the tailored clothing of both men and women. Nowhere have his taste and style been more emphatically retained than in riding apparel as it evolved for both men and women through the nineteenth century. The cut of the costume worn by the Scottish country gentleman George Harley Drummond in the portrait by Sir Henry Raeburn could be said to represent Brummell's ideal.

A glance at the series of French fashion illustrations that starts on page 72 showing nineteenth-century riding habits reveals the degree to which these costumes used the fashionable French silhouette and the extent of the conservative and masculine influence of Beau Brummel. The line of each habit reflects a simplification of cut and ornamentation when compared with fashionable day or evening counterparts. This is, of course, in keeping with the physical demands of riding horses, but it also reveals the sense of appropriateness and discipline associated with riding as a sport for women. This conservatism did not, however, prevent the sleeves and skirt from including a fashionable quantity of cloth.

One of the most beautiful and fashion-conscious horsewomen of the nineteenth century was the tall and slender Elisabeth of Austria (1837–1898). Not satisfied with a daily ride in Vienna, the Empress rode and hunted on an international scale, traveling by special train with her entourage (and forty tons of luggage!) to France, England, and Ireland, as well as to parts of the Austro-Hungarian Empire. On these trips she took at least sixteen riding habits and along the way bought new ones, preferably in dark blue, in the latest style. According to Brigitte Hamann, Elisabeth

had herself sewn into her riding habit every morning, and to the dismay of the prudish English aristocracy, she did not wear a petticoat under her habit; her only undergarment was a very soft chemise of the finest kid, which was as tight as a second skin. Naturally, she had herself sewn into that every morning too. . . . The severe, tight cut of the riding habit underlined her height. . . . Never before or after were ladies' riding habits as elegant or refined as in the 1880s, when Elisabeth set the pace for the fashion on the parcours. Never had riding been as fashionable for ladies of society. (The Imperial Style: Fashions of the Hapsburg Era [New York: The Metropolitan Museum of Art, 1980], pp. 148, 149.)

The inclination of women to have their riding skirts designed in the latest feminine style occasioned embarrassing as well as dangerous situations. Strong gusts of wind might play havoc with a carefully arranged skirt, and early in the nineteenth century various pins or straps, such as the one shown in the 1800 fashion plate, were suggested as remedies. Much more seriously, a fall from a horse might find the rider's skirts caught or entangled, adding to the risk of injury. Safety is a perennial concern, whether riding astride or sidesaddle, and keeping one's seat in a wide skirt took great skill and balance. The sidesaddle itself demanded skirts of sufficient width to allow for proper placement of the right leg. By 1855 a slight pouch on the right side of a full skirt had appeared as a remedy, but it was not until late in the nineteenth century that special tailoring was devised to accommodate the right knee, with a dramatic decrease in the volume of the skirt. An issue of *Cassell's Family Magazine* of 1879 describes a skirt such as too complicated to make at home, but by June 1893 *The Delineator* offered a detailed description and a pattern. The first "safety-skirt," which the rider could open up the back while in the saddle and fasten again when on the ground, was introduced in 1875, the idea being that this arrangement was less likely to catch during a fall. A later design for riding astride, resembling a modern culotte, is shown in the 1893 plate. Even then, there was as great a desire for a fashionable skirt shape when off the horse as for comfort and decorum when mounted. Women might wear the breeches and boots of the man's habit underneath, but few felt it proper to relinquish the look of the skirt entirely.

George Harley Drummond by Sir Henry Raeburn (British, 1756–1823), 1808. *The Metropolitan Museum of Art*

Special riding corsets underneath the habits gave the torso the current fashion shape and kept the spine erect for proper bearing, while petticoats and even bustles held the skirt in a stylish line. (The English found the simple kid chemise of Elisabeth of Austria a shocking lack of underwear!) Drawers of various kinds became trousers strapped under the foot, much like fashionable menswear of the mid-nineteenth century, and breeches were cut like a man's to below the knee. In breeches for sidesaddle, when made of traditional cloth, each leg was cut with regard to its position when mounted.

The guidelines for proper riding clothes developed later for women than for men. The formalization of women's sidesaddle attire seems to have come about with the specially cut skirt worn over breeches and boots. Thereafter, the corseted bodice shape and the style of sleeve became the only hallmarks of fashion found in formal riding apparel, and the influence of masculine style encompassed the whole look. The Belle Epoque, replete with traditions and a sense of propriety, determined the standard to which early twentieth-century equestrian activity adhered. Although sidesaddle riding went out of fashion by the end of the 1930s for most horsewomen, some ladies continued to ride sidesaddle to the hounds, and the style is now enjoying a revival, not only in the hunting field but also in the show ring. Sidesaddle habits retain the apron as a skirt, while women riding cross-saddle wear habits with a traditional masculine cut.

Jodhpur pants, cut to the ankle and worn with jodhpur boots, were introduced for women in the 1920s. Originally adopted by British colonials in India for the comfort they offered in hot weather, they are now worn primarily by children or those who ride American, gaited horses in the so-called saddle-seat style. Until the introduction of elastic fibers in fabric, a full cut above the knee for both breeches and jodhpurs for men and women was necessary, since the rider had to be able to flex the legs to mount the horse and to move athletically at the faster gaits. The material below the knee, usually reinforced with suede patches, had to remain snug to ensure a secure grip in the saddle and to prevent chafing. The slim appearance of riders today is in part due to a new breeches cut made possible by stretch fabrics.

Women riding *en cavalier,* such as Marie Antoinette, had, of course, imitated a man's boots as well as his costume. Some early stirrups had a kind of shoe-shaped box which fitted over a lady's slipper, but half boots were used from at least 1786. Some early nineteenth-century stirrups had a platform for the slipper, as illustrated in the fashion plate of 1800. Today, however, men's and women's boots are cut in the same style and differentiated only by regulations governing various activities, such as hunting and showing.

Riding hats have also become standardized over the course of time. Whereas fashion set the style for headgear during most of the eighteenth and nineteenth centuries, safety also played a part in the final development of the bowler, top hat, and riding or hunt cap styles designed and made specifically for riding. These specialized hats are made to be lightweight but close fitting and strong and hard enough to protect the wearer's head during a fall. They are sometimes attached to the neck of the riding coat by a cord, a further convenience for a rider experiencing an unplanned dismount or an extraordinary gust of wind.

Other accessories were also developed specifically for riding. Leather and string gloves provided an excellent grip on the reins when wet or dry and are still worn today. The hunting stock, a plain version of eighteenth-century neckwear adopted by the British, is still tied at the neck in a traditional style and fastened with a gold stock pin, while other scarves and ties are specified for other types of riding. Rainwear for use on horseback has a long history, beginning with capelike garments and progressing to the lightweight waterproof coat of today.

The choice of clothing and headgear deemed appropriate for different occasions is largely dictated by convention and special regulations. Following traditions begun in the seventeenth century, twentieth-century horsewomen conform to the specifics set forth by such authorities as Sydney D. Barry in *Clothes and the Horse: A Guide to Correct Dress for All Riding Occasions* (London: Vinton, 1953), the rule book of the American Horse Shows Association, or the regulations of individual hunt clubs. These regulations may be found in *Baily's Hunting Directory* (published annually) for British and American hunting and in the *Manuel de Vénerie* for French livery. (French hunts retain a decidedly eighteenth-century look, and the women still wear the tricorne hat.) Color is another carefully regulated area of attire. For example, in Britain and America red is often reserved for the coats worn by male members of the hunt and the hunt staff, who also have the privilege of wearing colored boot tops and, depending on the circumstances, white breeches. Only on special occasions are these rules broken. Women participating in events as members of the United States Equestrian Team, for instance, where they compete on an equal basis with men, wear identical uniforms, including a red coat for show jumping and a black cutaway and white breeches for dressage. Fashionable elements still affect the cut and fit of a contemporary habit, but are found only in very subtle degrees. Except for improvements in the cut of the breeches, which has allowed the skirt of the jacket to be shorter and less full, the basic silhouette for formal riding attire for women has not changed much since the 1920s.

The tradition of man-tailored garments for women, which had its origins at the end of the seventeenth century, has transcended sport and reached into every aspect of women's clothing today. No sooner was careful tailoring applied to riding apparel than the tailored suit for daytime wear became part of every woman's wardrobe. The ease and comfort of masculine apparel inspired Gabrielle Chanel early in her career, and the Chanel suit is very much with us today. The superb cut and tailoring of riding apparel are as attractive today as ever before and perhaps as influential in the fashion choices available to women.

Jean R. Druesedow

Vogue Magazine, "Busvine," 1927. Busvine was a London tailor whose designs for sidesaddle habits were unquestionably the most fashionable of his day. This habit is made of tan English whipcord and includes a Tattersall waistcoat, a white hunting shirt, and an English bowler hat.

In this handsome portrait by George Stubbs, the countess of Coningsby is wearing the colors of the Charlton hunt, which was based at the duke of Richmond's Goodwood House. Her habit includes a black, broad-brimmed beaver hat trimmed with white ermine, a black cravat, a blue riding habit with a coat that flares from the waist trimmed with ornamental gold buttons and froggings, a waistcoat, and a full skirt. This outfit was characteristic of British hunting clothes before the period when Englishmen took to jumping fences. *Yale Center for British Art, New Haven*

71

Journal des Dames et des Modes,
"Attitude d'Amazone," 1800.

Journal des Dames et des Modes, "Habit
Amazone en Drap," 1803.

Petit Courrier des Dames, "Habit Amazone
en Drap," 1826.

Les Modes Parisiennes, 1857.

Petit Courrier des Dames, "Modes de Longchamps," 1841.

Petit Courrier des Dames, "Costume d'Amazone en toile de laine," 1834.

75

Journal des Demoiselles, 1867.

Journal des Demoiselles, 1871.

La Mode Illustrée, "Amazone en drap" and "Amazone d'été en mohair," 1886.

La Mode Illustrée, "Amazones," 1893.

*Amazone devant le Château de
Pierrefonds* by Alfred de Dreux (French,
1810 – 1860), ca. 1850. *Hermès Collection,
Paris*

Vogue Magazine, "Correct Hunting Attire," 1927. "This Market-Harborough habit of dark-blue melton cloth, worn with a waistcoat of Tattersall, black butcher boots, and a silk or pique stock, is the correct out-fit for hunting or showing hunters. A high silk hat or the bowler is equally correct. . . . English habit imported by Saks-Fifth Avenue."

Vogue Magazine, "A Habit for Informal Cross-Saddle Riding," 1927. "Correct in every detail for summer shows and hacking is Miss Kitty Penn Smith's outfit, including well-fitted jodhpurs of brownish-beige gabardine, tan jodhpur boots, a coat of a rough brown tweed, and a brown felt hat. A swagger stick and canary string gloves complete the outfit; English habit imported by Saks-Fifth Avenue."

The grace and perfect form of this horse and rider, photographed about 1890, illustrate the ability of the sidesaddle rider to retain her seat even over a fence. Many women who are proficient in sidesaddle riding claim that the short-stirrup grip saddle provides a more comfortable and secure seat for jumping than the conventional cross-seat saddle.

The couturier Coco Chanel was an enthusiastic horsewoman who astonished her friends not only by riding astride but also by making her own jodhpurs based on a pair owned by a male groom. With her in this photograph from the 1920s is Boy Capel, a great sportsman of the day.

The hunting party of Madame la Duchesse
d'Uzes in the forest of Rambouillet, about
1905.

These two photographs taken on an early autumn morning in 1931 show the participants in a hunt with the pack of Lord Cowdray just before they departed for a day's sport. The guests lined up on the steps for their photograph are Oxford students wearing correct traditional hunting garb; the young women can be distinguished from the men by their bowler hats. Two of the ladies are obviously planning to ride astride, while the third wears the apron skirt appropriate to sidesaddle.

Although these members of the Myopia Hunt Club in Massachusetts were photographed recently, the riding habits give the scene a timeless quality.

These three photographs, displaying the apparel of the tailor Nardi and reproduced in a 1930s tack-shop catalogue for Kauffman & Sons Saddlery, show not only the correct dress for informal cross-saddle riding, left, and formal sidesaddle equitation, center, but also a feminine version of an outfit for playing polo, originally a game for men only.

This 1861 painting of the Prince Imperial, son of Napoleon III, by Bénédict Masson (French, 1819–1893) shows the young prince handsomely attired in the costume designed for *la Vénerie Impériale*; the distinctive green coat is decorated with red velvet and gold-and-silver braid and is worn with white breeches, black boots, and a tricorne hat. *Hermès Collection, Paris*

The prince's mother, the Empress Eugénie,
wears a version of the same habit. *Musée
de la Vénerie, Senlis*

Jodhpurs are usually worn today by children, but early in the century riding apparel for young horsemen was simply a reduced version of the habits worn by their elders. This charming portrait of Alan Harriman was painted in 1905 by George De Forest Brush (American, 1855–1941). *The Metropolitan Museum of Art*

This charming equestrian portrait photographed in 1903 shows (left to right) Lady
Diana Somerset on Maisie, Dyer the groom,
Lady Blanche Somerset on Darkie, the
duchess of Beaufort, and the marquess of
Worcester on his donkey, Minnie. The girls
are wearing their best hunting clothes,
while the young marquess sports a pair of
gaiters as he sits securely in his special
boxlike saddle.

This page from a sixteenth-century Nuremberg tournament book shows one of the fantastic chariots that took part in the procession preceding the tournament. No expense or flight of imagination was spared in making these vehicles, which are similar in spirit to the floats featured in some present-day parades. *The Metropolitan Museum of Art*

Fashion on Wheels

*S*ince antiquity, monarchs and princes have used various kinds of conveyances to dazzle their subjects. While some rode horses and others were carried in litters, it was the wheeled vehicle that offered the greatest possibilities for magnificent display. The rulers of Assyria and Egypt are depicted on ancient tombs and monuments riding on ceremonial occasions in ornate horse-drawn chariots, the symbols of power and authority. Nearer our own time, engravings and paintings by Albrecht Dürer and other artists show kings and princes riding in gala processions in highly decorated carriages.

The use of such carriages by lesser mortals was discouraged and, in some European countries, actually forbidden. One reason for this prohibition may have been to thwart the ambitions of potential rivals, but there was also the fear that knights and noblemen would become soft and unfit to lead their vassals on horseback in time of war if they were allowed to lounge through the streets in soft-cushioned coaches. At first only ladies and the old and infirm were permitted to use wheeled vehicles, but in time restrictions were lifted, and the use of carriages gradually increased. Different groups of specialized vehicles began to evolve, each group having its own style of decoration and of costume for occupants and attendants.

State coaches were always elaborately decorated, but this coach, built for King Ludwig II ("The Dream King"), of Bavaria, is perhaps the most elaborate ever constructed. *Nymphenburg Palace, Munich*

*B*eginning in the sixteenth century, coaches in which a monarch or a member of the royal family sat as though on his ornate throne were used for state ceremonies or for royal journeys through vassal territory. As time passed, the decoration of these state coaches became more splendidly lavish with gilded rococo carving, allegorical sculpture and painting, and heraldic devices. The height of fantastic grandeur was reached with the state coach of King Ludwig II of Bavaria, built in Munich in 1870 – 71. This coach, which can still be seen at the Nymphenburg Palace in Munich, has a trapezoidal body slung low to the ground on heavy leather braces, which are covered with embroidered blue velvet and suspended by C-springs mounted on the undercarriage. The body, wheels, and undercarriage are sumptuously decorated with gilded carving and figural motifs. The body panels are paintings on copper of scenes from the life of Louis XV of France and an allegory of the Christian Faith. On the roof are spritelike figures sounding trumpets, and the inside is lined with blue velvet heavily embroidered with gold thread. The coachman's seat is covered with an elaborately decorated hammercloth embroidered on the sides with the royal crown and monogram in gold.

The coachmen, postilions, and attendants who accompany state coaches are dressed in appropriately ornate livery coats, richly embellished with gold cords and strappings, worn with silk knee breeches, silk stockings, buckled shoes, and a cocked hat. The footman's dress suit differed from the coachman's only in having a coat of a more exaggerated cutaway style, fastened not with buttons but with a hook and eye at the point of the breast. The postilion, who rides one of the horses pulling the carriage, usually the near-side (left) horse, wears a full-dress livery with a short jacket reaching to the waist only and decorated with gold lace and gilt buttons. A white shirt and stock tie, white leather breeches, white gloves, decorated cap, boots with brown tops, and an iron leg-guard on the left leg to protect it from the battering of the carriage pole, complete the uniform. Full-dress livery became somewhat formalized toward the end of the eighteenth century, and it has been changed only in detail since then in surviving royal households.

In the more prosperous European countries, members of the nobility also had state carriages built for their use when attending the courts of their sovereigns or on various ceremonial occasions. Most of these were enclosed coaches carrying four persons, but similar, smaller carriages, called chariots in England, seated two persons inside. Open carriages, such as the landau, vis-à-vis, and barouche (called a *calèche* in

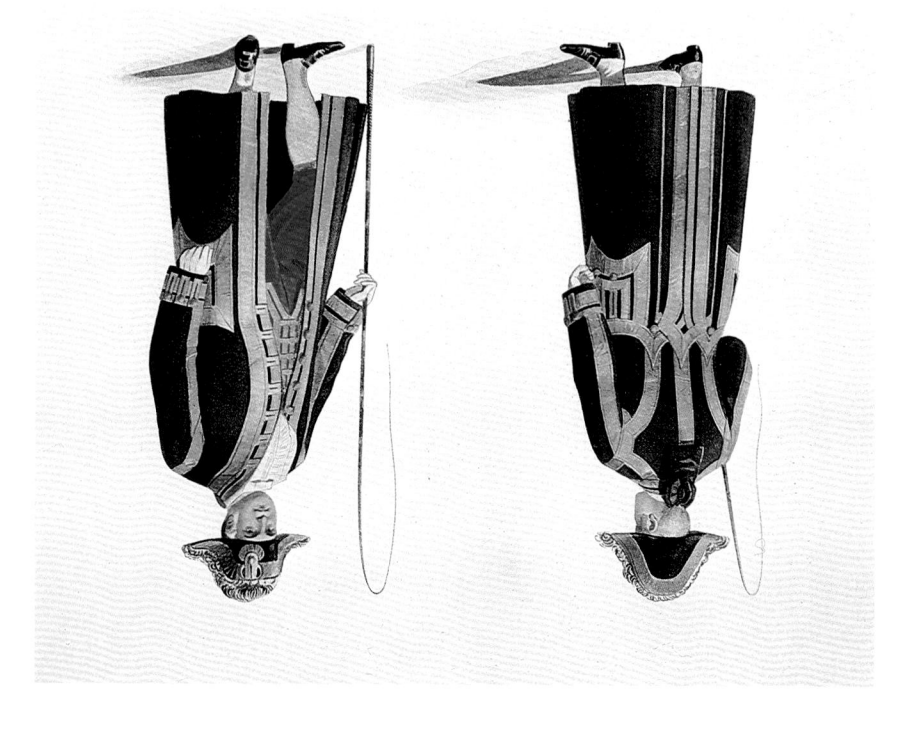

The coachmen, footmen, and postilions on state coaches wore ornate livery to match the grandeur of the coaches themselves. This plate, from an early twentieth-century French history of driving, shows the livery of the coachmen who drove for the French court.

D uring the latter half of the eighteenth century, noblemen, official envoys, and church dignitaries began to make long journeys in Europe by carriage with some frequency. Vehicles were specially equipped for such trips, and in some of them it was possible for the occupants to lie down and sleep. Some travelers would use their own carriages with

hammercloth like a throne."

without any apparent effort by an impassible coachman, seated on his delightful to mark the fiery, almost fierce action of the horses, restrained described by a contemporary French writer as follows: "It is truly for one of Her Majesty's "drawing rooms" at Buckingham Palace was early years of Queen Victoria's reign, and the picture of coaches arriving by the rich and powerful was a noteworthy feature of London life in the expensive luxury. The use of fancy horses and coaches for public display team of such horses, matched for color, size, and action, was an stylishly, wearing with suitable dignity their heavy, ornate harness. A these ponderous vehicles but they were also expected to step along State carriage horses needed not only size and strength to draw somewhat similar to that worn by the royal carriage servants. vants who, on occasions of appropriate importance, wore state livery state coaches of royalty. Accompanying these state carriages were ser- carving was common but on an altogether more modest scale than the and the badges of the orders of chivalry on the side panels. Some gilded normally decorated with their owners' coats-of-arms on the door panels France) were also used in some noble stables. These state carriages were

This handsome state coach design was produced by a London carriage-maker, who
constructed vehicles for noblemen and
decorated them with appropriate coats-of-
arms and badges. The enclosed coach
(called a "glass coach" because it has win-
dows on each side) was designed to carry
four people. Similar coaches were made to
carry two people; in England this type was
called a state chariot and in France a coupé
(from the word couper, "to cut," since it
was effectively half a coach). Museums at
Stony Brook

This two-wheeled post chaise in a plate from a 1763 British book was probably drawn by one horse, with a second horse, outside the shafts on the left, ridden by a postilion who controlled both horses in the absence of a coachman. Until the eighteenth century, men riding horses sat the trot, a fairly uncomfortable gait, but postilions developed the habit of rising in their stirrups at each stride, which enabled them to ride more comfortably over distance. Today most riders adopt this technique, which is called "posting."

horses hired at posting inns or stations, a service that had been organized under government regulation in many countries during the seventeenth century to speed the movement of messengers. Some of these posting carriages were two-wheeled; for example, the original form of post chaise was a two-wheeler. The post horses were often ridden by a postilion and not driven from the carriage. In France important people traveling "post" were often accompanied by a courier on horseback who saw to accommodation at inns on the route. The journalist C. J. Apperley (known as Nimrod) in *Nimrod Abroad* has given us the following description of such a courier in about 1825:

> *A French courier must be seen to be believed.... No butcher in England is ever seen on so miserable an animal.... Of the rider, on his head—on the very top of it — is stuck a cap* à la militaire, *whilst his nether parts are cased in very thick, very tight, yellow or green breeches, and, of course, jackboots with spurs of some inches in length. Then away he goes, sitting back in his saddle, flourishing his whip above his head with no small degree of skill, the smacking of which, together with the jingling of bells (around the horse's neck), produces a musical medley of no common order.*

The French postilions wore a similar outfit, as well as a pair of very heavy, high boots designed to protect the legs from the carriage pole, so heavy, in fact, that the boots were often fastened to the saddle and the postilion was lowered into them in his stockinged feet. In Britain, the post-boys, so called whatever their age, were said to be generally neatly dressed in short bright-blue or yellow jackets with a single row of metal buttons, breeches of white corduroy, and brown-topped riding boots. They usually wore high beaver hats, light in color, in which they stored a handkerchief, their tobacco, matches, and other small necessaries. In case of bad weather, they often took along overcoats, which would be rolled and strapped onto some part of the carriage, perhaps the front C-spring.

*T*he first wheeled conveyances for the general public were slow stage wagons, but early in the eighteenth century, faster coach service began to be organized. The coaches and the kind of service offered differed according to country, but it is generally acknowledged that the British coach service was the ne plus ultra before the coming of the railways.

There were two kinds of public coach in Britain—the crack mail coaches and the stage coaches. The mail coaches were horsed by contractors who also employed the drivers, but the guards were employees of the Post Office and wore a uniform of trousers, top boots,

This model of a French postilion wears the livery of members of the official messenger service for the French court in about 1825. His dark wool coat has a red collar, lapels, and cuffs, richly ornamented with silver galloons and brass buttons engraved *Poste aux chevaux*. His breeches are of buff calfskin, his hat of black leather, and his boots of exceptionally heavy leather. The horse's saddle is especially designed for the postilion: under the saddle tree is a case for carrying gold coins; at the pommel is a leather case for blankets; and behind the cantle is a leather trunk in which the mail was carried. The French royal coat of arms is engraved in silver on the horse's bridle. *Musée de L'Empéri, Salon de Provence*

97

This lithograph based on an early nineteenth-century painting called *The Last Change-in* shows a typical British mail coach stopping at its final stage between York and London to pick up a fresh team of horses. The coachman wears a heavy top-coat and has a Tattersall blanket wrapped around his legs; the guard at the back adjusting the luggage wears a Post Office uniform, which includes a scarlet coat decorated with gold and a black top hat.

scarlet coat with strappings of gold lace, and a gold-braided, black top hat. They were armed with a blunderbuss, which was carried in a box affixed to the coach roof in front of their seat. The coachmen had no uniform attire but were dressed according to season in a low-crowned hat, a heavy, many-layered topcoat, with scarves and comforters as well in bad weather. Breeches and boots usually completed the outfit, but in later years many coachmen favored trousers instead.

Like the mail coaches, many of the stage coaches also carried guards who rode on the back seat of the coach. They were first put there solely to guard the coach, but later they took on other duties connected with the passengers and cargo. Some form of official garb was normal and usually consisted of a beaver hat and long frock coat of some brightly colored cloth with metal buttons and strappings like those on a mail guard's coat. Breeches and boots were also worn. Some of the coach proprietors may have provided the uniforms for the guards on their coaches, but evidently some individual preference in matters of dress was tolerated. There was, for instance, the case of Bob Hadley's hat. Hadley was the guard of the "Unicorn" coach that ran from Manchester to the pottery-making towns in the south, and his outsized hat was described as resembling "an umbrella in extent, and Bob, as he luxuriated under its broad leaf, looks like an orang-utang under a banyan tree."

It had long been customary for the guards to carry a horn of some kind to give warning of the coach's approach to the hostlers at staging inns, the turnpike keepers, and other vehicles or road users. Some guards came to pride themselves as performers on the coach horn and on occasion would entertain the passengers with such traditional and popular airs as could be sounded in the limited musical range of a standard coach horn that was thirty-six inches in length. To add to their musical repertoire, a few guards used key bugles, but these were frowned on by officials at the Post Office, and the guards on mail coaches were forbidden to use them.

*I*n the days of poor roads and of coaches without springs pulled by underbred horses, driving as a pastime for the amateur had few attractions, but in the eighteenth century conditions began to improve, and about 1750 people began driving for pleasure. Carriages designed for the amateur driver began to appear, the four-wheeled types being called phaetons. The name, probably first used in France in this connection, was taken from the classical myth of Phaeton, the son of Helios (the sun), who persuaded his father to allow him to drive the sun chariot across the sky but was so erratic as a driver that he threatened to set heaven and earth on fire.

Although this amusing eighteenth-century print is hardly a realistic depiction of a highflyer phaeton, it does reflect the extremes to which fashionable drivers went in selecting their vehicles.

In England the prince of Wales, the future George IV, and the young bloods of his entourage took to driving phaetons of a type known as the "highflyer," built with a seat raised to an incredible height. Such was their fascination with driving that some of these amateur reinsmen would bribe the coachmen on the public coaches to let them take the reins. For those amateur coachmen who aspired to "take a handful" on a public coach, Donald Walker in *British Manly Exercises* (1837) offered the following suggestions:

> *When traveling with a coachman you do not know, always adopt the following plan. Never get upon a coach-box wearing a black handkerchief around your neck, or in blue pantaloons. Always take care to have a look of the drag about you: a neat pair of boots, and knee-caps if cold weather; a good drab surtout [a close-fitting overcoat] . . . a benjamin [a coat consisting of as many as six capes, often with large pearl buttons] or two about the coach, and a little of the spot [a colored tie] about the neck. For the first mile I always observe a strict silence, unless broken by coachee. . . . Leave him alone for a short while and when his mind is at ease, he will look you over as you sit beside him. He will begin with your boots, proceeding upwards to the crown of your hat, and if he likes you and you make a remark or two that pleases him, and shows you to be a judge of the art, the first time he stops he will say, "Now, sir, have you got your driving gloves on? Would you like to take 'em?" Coachmen's expenses on the road being heavy, you must not forget to reward him. They are generally satisfied with one shilling for under and two shillings for anything over thirty miles.*

This small four-wheeled carriage dating from the 1760s is called a phaeton and was designed so that amateurs could drive without relying on a professional coachman.

By 1800 driving had become a fashionable sport, and notices appeared in the press, such as the following extract from *The Sporting Magazine* in 1801: "Lord Sefton takes the lead among our modern 'whips' and is very nice in his selection of coach and curricle horses. His lordship purchased six carriage horses the other day at the sum of seven hundred guineas."

In 1807 Lord Chesterfield organized the Kensington Driving Club whose members drove together from London to certain hostelries about fifty miles away, where they would dine, afterwards driving home again by lamplight. As to dress, his lordship adjured club members to "drive like coachmen but dress like gentlemen." His advice was not followed by other clubs that came into being about this time. Some young amateurs adopted the dress, manners, and speech of the professional "knights of the road," even to the extent of having their teeth filed so that they could expectorate with the same proficiency. Members of the Whip Club drove yellow-bodied barouches, wearing ankle-length drab-colored coats with three tiers of pockets and large mother-of-pearl buttons, blue waistcoats with one inch-yellow stripes, and plush breeches with strings and rosettes to the knee.

Most of the original driving clubs had disappeared by 1850, but at the end of the Crimean War in 1856 an interest in driving revived among the well-to-do. The Four-in-Hand Driving Club in England was formed in that year for drivers of private four-in-hand coaches, and membership was limited to thirty. The new club was conducted in a more polished fashion than those of a quarter century earlier. Members all drove private coaches, usually called park drags, built to the same general pattern as the mail coaches but finished in discreet colors, brilliant with many coats of fine varnish. The members' driving attire consisted of a single-breasted morning coat, black silk hat, and trousers. A blue cornflower buttonhole was customary as a tribute to the duke of Beaufort, president of the club, whose family color was blue. Official meets were held in London's Hyde Park. Driving a coach and four became the rage among the sporting set in England and a new group, the Coaching Club, was formed in 1870 when the Four-in-Hand Club resolutely refused to increase its membership.

At about the same time other coaching enthusiasts started a revival of public coaches on certain routes. Often financing was provided by a syndicate of coaching men who shared the pleasure of driving. The road coaches, as they were called, were built much like the park drags but were somewhat heavier and finished in brighter colors, lettered with the names of places along the route. One of the early figures in this coaching revival was an American, George William Tiffany of Baltimore, who ran a coach on the road from London to Brighton in the summer of 1873. The verdict of British critics of this intrusion into one of the national institutions was that "he did the thing very well."

Driving for sport and pleasure in America did not become widespread until the second half of the nineteenth century. The first park drag built on the English pattern here was owned by T. Bigelow Lawrence of Boston in 1860. Leonard K. Jerome had one specially built by Wood Brothers of Bridgeport in 1863, and he and others regularly drove with their coaches to watch the races at Jerome Park. Jerome occasionally drove a six- or even eight-horse team hitched to his coach, but such flamboyant behavior was dismissed by his English counterparts with the comment "No gentleman drives more than four horses." Jerome was one of the founding members of the first American driving association, the Coaching Club, which was formed in New York in 1875. The official dress for members was a dark-green cutaway coat, yellow striped waistcoat, trousers of black cloth, and a black silk hat. The annual spring meet took place in Central Park on a Saturday in April or May, and a summer meet was held at Newport, Rhode Island, in August.

*C*arriages became increasingly popular during the nineteenth century in Europe, England, and America, for social as well as sporting reasons. Prominent families that did not include an enthusiastic amateur coachman would nevertheless own one or more four-wheeled carriages, which would be driven by a coachman in livery. Although often modest on the exterior, these private carriages were finely upholstered and appointed for the comfort and stylish appearance of the occupants inside. There were many different types of private carriage, open and enclosed, and each type had its own name, often borrowing the proper name of the owner to whose specifications it was built. Open carriages included the landau, calèche (known as a barouche in England), victoria, and vis-à-vis or sociable. Closed carriages were the brougham or coupé, town coach, clarence, and opera bus. A private hansom cab was kept in many private stables, and this, too, was driven by a professional coachman. As carriage design became more complicated, the names became more confusing. A writer for *The Hub and New York Coach-Makers' Magazine* noted in 1872:

This portrait by Alfred de Dreux (French, 1810–1860) of the Mosselman family, painted in 1848, shows Mme Mosselman driving her own carriage, which is of the type called a park-chaise. Queen Victoria drove a similar vehicle, which in England was called a pony phaeton. *Petit Palais, Paris*

Jerome Park, just outside New York, was established in 1866 by Leonard K. Jerome, who was a founder of the American Jockey Club along with August Belmont and who later became the grandfather of Winston Churchill. The park was the site of horse races and polo matches, and the fashionable attended in great numbers, often driving their own carriages. As a contemporary writer put it: "Racing was a social function. Jerome Park was in its glory, and the racehorses all belonged to one's friends." In the right foreground of this painting (ca. 1866) by J. H. Beard is a lady's phaeton and, to the left, a high-wheeled sulky or racing carriage. *National Racing Museum, Saratoga Springs, New York*

The difference in the names given to carriages is often perplexing to the public, and, in some cases, even to the manufacturer. One and the same vehicle goes frequently by different names, not only in different cities, but sometimes even in different shops in the same city. We do not wish to be understood to assert that a uniform denomination of carriages is an object of particular importance; yet it can not be denied that it would be more convenient if there were a little more harmony.

When a carriage was pulled by a single horse, the coachman would drive alone, but if a pair was used, it was normal for a groom, also wearing livery, to sit beside him. In park drags, two grooms were always carried on the rear seat. The livery of these servants would vary from one family to another, but certain standards prevailed. In a manual called *Driving for Pleasure,* published in New York in 1896, the author, Francis T. Underhill, recommended that each servant should be equipped with the following:

One silk hat; one felt storm hat, or second hat dressed for the purpose; one Derby; one suit of stable clothes, made either of whipcord or tweed; one sleeved waistcoat; one heavy cover coat; one stable cap; one mackintosh (or an

For many years, starting in the late nineteenth century, an annual coaching event was held on a special race day at Auteuil, the great course in the Bois de Boulogne. Called the *Prix des Drags,* the race would attract many fashionable coaching enthusiasts who would drive their park drags, each one more impressive than the next, from the Place de la Concorde to the racecourse. This scene was photographed in 1921.

upper benjamin); one dozen collars; one dozen neck-cloths; one livery body coat; one striped valencia waistcoat (with sleeves); one livery great coat; one pair of trousers to match same (for occasional use in the morning or at night); one pair leathers (or cloth breeches); one pair top boots, with trees for same; one pair dogskin gloves; one pair heavy wool-lined gloves; one pair woolen gloves; one pair breeches trees.

Since each household coach was likely to have a coachman as well as a groom or footman, to say nothing of a team of horses and its requisite harness, outfitting a private carriage obviously involved a sizable investment.

In the second half of the nineteenth century, the public parks in many large cities were filled during the "season" by ladies taking the air in their carriages. Gentlemen in the park would often drive themselves in their gigs and phaetons, or in that most splendid of all two-wheeled carriages, the cabriolet. The cabriolet required only a single horse, but one of great size and beauty of form and action. One groom was carried, preferably small in stature; he stood on a small platform behind the body of the cabriolet, bobbing up and down with the motion of the horse.

Overleaf:
Fairman Rogers of Philadelphia taught engineering at the University of Pennsylvania but is best remembered as a superb horseman. He was a contestant at the first polo game played in America, held at Jerome Park in 1876, and was a leader in the revival of coaching as a sport. This painting by Thomas Eakins (American, 1844–1916) shows Rogers driving his park drag in 1879 shortly before the Coaching Club of Philadelphia was founded. *Philadelphia Museum of Art*

Even in winter, it was fashionable for ladies in society to take the air in open carriages driven by their coachmen. This watercolor sketch by Constantin Guys (French, 1805 – 1892) shows a particularly elegant turn-out. The lady rides in a *milord* (which in England would be called a victoria) drawn by a horse wearing a blue caparison with yellow trim. *The Metropolitan Museum of Art*

This handsome print, dating from 1834, shows a cabriolet drawn by a large horse, held by an appropriately small groom, as was the fashion of the day. Grooms such as this one were called "tigers," because of their distinctively striped waistcoats.

Overleaf:

Thomas Worth (American, 1834–1917) was a master of caricature whose works were reproduced and sold by Currier & Ives during the late nineteenth century. He depicted the whole range of equestrian activity, from foxhunting and trotting races to carriage scenes, such as this one entitled *Fashionable Turnouts in Central Park,* published in 1869. The picture is a veritable catalogue of pleasure carriages: in the foreground is a victoria with a rumble for the carriage groom; behind it, moving left, is a Stanhope phaeton and behind that is a town coupé driven four-in-hand; to the left of the coupé is a Sefton (or canoe-shaped) landau; on the right, coming down the hill, is a Stanhope gig; above on the right is a pair-horse brougham or coupé; and at the top, moving left to right, are a lady's park phaeton with an English canopy (*left*) and a dog-cart phaeton (*right*).

*I*n the middle of the nineteenth century, while the amateur reinsmen of Europe were driving their stylish phaetons and drags in the city parks, their counterparts in the United States were becoming more and more fascinated by the lure of the fast trotter. The development of a superior breed of trotters in America began early in the nineteenth century. In 1818, Major William Jones's black gelding, Boston Blue, trotted a mile in three minutes flat at Jamaica, Long Island, to win a bet of two thousand dollars, and thereafter interest grew apace. It appears that Jamaica was the location of the first trotting track in the country, and racing at a track near Philadelphia was started a few years later. By 1830 organized racing had spread to other parts of the country, and ownership of the fastest trotter in town became the ambition of many a young gentleman.

In New York, the owners of fast trotters would drive along Harlem Lane on weekends, and many an impromptu "brush" between rivals took place there. William H. Vanderbilt and Robert Bonner owned the fastest trotters at that time. Bonner, an Irishman, made a fortune as the publisher of the *New York Ledger* and other periodicals. He paid the incredible sum of thirty-five thousand dollars for a horse named Dexter, the king of the trotters.

By the 1890s several racing clubs had been formed in Buffalo, Cleveland, Boston, and other places. Membership was restricted to amateurs who were encouraged to drive their own horses. Wearing trousers, lightweight jackets, and caps, but not racing colors, these amateurs competed in "matinee" races throughout the summer. The professional race drivers used high-wheeled sulkies, built by American craftsmen who achieved miracles of lightness and strength, but the amateur reinsmen for the most part used four-wheeled speed wagons. Following the success of pneumatic tires in professional racing in the early 1890s, special matinee wagons were designed with wire wheels and inflated tires.

*T*he coming of the automobile did not drive horses from the streets for many years, but in the United States the largest private stables in the big cities soon closed. The Coaching Club held its last meet in New York in 1910, and coachman-driven carriages were no longer seen in Central Park. Harness classes for gigs, highflyers, and other phaetons continued to be well supported at the National Horse Show in New York and elsewhere, and they continued to be turned out as impeccably as ever with grooms in livery. World War II practically ended the days of the gracious carriage, and for some years it seemed that the art of the coachman was ended.

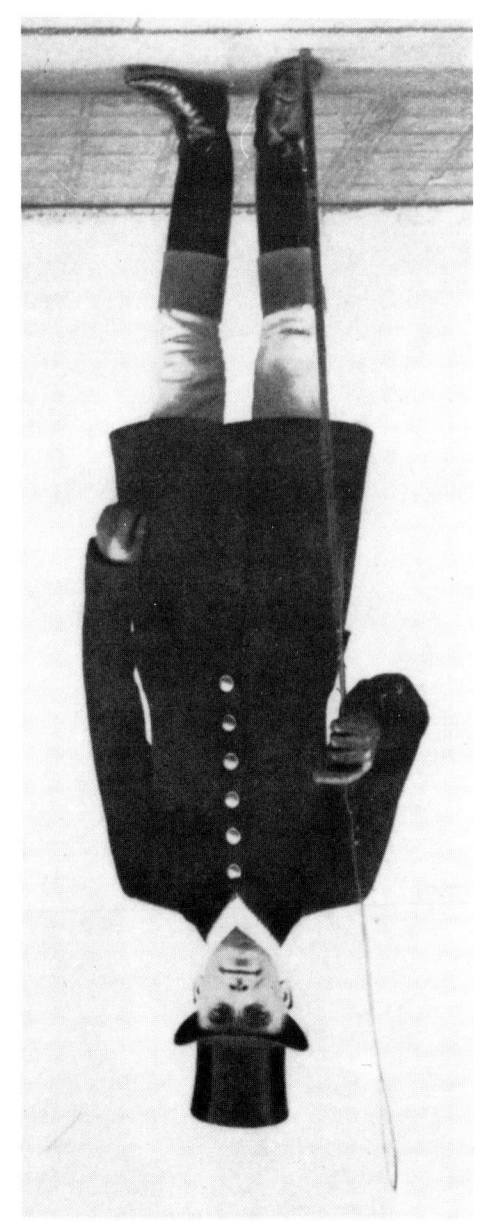

These photographs from Francis T. Underhill's 1896 manual *Driving for Pleasure* show the typical livery of a coachman employed by an American family in the late nineteenth century.

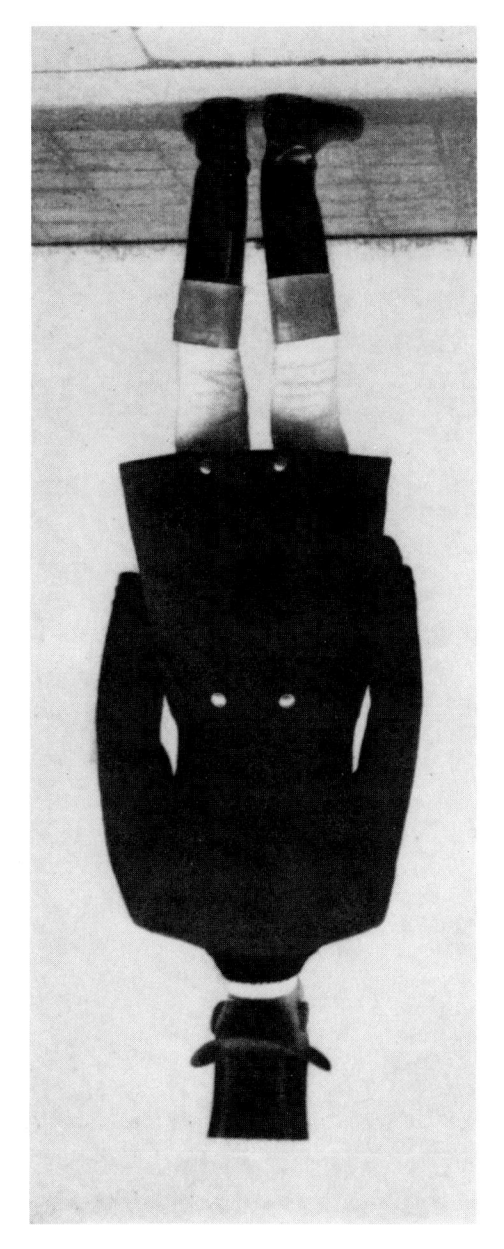

Thomas Ryder

Then in 1960, at the invitation of the late Ward Melville, a few carriage collectors gathered at Stony Brook on Long Island, and the Carriage Association of America came into being. The main objective of the new society was to save what relics remained of the horse-drawn era; it also sought to preserve the techniques of driving and the proper use of horses in harness. Interest in carriages and driving has grown at a steady pace since then, and driving activities of various kinds now take place in many parts of the country—as well as in England and Europe. One of the most popular events is the annual Carriage Marathon at the Devon Horse Show in Pennsylvania on the last Sunday in May. More than a hundred carriages appear at this event, most of them turned out as immaculately as those of the *haute monde* at the height of the season in Central Park at the turn of the century. There are also classes at Devon for coaches driven four-in-hand. A few other shows in different parts of the world offer classes for coaches, including obstacle courses, and more would do so if enough participants could be found.

In recent years coaching weekends have been held at Newport, reviving a summer tradition of the old Coaching Club, and a carriage drive is now held each August at Saratoga Springs, New York. Fashions may have changed somewhat, but old-timers assert that the standard of turnout at these events compares favorably with days gone by. One old hand wistfully added that he would willingly barter his soul, supposing he had one, for the privilege of sitting on the box once again behind four smart steppers.

A popular activity for those who could not resist the idea of outracing their neighbors even

in wintertime was to hitch their trotters to a sleigh and take a turn through the snow.

Carriage driving is enjoying a revival today, and amateur coachmen take pleasure in showing off their well-trained horses and their painstakingly restored vehicles at meets and horse shows throughout the United States and Britain. This handsome hackney pony is pulling a Stanhope gig. Stanhope was an English gentleman who had a number of carriages designed to his specifications by Tilbury, the London carriage-maker, and his name became attached to carriages of the same design.

William H. Vanderbilt owned some of the
fastest trotters in New York during the late
nineteenth century; here he is driving a
pair of fine mares, from a print published
in 1884.

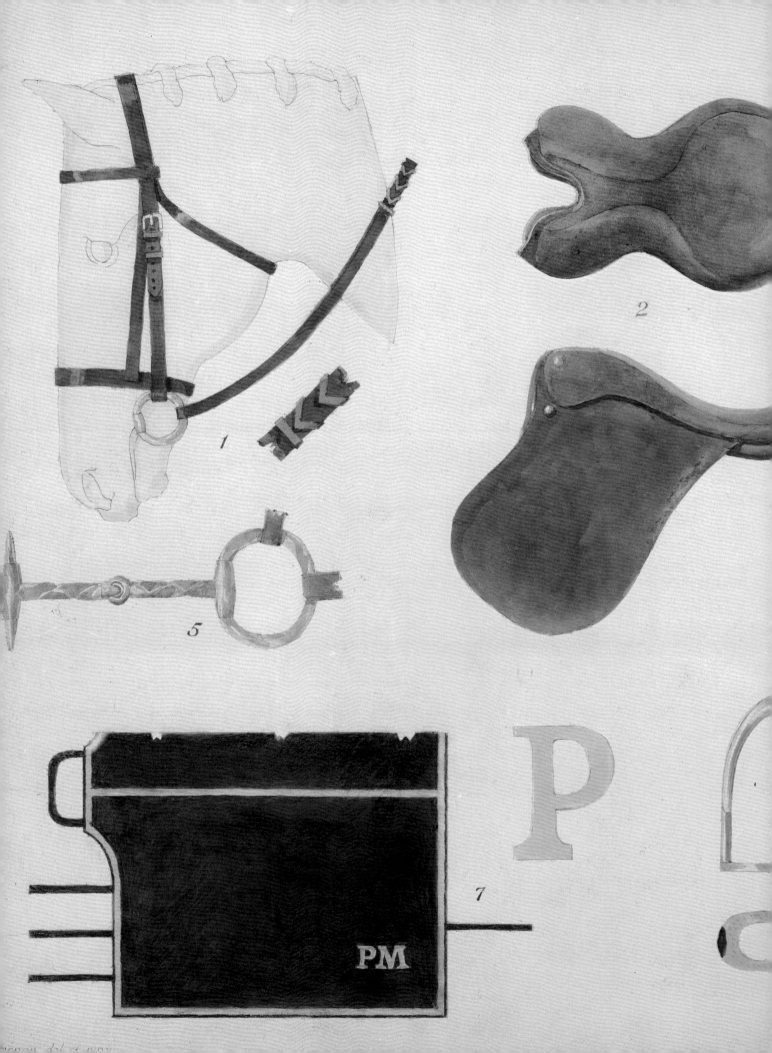

1

2

5

7

P

PM

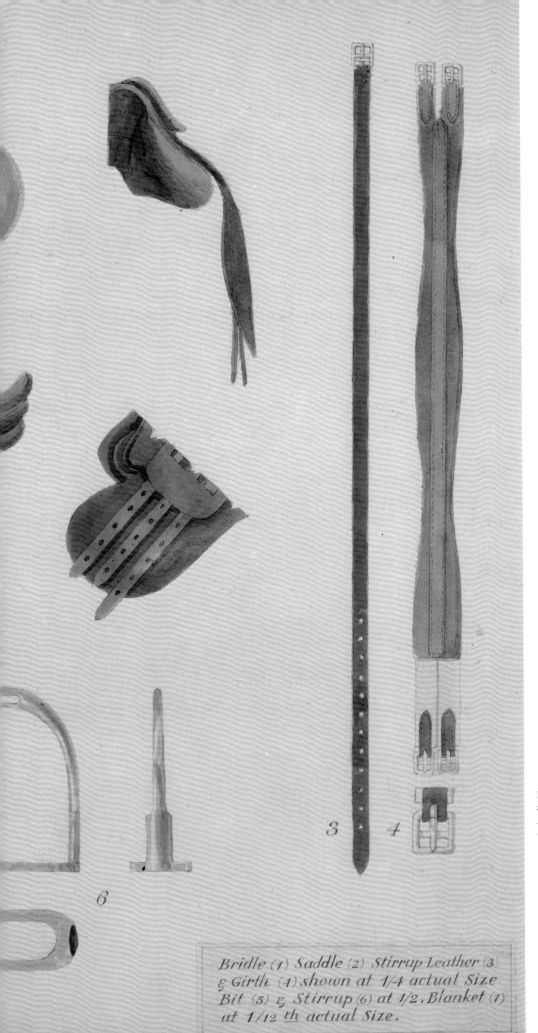

3   *4*

Bridle (1) Saddle (2) Stirrup Leather (3)
g Girth (4) shown at 1/4 actual Size
Bit (5) g Stirrup (6) at 1/2. Blanket (7)
at 1/12 th actual Size.

6

Paul Mellon's hunting equipment
as painted by Harold Sterner.
Paul Mellon Collection,
Upperville, Virginia

Glossary

Like any other field in which specialized equipment, apparel, and methods are used, the world of the horse has its own language. Some of the words and phrases that follow will be familiar to the general reader but have quite specific meanings when used in reference to horses, and these definitions are the ones given below.

Airs above the ground: Various movements in advanced dressage in which the horse's forehand, hindquarters, or both are raised above the ground, such as the *levade*, *capriole*, and *courbette*

Amazone: The French term for a woman who rides sidesaddle; also refers to her riding habit

Amble: See Pace

Arabian: A breed of light horse originally developed in Arabia; an important contributor to other light-horse breeds, including the thoroughbred

Barouche: An open four-wheeled carriage that seats four people, with an elevated seat in front for the driver; called a *calèche* in France

Benjamin: A close-fitting coat with several capes, worn by a coachman

Bicorne: See Cocked hat

Bit: A piece of metal (or rubber or bone) held in the horse's mouth by a bridle, used to control and steer the horse in riding or driving. See Bridle

Boot tops: Originally that part of the high boot worn over the knee; now refers to the band of leather, usually of a different color, sewn around the top of hunting boots

Bouton: The French word for button; refers to distinctive costumes worn for hunting by different groups or families in France

Bowler: A narrow-brimmed, dome-shaped, hard felt hat worn in the hunting field by men or women, named after a nineteenth-century London hat-maker; also called a derby, after the twelfth earl of Derby

Breeches: Riding trousers that button below the knee, to be worn with high boots

Bridle: An arrangement of leather straps devised to hold the bit in a horse's mouth. See Bit

Brougham: A closed carriage seating two people, with an elevated seat outside for the driver; in France called a *coupé* ("cut") for its resemblance to a closed four-passenger carriage cut in half

Browband: A bridle strap placed across the horse's face just in front of the ears and above the eyes

Cabriolet: An open, two-wheeled carriage that has a folding leather hood and holds two people; drawn by one horse placed between the upward-curving shafts, driven by a coachman, and attended by a groom who rides in back; term also used in England and France to describe an open four-wheeled carriage similar to a victoria

Calèche: See Barouche

Camlet: A fine fabric of mixed materials, including wool, silk, and goat or camel's hair, closely woven and nearly waterproof

Canter: A three-beat gait

Cantle: The back part of the saddle, often raised to give the rider a secure position

French eighteenth-century spurs designed for a musketeer.

Caparison: A decorative covering or trapping worn by a horse

Capriole: One of the airs above the ground in which the horse leaps into the air

Carrousel: A procession or ballet performed on horseback

Carriage: A horse-drawn two-passenger vehicle intended for private use

C-spring: A suspension spring for a carriage formed like the letter c

Chamfron: Plate armor designed to protect a horse's head

Chaps: An article of protective clothing worn on a rider's legs; derived from the Spanish word *chaparejos* or *chaparreras*, meaning leather breeches

Chariot: In the ancient world, a two-wheeled horse-drawn vehicle used for battle, racing, or processions; in eighteenth-century England a four-wheeled private or state carriage

Chasse à courre: The French term for hunting, usually for stag or roebuck

Chivalry: From the French word for *horseman*, refers to the customs of knighthood

Chukker: One of four or five periods of seven and one-half minutes each in a game of polo

Clarence: A closed, four-wheeled carriage seating four people, named for the duke of Clarence, later William IV of England

Coach: A large, four-wheeled enclosed carriage driven by a coachman seated outside in front

Coach-and-four: A coach drawn by four horses

Coachman: The driver of a coach, usually a professional

Cockade: An ornamental badge worn on a hat by a servant in livery

Cocked hat: A hat with a turned-up brim with two or three horn-shaped projections (bicorne or tricorne), still worn by Frenchwomen who hunt on horseback and by riders who perform in the classical tradition

Colors: A reference in England and the United States to the distinctive collars worn by members of different hunts

Conformation: The structure or shape of a horse

Coupé: See Brougham

Courbette: One of the airs above the ground in which the horse raises both forelegs and, as they fall, raises his hindlegs into the air; also called a curvet

Crinet: Plate armor to protect a horse's neck

Croup: The upper line of a horse from the loin to the root of the tail

Crupper: A piece of harness in the form of a padded loop that passes under the tail

Crutch: On a sidesaddle, one of the two projections that support the legs; the lower crutch is also called a leaping-head

Cuirass: A piece of body armor to cover the rider's upper torso

Curb: A type of bit with a high port inside the horse's mouth and a strap or chain beneath the jaw

Curricle: A small, two-wheeled, open carriage drawn by a pair of horses

Cutaway: A coat with the skirts cut away at the waist to form long tails at the back, worn in formal fox hunting and modern dressage competition

Derby: See Bowler

Dog-cart: A two-wheeled carriage drawn by one horse usually with seats for four seated back to back; also a four-wheeled version drawn by one horse or a pair

Drag: A heavy coach drawn by four or more horses, with seats on top; see also Park drag

Dressage: The modern term for classical riding as developed in the Renaissance; from the French word for *training*

Épaule en dedans: See Shoulder-in

Equitation: The art of riding on horseback

Footman: A liveried servant attending a rider or a carriage on foot

Boots worn by the Prince Imperial Jean-Joseph-Eugène-Louis Napoléon Bonaparte, France, nineteenth century.

Forehand: The forequarters of a horse

Forward seat: A modern style of riding developed by the Italian cavalryman Federigo Caprilli in which the rider balances over the horse's forehand at the gallop or over a jump to enable the horse to move freely

Four-in-hand: A team of four horses driven by a single coachman

Gait: One of several ways in which a horse can move, determined by the sequence of footfalls, including the walk, trot, canter, gallop, pace, rack, and so on

Gallop: A fast four-beat gait

Galloon: A band of trimming on an article of clothing, usually embroidered or braided, often with metallic thread

Gelding: A castrated male horse

Gig: A small, two-wheeled, open carriage drawn by one horse between shafts or by two horses in tandem (one in front of the other)

Girth: A strap that passes beneath the barrel of a horse to hold a saddle or pad in place on his back

Groom: A servant, often liveried, who cares for a horse; also a verb meaning to clean a horse

Hacking: Informal riding for pleasure; derived from the word *back* meaning a rented horse

Hammercloth: A decorated cloth draped over the coachman's seat

Hansom: A closed, two-wheeled carriage driven by a coachman who sits on an elevated outside seat at the back of the carriage

Hauberk: A type of medieval armor

Haute école: A French term meaning *high school*, refers to advanced levels of dressage

Highflyer: A phaeton with an elevated seat for the driver

Hobby: A type of riding horse bred in England and Ireland before the development of the modern-day thoroughbred

Hostler: A groom at an inn or stable; often spelled *ostler*

Hunt cap: A dome-shaped, stiff cap, often covered with black velvet, with a short brim in front; traditionally worn only by members of the hunt staff and children in the hunt field but now worn by many riders as informal protective gear

Huntsman: A professional member of the hunt staff whose task it is to manage the hunt and care for the hounds

Jabot: A piece of lace or cloth hanging from a collar in front

Jackboots: High boots with tops covering the knee; originally a military form but adapted for riding in the seventeenth century

Jodhpurs: Riding breeches that extend to the ankle, often with a foot strap, to be worn with short boots; derived from the name of the state in India where British colonials are said to have adopted them for playing polo

Jousting: One of the contests in a tournament in which two mounted knights in armor charge each other with lances

Landau: A four-wheeled carriage with a divided top that can be folded down; driven by a coachman on an elevated seat in front

Lariat: A rope with a noose, used in herding livestock; also called a lasso

Leaping-head: See Crutch

Leggings: A protective covering of leather or fabric for the rider's legs

Levade: One of the airs above the ground, in which the horse's forehand is elevated for a few moments with the hindquarters directly beneath the horse's body

Lipizzan: A breed of horse used at the Spanish Riding School, Vienna, derived from Andalusian stock originally bred at Lipizza, near Trieste, in the seventeenth century; also used as a carriage horse

Livery: A uniform worn by servants; also refers to a stable where horses are rented out for riding or driving

Embroidered saddle cloth, France, eighteenth century.

Master of Foxhounds: The man (or woman) in charge of a hunt by whose permission members and guests are allowed to participate; usually not a professional position; also called Master of Hounds

Melton: Melton Mowbray in England was once an important center of the cloth industry that gave its name to a type of heavy woolen cloth manufactured there used in making hunting coats

Pace: An intermediate two-beat lateral gait performed by the horse in which the legs on one side move together rather than diagonally, as in the trot

Pack: A group of hounds used for hunting; also refers to the riders who participate in a hunt

Padron: A Spanish word meaning *landowner*

Pair: Two horses driven side by side

Palfrey: A horse used for pleasure riding or processions rather than battle, usually a pacer

Park drag: A private coach drawn by four or more horses and driven by a single coachman

Petasos: A flat-brimmed Greek hat

Phaeton: An open, four-wheeled carriage driven by an amateur rather than a professional coachman

Piaffe: A movement in advanced dressage in which the horse trots in place

Picador: A mounted participant in a bullfight

Piebald: A white horse with black patches (a skewbald is white with any other color)

Pillion: A cushion or pad worn behind a man's saddle to support a woman; also refers to the style of riding double

Pink: A term occasionally applied to a scarlet hunting coat, once thought to have been the name of a London tailor but most likely a slang reference to the color of a well-worn hunting coat

Poitrel: A piece of plate armor made to cover a horse's chest and body

Poll: The area just behind the horse's ears where the top of the bridle rests

Polo: A stick-and-ball game, usually played on horseback, with four members to each team

Pommel: The front of a saddle, often raised to enable the rider to remain securely in position

Postboy: See Postilion

Post chaise: A vehicle originally used for carrying mail or messages and drawn by a horse ridden by a postilion rather than driven by a coachman

Postilion: One who rides as a guide on the near (left) horse of a pair that draws a post chaise or coach

Posting: Rising in the stirrups at the trot

Quintain: A device used by knights on horseback as a battle exercise or in a tournament contest

Racing silks: A uniform jacket and cap cover of lightweight fabric, worn by the professional jockey or driver of a racehorse, with colors or patterns that indicate a horse's owner; originally derived from the word *silk* referring to a gown worn by an advisor to the crown, indicating rank

Rack: A four-beat lateral gait or "broken pace," in which the horse's legs on each side move together but do not hit the ground simultaneously

Reins: Straps that attach to the bit rings on a bridle at one end and are held by the rider at the other in order to control and steer the horse

Rowel: A small wheel with radiating spokes attached to a spur

Rumble: A seat outside a carriage on the back to hold a guard, groom, or footman

Saddle-seat: An American style of equitation used in riding certain types of horses, including saddlebreds, Tennessee walking horses, and Morgans

Saddle tree: The frame of a saddle, made of wood or fiber glass

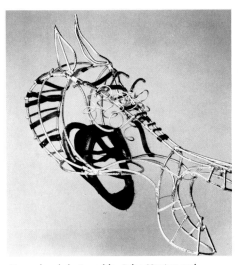

Horse head designed by John Napier and made by Hector Pascual for the play *Equus* by Peter Shaffer, Paris, 1977.

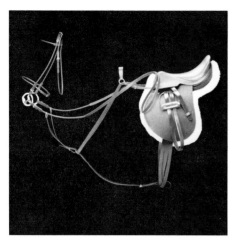

Snaffle bridle and forward-seat saddle by Hermès, French, twentieth century.

Seat: A rider's position on a horse's back

Sefton: A type of landau, named for an English nobleman

Shoulder-in: A lateral dressage movement in which the horse moves on two tracks, the forelegs on one, the hindlegs on another

Sidesaddle: A saddle with two crutches or pommels on the left side to support a woman's legs

Silks: See Racing silks

Singlefoot: A slow version of the rack

Snaffle: A simple bit with a straight or jointed bar

Sociable: An open, four-wheeled carriage in which four people may sit, two facing the other two; also called a vis-a-vis

Spur: A metal device worn on each boot to reinforce the pressure of the rider's leg

Stage coach: A closed public coach drawn by four or more horses that work in relays, being replaced at various stages along the route

Stanhope gig: A small, open, one-horse carriage, originally designed to the specifications of an English gentlemen named Stanhope in the nineteenth century

State coach: A closed, four-passenger coach drawn by four or more horses for use by royalty or nobility

Stirrup: A metal or wooden device suspended by straps from a saddle to support the rider's feet

Stock: A simple white cravat or neckcloth worn in the hunt field; for formal wear, the stock must be tied in a specific manner and fastened with a gold stock pin

Stud: A breeding stallion; also a breeding farm

Sulky: A small, open, two-wheeled carriage used for racing a harness horse

Surcingle: A three-inch strap of leather or webbing passing over the saddle and under the horse's body, secured with a buckle

Surtout: A long overcoat or frockcoat, close fitting to the waist and usually doublebreasted

Tack: Equipment worn by a horse, such as a bridle or saddle

Tandem: A method of driving two or more horses, one in front of the other

Tattersall: A bright, solid fabric with colored lines forming squares, often used for waistcoats; the name of a London horse market where such material was used for horse blankets

Thoroughbred: A breed of light horse developed for racing; also widely used for hunting, showing, and pleasure riding

Throatlatch: A strap on the bridle that passes under the horse's throat; also refers to that part of a horse's head

Tournament: An event in which knights on horseback compete in various contests to show skill and courage

Tricorne: See Cocked hat

Trot: A two-beat diagonal gait

Undercarriage: The framework supporting a carriage to which the wheels are attached

Valencia: A kind of woven fabric used for waistcoats

Vaquero: A Spanish word meaning *cowboy* or *herder*

Vénerie: The French term for hunting; *la grande vénerie* refers to hunting for stag, roebuck, or boar, a royal or noble privilege; *la petite vénerie* refers to hunting for lesser quarry, such as rabbit, hare, or fox

Victoria: An open, four-wheeled carriage with a folding top, driven by a coachman in front and carrying two passengers

Vis-à-vis: See Sociable

Whip: A stick used as an aid in riding or driving; there are many different sizes and types, including the crop, fly whisk, and jumping or racing bat

Whipper-in: A huntsman's assistant whose job it is to control the hounds during a hunt, usually a professional member of the hunt staff

Photo Credits

Frontispiece "Philippe, duc d'Orléans, dressed as the king of Persia," engraving by François Chauveau, illuminated by Jacques Bailly, from *Courses de testes et de bague faites par le Roy et par les princes et seigneurs de sa cour en l'année M.DC.LXII*, published in Paris, 1670. Library at Versailles. Photograph courtesy Franco Maria Ricci

Page 10 Saint George. The Metropolitan Museum of Art, New York. Gift of Humanities Fund, Inc., 1972. 1972.145.13

Page 11 Caucasian tympanum. The Metropolitan Museum of Art, New York. Rogers Fund, 1938. 38.96.
Greek vase painting. Staatliche Antikensammlung, Munich

Page 13 Marcus Aurelius. Piazza del Campidoglio, Rome. Photograph Alinari/Art Resource

Page 14 T'ang horse and rider. Shaanxi Provincial Museum, China. Photograph Robert Harding Picture Library

Page 15 Carved staghorn saddle. The Metropolitan Museum of Art, New York. Gift of James Hazen Hyde, 1953. 53.50.
Scene from the Bayeux tapestry. Cathedral at Bayeux, France.
Pur-I-Vahman silver plate. Hermitage, Leningrad. Photograph by Pieter Meyers

Page 16 Plate 9, engraving by Crispin de Pas, from *L'Instruction du Roy en l'exercise de monter à cheval* by Antoine de Pluvinel, published in Paris, 1625. The Metropolitan Museum of Art, New York.
Armor for rider. The Metropolitan Museum of Art, New York. Gift of William H. Riggs, 1913. 14.25.717a-r.
Armor for horse. The Metropolitan Museum of Art, New York. Fletcher Fund, 1921. 21.139.2

Page 17 "Epaule en dedans," engraving by Charles Parrocel, from *L'Ecole de Cavalerie* by François Robichon de La Guérinière, published in Paris, 1733. Photograph courtesy Alexander Mackay-Smith.
Louis XV on Horseback by J. B. van Loo and Charles Parrocel. Musée de Versailles.
Photograph of Spanish Riding School horseman performing the *levade* courtesy The Spanish Riding School, Vienna

Page 18 "Le sauteur aux piliers," engraving after a design by Albert Adam and Tom Drake, from *Ecole de Cavalerie*, published in Saumur, 1869. Photograph courtesy Ecole Nationale d'Equitation, Saumur.
The Hunt by Paolo Uccello. Ashmolean Museum, Oxford

Page 19 English fox hunters, engraving by Henry Alken, from *Illustrations for Land-Scape Scenery*, published in London, 1821. The Metropolitan Museum of Art, New York

Page 20 Battle Scene: Arabs Making a Detour by Adolph Schreyer. The Metropolitan Museum of Art, New York. Gift of John Wolfe, 1893. 94.23.2

Page 21 Photograph of Peruvian paso fino horse courtesy Alexander Mackay-Smith. *The Outlaw* by Frederic Remington. The Metropolitan Museum of Art, New York. Bequest of Jacob Ruppert, 1939. 39.65.50

Page 22 Monument to Gattemalata by Donatello. Piazza San Antonio, Padua. Photograph Alinari/Art Resource

Pages 22-23 The Procession of the Magi (detail) by Benozzo Gozzoli. Palazzo Medici Riccardi, Florence. Photograph Scala/Art Resource

Page 24 Henry II, King of France by Workshop of François Clouet. The Metropolitan Museum of Art, New York. Bequest of Helen Hay Whitney, 1944. 45.128.12

Page 25 Prince Maurice of Orange by Pauwels van Hillegaert the Elder. Rijksmuseum, Amsterdam

Page 26 Duke of Buckingham by Peter Paul Rubens. Kimbell Art Museum, Fort Worth, Texas

Page 27 Don Gaspar de Guzman, Count Duke of Olivares by Diego Rodriquez de Silva y Velázquez. The Metropolitan Museum of Art, New York. Fletcher Fund, 1952. 52.125

Page 28 The Polish Rider by Rembrandt van Rijn. Copyright The Frick Collection, New York

Page 29 "La Guerra di Bellezza," engraving by Jacques Callot. The Metropolitan Museum of Art, New York. Harris Brisbane Dick Fund, 1940. 40.52.20.
Spanish Riding School quadrille. Photo courtesy The Spanish Riding School, Vienna

Page 30 "Louis XIV dressed as a Roman emperor with his attendants," engraving by François Chauveau, illuminated by Jacques Bailly, from *Courses de testes et de bague faites par le Roy et par les princes et seigneurs de sa cour en l'année M.DC.LXII*, published in Paris, 1670. Library at Versailles. Photograph courtesy Franco Maria Ricci

Page 31 Shah Jahan on Horseback. The Metropolitan Museum of Art, New York. Purchase, Rogers Fund and The Kevorkian Foundation Gift, 1955. 55.121.10.21

Page 32 Plates 43 and 47, engravings by Crispin de Pas, from *L'Instruction du Roy en l'exercise de monter à cheval* by Antoine de Pluvinel, published in Paris, 1625. The Metropolitan Museum of Art, New York

Page 33 Hand-colored plate from a Nuremberg tournament book. The Metropolitan Museum of Art, New York

Page 34 August by the Limbourg Brothers and Jean Colombe, from *Très Riches Heures du Duc de Berry*. Musée Condé, Chantilly. Reproduction of the first complete and exact facsimile edition of "Les Très Riches Heures du Duc de Berry" (1984) printed by the authority of Faksimile-Verlag, Luzern, Switzerland. Facsimile edition with English commentary may be obtained from Harry N. Abrams, Inc., New York. For understandable reasons the present illustration

cannot be compared with the quality of the facsimile edition.

Page 35 Tapestry, after a design by Jean-Baptiste Oudry. Musée de Versailles. Photograph Roger-Viollet

Page 36 Sir Roger Burgoyne Riding His Grey Hunter Badger, with the Bitch, Juno, in the Grounds of Sutton Park by James Seymour. Yale Center for British Art, New Haven.
George, Marquess of Huntly (later Fifth Duke of Gordon) on Tiny by Benjamin Marshall. Yale Center for British Art, New Haven

Page 37 Two Busvines and a Cutaway by Sir Alfred Munnings. Private collection. Copyright The Sir Alfred Munnings Art Museum, Dedham, England

Pages 38-39 Watercolor by Harold Sterner. Paul Mellon Collection, Upperville, Virginia

Page 40 The Race of the Palio by Giovanni di Francesco Toscani. The Holden Collection, The Cleveland Museum of Art, Cleveland, Ohio.
Panathenaic amphora. The Metropolitan Museum of Art, New York. Purchase, 1907. 07.286.80

Page 41 The Start of the Race of Riderless Horses by Emile-Jean-Horace Vernet. The Metropolitan Museum of Art, New York. Bequest of Catharine Lorillard Wolfe, 1887. Catharine Lorillard Wolfe Collection. 87.15.47

Pages 42-43 Flying Childers with Jockey Up by James Seymour. Private collection. Photograph Bridgeman Art Library, Ltd.

Pages 44-45 Racehorses Belonging to the Duke of Richmond Exercising at Goodwood by George Stubbs, A.R.A. Goodwood House, England. Photograph Bridgeman Art Library, Ltd.

Page 46 Before the Start by Sir Alfred Munnings. Mrs. John Hay Whitney Collection, New York. Copyright The Sir Alfred Munnings Art Museum, Dedham, England

Page 47 Photograph of steeplechasers by Raymond G. Woolfe, Jr.
Photograph of point-to-point courtesy Simon Blow

Page 48 John and Sophia Musters Out Riding at Colwick Hall, Nottingham by George Stubbs, A.R.A. Major Musters Collection, Nottingham. Photograph Bridgeman Art Library, Ltd.

Page 49 Man on Horseback and Study of Horse's Head by Théodore Géricault. The Metropolitan Museum of Art, New York. Bequest of Walter C. Baker, 1971. 1972.118.215.
Portrait de Guillaudin à Cheval by Edouard Manet. Private collection

Page 50 Page 180 verso from the *Shah-nameh of Shah Tahmasp*. The Metropolitan Museum of Art, New York. Gift of Arthur A. Houghton, Jr., 1970. 1970.301.2

Page 51 Polo by George Bellows. The Metropolitan Museum of Art. Bequest of Emma A. Sheafer, 1973. 1974.356.19.
Photograph of the Greentree polo team

courtesy Mrs. John Hay Whitney, New York

Pages 52-53 Photograph of polo game by Raymond G. Woolfe, Jr.

Page 53 Photograph of the most honorable marquess of Cholmondeley courtesy the dowager marchioness of Cholmondeley

Page 54 Arab Horseman Giving a Signal by Eugène Delacroix. The Chrysler Museum, Norfolk, Virginia

Page 55 Plate 11 from *Tauromachia* by Francisco Goya. The Metropolitan Museum of Art, New York. Rogers Fund, 1921. 21.19.11

Page 56 Vaquero by James Walker. The Bancroft Library, Berkeley, California

Page 57 Padron by James Walker. The Bancroft Library, Berkeley, California

Page 58 Marie Antoinette by Louis-Auguste Brun. Musée de Versailles. Photograph Documentation photographique de la Réunion des musées nationaux

Page 59 Wife of Bath, from the Ellesmere manuscript of Chaucer's *Canterbury Tales.* Huntington Library, San Marino, California

Page 60 Saddle, Hermès Collection, Paris. Falconry scene by Claude Deruet. Musée de Chartres

Page 61 "Dame en habit de chasse," 1676. Musée de la Vénerie, Senlis

Page 62 Départ pour la Chasse à Courre, artist unknown. Location unknown. Photograph Roger-Viollet

Page 63 Halte de Chasse by Carle van Loo. Musée du Louvre, Paris. Photograph Documentation photographique de la Réunion des musées nationaux

Page 64 La Duchesse de Bourgogne by Pierre Gobert. Musée de Versailles. Photograph Documentation photographique de la Réunion des musées nationaux

Page 65 Lady Worsley by Sir Joshua Reynolds. Earl of Harewood Collection, Harewood House, Leeds

Page 66 Plate from *Galerie des Modes,* 1779. The Metropolitan Museum of Art, New York.
Plate from *Galeries des Modes,* 1787. The Metropolitan Museum of Art, New York

Page 67 George Harley Drummond by Sir Henry Raeburn. The Metropolitan Museum of Art, New York. Gift of Mrs. Guy Fairfax Cary in memory of her mother, Mrs. Burke Roche, 1949. 49.142

Page 69 Vogue Magazine, 1927

Pages 70-71 The Countess of Coningsby in the Costume of the Charlton Hunt by George Stubbs, A.R.A. Yale Center for British Art, New Haven

Page 72 Journal des Dames et des Modes, 1800. The Metropolitan Museum of Art, New York.
Journal des Dames et des Modes, 1803. The Metropolitan Museum of Art, New York

Page 73 Petit Courrier des Dames, 1826. The Metropolitan Museum of Art, New York

Page 74 Petit Courrier des Dames, 1834. The Metropolitan Museum of Art, New York

Page 75 Les Modes Parisiennes, 1857. The Metropolitan Museum of Art, New York. *Petit Courrier des Dames,* 1841. The Metropolitan Museum of Art, New York

Page 76 Journal des Demoiselles, 1867. The Metropolitan Museum of Art, New York. *Journal des Demoiselles,* 1871. The Metropolitan Museum of Art, New York

Page 77 La Mode Illustrée, 1886. The Metropolitan Museum of Art, New York

Page 78 La Mode Illustrée, 1893. The Metropolitan Museum of Art, New York

Page 79 Amazone devant le Chateau de Pierrefonds by Alfred de Dreux. Hermès Collection, Paris

Page 80 Vogue Magazine, 1927

Page 81 Vogue Magazine, 1927

Page 82 Photograph of lady jumping courtesy The Valentine Museum, Richmond, Virginia.
Photograph of Chanel on horseback courtesy Chanel Archives

Page 83 Photograph of French hunting party Roger-Viollet

Page 84 Photographs Roger-Viollet

Page 85 Photograph of Myopia Hunt Club by Alix Coleman

Page 86 Photograph courtesy Charles Kauffman

Page 87 Photographs courtesy Charles Kauffman

Page 88 Prince Impériale by Bénédict Masson. Hermès Collection, Paris

Page 89 Empress Eugénie in Imperial Hunting Livery by Albert Adam. Musée de la Vénerie, Senlis

Page 90 Alan Harriman by George De Forest Brush. The Metropolitan Museum of Art, New York. Gift of General Boykin C. Wright, 1953. 53.177

Page 91 Photograph courtesy Simon Blow

Page 92 Page from hand-colored Nuremberg tournament book. The Metropolitan Museum of Art, New York

Page 93 Carriage of Ludwig II of Bavaria. Nymphenburg Palace, Munich

Page 94 Coachman livery, illustration from *L'Art de Conduire et d'Atteler,* published in Paris, 1903. The Museums at Stony Brook, New York

Page 95 "Chariot," colored engraving published in London, 1837. The Museums at Stony Brook, New York

Page 96 "Post chaise," plate 32 from *The Nobleman and Gentleman's Director and Assistant in the True Choice of their Wheel-Carriages,* published in London, 1763. The Museums at Stony Brook, New York

Page 97 Restoration of a postilion. Musée de l'Empéri, Salon de Provence

Page 98 "The Last Change-in." The Museums at Stony Brook, New York

Page 99 "Phaetona, or Modern Female Taste, 1776," illustration from *Carriages and Coaches: Their History and Their Evolution* by Ralph Straus, published in London, 1912. The Museums at Stony Brook, New York

Page 100 "Phaeton," plate 6 from *The Nobleman and Gentleman's Director and Assistant in the True Choice of their Wheel-Carriages,* published in London, 1763. The Museums at Stony Brook, New York

Pages 102-3 Mme et M. Mosselman et leurs filles by Alfred de Dreux. Petit Palais, Paris. Photograph Bulloz

Page 104 Jerome Park by J. H. Beard. The National Museum of Racing, Inc., Saratoga Springs, New York

Page 105 Photograph Roger-Viollet

Pages 106-7 The Fairman Rogers Four-in-Hand by Thomas Eakins. Philadelphia Museum of Art, Philadelphia, Pennsylvania

Page 108 Winter Drive by Constantin Guys. The Metropolitan Museum of Art, New York. Rogers Fund, 1937. 37.165.95

Page 109 "A Cabriolet," aquatint engraving by Robert Havell, published in London, 1834. The Museums at Stony Brook, New York

Pages 110-11 "Fashionable Turn-outs in Central Park," lithograph after a painting by Thomas Worth, published in New York, 1869. The Museums at Stony Brook, New York

Pages 112-13 Coachman's livery, illustration from *Driving for Pleasure* by Francis T. Underhill, published in New York, 1896. Private collection

Pages 114-15 "Trotting Cracks in the Snow," lithograph published in New York by Currier & Ives. The Metropolitan Museum of Art, New York

Page 116 Photograph loaned privately

Page 117 "The Celebrated Trotting Mares Maud S. and Aldine Driven by Wm. H. Vanderbilt, Esq., at the Gentlemen's Driving Park, Morrisiana, N.Y.," published in New York, 1884. The Museums at Stony Brook, New York

Pages 118-28 Watercolor by Harold Sterner. Paul Mellon Collection, Upperville, Virginia.
Spurs, Musée de la Chaussure, Romans, France.
Prince Imperial boots, Musée de la Chaussure, Romans, France.
Saddle cloth. The Metropolitan Museum of Art, New York. Gift of James Hazen Hyde, 1953. 53.50.
Equus horse head. Pierre Bergé Collection, Paris.
Bridle and saddle, Hermès Collection, Paris.
Plate from *The Triumph of the Emperor Maximilian I* by Hans Burgkmair (German, ca. 1473-ca. 1559). The Metropolitan Museum of Art, New York. Harris Brisbane Dick Fund, 1932. 32.37

Endpapers Engravings by Henry Alken from *Illustrations for Land-Scape Scenery,* published in London, 1821. The Metropolitan Museum of Art, New York

Staff of The Costume Institute

Diana Vreeland, Special Consultant
Jean R. Druesedow, Associate Curator in Charge
Paul M. Ettesvold, Associate Curator
K. Gordon Stone, Associate Museum Librarian
Judith Jerde, Associate Conservator
Anne H. Schirrmeister, Assistant Curator

Lillian A. Dickler, Senior Administrative Assistant
Jean Lawson, Senior Administrative Assistant
Dominick Tallarico, Principal Departmental Technician
Karen Meyerhoff, Assistant for Study Storage
Mavis Dalton, Associate Curator, part-time

Exhibition Staff

Exhibition conceived and organized by Diana Vreeland
Assistant to Mrs. Vreeland/Exhibition Coordinator: Stephen Jamail
Research Associate: Katell le Bourhis
Advisor for the Installation: Stephen de Pietri

Assistants for the Exhibition:
Sarah Richardson, Richard de Gussi-Bogutski, Kirk Allan Adair, June Bove, Natasha Grenfell

Designers: Jeffrey Daly, David Harvey
Lighting: Willian L. Riegel

About the Authors

Alexander Mackay-Smith is the author of a number of books, including *The Colonial Quarter Race Horse* and *The Race Horses of America: Portraits and Other Paintings by Edward Troye,* and was for years editor of the weekly *Chronicle of the Horse*. He was the founder and curator of the National Sporting Library in Middleburg, Virginia, and has been associated with the United States Equestrian Team, the American Horse Shows Association, the Masters of Foxhounds Association of America, the U.S. Pony Clubs, the U.S. Combined Training Association, and the International Alliance of Equestrian Journalists. He was, for twenty seasons, the Master of two Virginia hunts, and he still rides regularly to hounds.

Jean R. Druesedow is Associate Curator in Charge of The Costume Institute, The Metropolitan Museum of Art. She taught speech and theater arts at Miami University, Eastern Kentucky University, and the Mediterranean Division of the University of Maryland, and she joined the staff of The Costume Institute in 1978. She lectures widely on fashion and costume history and is Vice President of The Costume Society of America.

Thomas Ryder has been the editor of *The Carriage Journal* since 1975 and is actively involved in coaching, both as a participant and as a judge. He was born in England, where he learned to drive at an early age from an uncle who refused to drive an automobile; he moved to Canada in 1954 and to the United States in 1963. He is the author of several books about driving, including *On the Box Seat, The High Steppers,* a history of hackney horses, and *The Road and the Ring*, the coaching memoirs of an English horsewoman.

The Metropolitan Musem Of Art

Man and the Horse